D1320143

SACRIFICE AND SACRAMENT

By the same Author

SACRIFICE AND
SACRAMENT

by

E. O. JAMES

Professor Emeritus of the History of Religion in the
University of London
Chaplain of All Souls College, Oxford
Fellow of University College
and Fellow of King's College, London

BARNES & NOBLE, Inc.
New York

© THAMES AND HUDSON LONDON 1962
PRINTED IN GREAT BRITAIN BY
WESTERN PRINTING SERVICES LTD BRISTOL

CONTENTS

5

Contents

Contents 9

PREFACE

IT is a quarter of a century since I last undertook an investigation of the institution of sacrifice in the light of the anthro-
pological, archaeological and documentary evidence then
available. Since then the cultus has constantly been under
review. Most modern investigation, especially that into the
very closely allied principle of sacrament, has been in terms of
Christian theological conceptions and interpretations: this is
hardly surprising, since the self-offering of Christ as a propitiatory victim, together with the Incarnation, has always been
a cardinal doctrine of a faith finding expression in a sacrificial
tradition and a sacramental system. This theological approach
has meant that the very considerable literature has largely
concentrated on the doctrinal, apologetic and devotional
aspects of sacrifice in their Christian manifestations and interpretations, and little, if any, reference has been made to the context in which the institution emerged, and to the long and
complex history that lies behind what are, after all, higher and
specialized spiritual developments.

Sacrifice and sacrament are not part only of Christianity.
They have arisen as a result of man's attempt to establish and
maintain right relations with the spiritual powers upon which
he feels himself and his natural environment to be dependent
for well-being and survival, and to secure protection from the
forces of evil. It is in this context, basic and natural for all men
at all times, that I have examined the rites, beliefs, principles
and themes of sacrifice and sacrament in this volume, to determine the nature, function and meaning of the elements in the
cultus at different cultural levels. It then becomes possible to obtain

a clearer view of these fundamental and recurrent phenomena in the history of religion, so that anomalies and crudities may be purged, and what is of value in the higher living faiths of mankind, especially Christianity, be established.

E. O. JAMES

CHAPTER I

The Institution of Sacrifice and the Sacramental Principle

THE DEFINITION OF SACRIFICE AND SACRAMENT

Sacrifice

IN opening an investigation of two complementary ritual institutions which have occupied a fundamental position in the history of religion throughout the ages some explanation is required of the terms by which they have come to be known, and which have acquired particular theological connotations. In its broader interpretation 'Sacrifice' (from the Latin *sacrificium*; *sacer*, 'holy' and *facere*, 'to make') involves the destruction of a victim for the purpose of maintaining or restoring a right relationship of man to the sacred order. It may effect a bond of union with the divinity to whom it is offered, or constitute a piacular expiation and propitiation to 'cover', 'wipe out', neutralize or carry away evil and guilt contracted wittingly or unwittingly. Hubert and Mauss have pointed out that the consecration of the victim may 'modify the moral state of the sacrificer or of certain material objects he has in view' by removing sanctity through a sacrificial process of desacralization. Secondary aims have also arisen such as the desire to secure the favour of an offended god by the offering of bribes on the utilitarian principle of *doutdes*, 'I give that thou mayest give'; or as the freewill thankofferings made in grateful recognition of benefits received. That these two principles are very closely related, can be seen in the donations of the firstfruits of the crops, the firstlings of man and beast, and many other gifts of a similar nature; which though conceived as honoraria are not far removed from bribes. In fact the *doutdes* notion is seldom entirely absent in any piacular sacrifices however refined and sublimated may be the form in which it appears.

The Sacramental Principle

The word *sacramentum* was employed in Roman law to signify the pledge deposited in public keeping by parties engaged in a lawsuit, and which the loser forfeited. From being a legal and religious sanction in which a man placed his life and property in the hands of the supernatural powers upholding justice, it became a dedicatory oath of allegiance taken by soldiers to their commander on embarking on a new campaign. The pledge might be sworn in a sacred place using a formula with a magico-religious significance, as in Mithraism where the ini-tiate promised loyalty to Mithras in his *sacramentum*. When it was adopted by the Christian Church these earlier interpretations of the term were retained. Thus, Pliny affirms that in his pro-vince the Christians assembled for worship *seque sacramento non in scelus aliquod obstringere, sed ne furta, ne latrocinia, ne adulteria committerent, ne fidem fallerent, ne depositum appellati abnegarent* ('having bound themselves by a solemn oath, not to become guilty of wicked deeds, never to commit fraud, theft or adultery, never to falsify their word, nor deny a trust when they should be called upon to deliver it up').[1] Whether anything of the kind ever actually occurred is not known, but it would seem that Pliny must have heard the word *sacramentum* used to des-cribe the oath that Christians were thought to take at their weekly assemblies. Similarly, Arnobius, having in mind the military oath,[2] says that it is better for Christians to break their worldly contracts than to break the *fides Christiana, et salutaris militiae sacramento deponere*.[3]

Under the influence of the Greek derivation μυστήριον, the symbolic value of the legal deposit, pledge or oath by a litigant was interpreted as a ritual act or object employed as a means of conveying supernatural grace and specific spiritual benefits. This conception of the Greek μυστήριον is not very far re-moved from the Latin *sacer* with its compounds *sacrificium* and *sacramentum*, since both signify that which is set apart, or tabu because it belongs to the sacred order distinct from the profane and commonplace. Thus, St Thomas Aquinas says that any, thing that is called sacred may be called sacramentum.[4] From being that which is made sacred by consecration, a sacrament may readily become an 'effective sign' of that which has been sanctified and made efficacious by virtue of Dominical institu, tion, becoming the bearer of supernatural power or divine grace and thus a bond of union between God and man. With such natural actions as eating, drinking, lustration, nuptial intercourse, and ritual techniques regarded as 'means of grace' and the pledge of a covenant relationship with the sacred order, the two worlds can be brought into conjunction. In this way the material becomes the vehicle of the spiritual through the agency of 'outward and visible signs'.

Taking the word 'sacrament' in its broadest sense as the sign or symbol conveying something 'hidden' and mysterious—a numinous element spiritually perceived and made efficacious— the entire universe has a sacramental significance. 'For the in, visible things of God from the creation of the world', as St Paul maintained, 'are clearly seen, being understood by the things that are made, even his eternal power and Godhead.'[5] Thus the evolutionary process appears as a graded series in which each lower level provided a basis for the one next above it. The lower, indeed, seems to be necessary to the growth of the higher. This is shown by the living cell which builds up its structure from certain complex inorganic compounds to pro, vide a foundation for the organism, which itself arises from a whole series of molecules of increasing complexity. The emer, gence of life in the universe represents a synthesis of molecules introducing new powers and potentialities in organic evolu, tion and thus building up more and more complex organisms in an ascending series culminating in Man. Man possesses a new synthesis of mind which enables him to transcend the organic series of the universe, and to apprehend an order of reality that lies beyond the cosmic order and is independent of the changing conditions of time and space.

The intercourse between the human spirit and its God,

however, is always an 'I-and-Thou' relationship, sacramental in character and purpose. To think of the universe as the expression of the divine acting dynamically and immanently in all the processes of nature is a sacramental conception inasmuch as it assumes divine action and control through material forms to effect some cosmic purpose and spiritual reality. But if a divine principle is to be found in the universe at all, it is in human nature and its relations that it can be most completely apprehended. Therefore, the action of the divine upon man has tended to be conceived as the influence of a Person upon a person rather than as the impact of a pantheistic immanental principle upon things. Immanence and transcendence are correlatives. The self is immanent in the body because it transcends it, and transcends the body because it is immanent in it. As Dr Quick has pointed out, 'the pantheism which denies transcendence wholly makes immanence equally impossible, since it leaves no room for any distinction between the Godhead and the totality of that in which it dwells.'[6]

If, on the other hand, the Deity is regarded theistically as supra-personal, revealing himself to and acting upon mankind without any material alteration of natural laws and processes in order to unite that human spirit to himself, a sacramental relationship consistent with these operations in the universe can be established. So conceived, the 'inward' and 'outward' experience meets in a higher unity which guarantees for the latter its full validity, so that the purposive order holds its own against the merely causal. In this sacramental context no hard and fast distinction can be drawn between the 'inward' and the 'outward', the spiritual and the material; this the ancients, like their modern counterparts in primitive states of culture, were not slow to recognize. They invested natural functions with a supernatural authority and significance because for them the natural and human order of reality did not stand in opposition to the sacred order.

Natural phenomena, human experience, cosmic events and divine activity were interrelated in an 'I-and-Thou' relationship *sui generis*, like that between subject and object. This was dynamically operative through an organized ritual technique in which the outward things in the natural environment perceptible to bodily senses were sublimated, especially for the purpose of dealing effectively with the incalculable and unpredictable elements in human experience, to promote the common weal and to secure protection against and release from evil. Thus, the sacred meal is at once a sacramental communion and a sacrificial oblation in which the two fundamental and complementary rites have been so very intimately associated throughout their long and varied history.

The Communion Theory of Sacrifice

In his *Lectures on the Religion of the Semites* in 1899 Robertson Smith based the institution of sacrifice on a communal meal in which the gods and the worshippers together eat the sacred flesh of a 'theanthropic animal', at once god and kinsman, to absorb its nature and life.[7] This totemic interpretation of the origin of the institution encounters at once the initial difficulty that the totem has never been a sacrificial victim in the proper sense of the term. The sacred species, in the form of an animal or plant, is eaten in a common meal by those belonging to a clan of which it is regarded as the ancestor and supernatural ally, for the purpose either of sharing in the source of its life and animating essence, or of ensuring its abundance for the benefit of other tribes for whom it is not tabu.[8] This second aspect is more in accord with the eating and desacralization of the first-fruits than with a sacrificial or sacramental communion with a god since the totem is neither a deity nor an intermediary effecting union with a divinity. The strengthening, by sharing in a common meal, of kinship with a totem from which members of a clan believe themselves to be descended is by no means the same thing as establishing a vital relationship with a god by partaking of his flesh and blood, or by the oblation and consumption of a sacrificial victim consecrated and immolated for this purpose.

Totemism is a specialized institution which certainly is not of universal occurrence and it is very doubtful whether it was ever practised to any extent, if at all, among the Semites, as Robertson Smith contended. In Palestine, as elsewhere, some clans and cities bore the names of animals or plants,[9] but it does not follow that thereby they assumed a specific totemic relationship with the species. Nor is there any convincing evidence of this in their religious or social organization.[10] Nevertheless, as Hubert and Mauss have stressed, the fact remains that sacrifice in one of its aspects is a *communio* by virtue of the mystic power inherent in the victim destroyed in the immolation and consumed by the priest or the worshippers, this intermediation establishing a communication between the sacred and the profane.[11] Concentrating attention upon the Hebrew and Hindu evidence, they agreed with Robertson Smith that the main purpose of sacrifice was to effect a union with the god, and in so doing to bring into conjunction the human and divine orders. Divine life having been infused into the victim by its consecration, this was released by its immolation and consumed by the offerer sacramentally, whereby he was raised to a higher moral state and brought into touch with the spiritual world. But this can hardly be made applicable to the situation as it obtains and has obtained in primitive society.

It remained for Durkheim to go behind the Semitic and Hindu data to the more primitive rites of increase known as Intichiuma among the native tribes of Central Australia. In them he thought he detected an act of oblation to make the totemic species more prolific. Thus, the men of the Undiaro kangaroo totem pour out their own blood upon a rock in which the ancestral kangaroos are believed to reside, in order to drive them out in all directions, and so to increase their numbers.[12] But this is done essentially to facilitate their increase rather than as an act of oblation. Similarly, the members of the witchetty grub totem go at the breeding season to their sacred sites at Emily Gap near Alice Springs in the Arunta country to perform their Intichiuma ceremonies in order to produce food for general consumption, though the grubs may be eaten by them only very sparingly.[13] When the emu clan makes Intichiuma several men open veins in their arms and allow the blood to stream on the ground till it is saturated. When the serum has coagulated they trace designs in it in white, yellow, and black, representing different parts of the body of the emu. A song is sung to the figure during the dance that follows. The effect of the rite is to prevent the sacred species from disappearing by quickening the embryos of the new generation.[14] Similarly, in the Unjiamba and Hakea-flower totems a young man opens a vein in his arm during the ceremonies to allow the blood to sprinkle on a stone which represents a mass of Hakea flowers in the centre of the oval-shaped pit where the rite is performed. This stone is a *churinga* because it is thought to embody the soul-substance of the totem, and, therefore, the sacred place is tabu to women and children and the uninitiated.[15]

The prominence of the shedding of blood in these ceremonies may be explained by the fact that it is the vehicle of life and consciousness, efficacious alike to the living and the dead, to supernatural beings and to men, and capable of establishing a vital union between a human group, its totemic ally, and all the members of the fellowship. Hence the belief that Intichiuma is a ritual revivification causing the sacred species to increase and multiply and so to exercise a magico-religious control over the source of the food supply. The life-giving essence is poured out on the sacred stones to promote and conserve life, and to constitute a mystic bond with the source of all beneficence sealed in the vital shedding of blood. In a state of culture where the food supply is always precarious and natural means of hunting animals and collecting insects and plants do not meet the needs of every emergency, the will to live finds practical and emotional expression in the ritual control of the means of sub-sistence and increase, promoting at the same time the con-solidation of the group.

Although Robertson Smith was mistaken in regarding the totem as a sacrificial victim, it is nevertheless, by virtue of its central position, at once human and divine, in the tribal fellowship, a potent agent in effecting intercommunion with the sacred order. So intimate is the relationship between the totem and the totemite that to consume its holy flesh, or certain parts of it especially impregnated with its soul-substance, is to share in the common life-principle and to make all the members of the clan 'one flesh'. To eat is to live, and as in primitive society food is the main link between man and his environment, by receiving it, as Malinowski says, he feels the forces of destiny and providence.[16] Dependent as he is on the precarious means of subsistence at his disposal, he must at all costs be in a right relationship with the powers and forces controlling the supply. This is accomplished by a ritual technique which is fundamental in the institution of sacrifice and in the sacramental principle, and which has found a particular mode of expression in totemism, even though the totem is neither a theanthropic or theriomorphic victim in a sacrificial sense of the term, nor a slain god eaten sacramentally.

The Palaeolithic Sacrificial Communio

In the light of present-day archaeological evidence it appears that seasonal ceremonies were held in the decorated cave sanctuaries of the Upper Palaeolithic, under conditions and for purposes similar to those of which the Intichiuma rites are a typical example. In both cases the aim seems to have been to facilitate effective hunting, to promote the food supply, and to enter into a mystic beneficial relationship with the supramundane sources of providential bounty when the animals and plants were prolific and required to be conserved. But here again it is most unlikely that the Palaeolithic ritual can be interpreted in terms of totemism, as was formerly suggested by Reinach and his contemporaries. The representation of such a variety of different animals is against this theory, as each totem almost certainly would have had its own sanctuary. It is true, as the Abbé Breuil has pointed out, that the bones of the animals depicted in the cave paintings are absent from the midden-heaps.[17] But in the great sanctuaries like Niaux, Les Trois Frères, and Lascaux the ceremonies seem to have involved the whole community in a collective attempt to control the chase by supernatural means directed to the common good rather than confined to single food groups, and independent of the socio-religious technicalities of totemism. Moreover the animals depicted do not seem to have been tabu as food, as is the totem, for spears or wounds in the vital parts are frequently painted or engraved upon them. These would ensure successful hunting by casting a spell on the quarry in the chase.

A complex cultus developed around the mysterious forces of nutrition and propagation to promote plenty by stimulating the fecundity of the species and to bring the food supply under human control by observing prescribed hunting rites. Thus, about four-fifths of the objects depicted in the cave paintings and parietal art of the Upper Palaeolithic in France and Spain are representations of animals, mostly edible, because probably it was they which constituted the principal source of the means of subsistence. Excellent as is the execution of many of the designs (e.g. the bison at Altamira in Cantabria in northern Spain, the great polychromes at Font de Gaume and at Lascaux in the Dordogne), the conclusion that cave paintings primarily were works of art is precluded by their having been created usually in the most inaccessible and distant chambers, nooks and crannies of tortuous caverns; a painting of a rhinoceros at Font de Gaume was found high up on a vertical wall of a narrow crevice, and the engravings on the steep walls of the chamber of felines at Lascaux are often exceedingly difficult or dangerous of access. Furthermore, the inner depths were far too damp, dark, cold and sinister to be inhabited, and many of them show no trace of occupation even at the mouth of the cave.

Another feature of the art is the practice of superposition. In spite of adequate wall space paintings or engravings often have been made one above the other, as at the cave of Teyat adjoining Les Eyzies in the Dordogne, presumably because the particular spot was thought to have especial magic powers. This runs contrary to the theory that aesthetic decoration is the motive of cave art but is understandable as a cult device, and when a regular sequence of superposed figures occurs it is possible to work out a relative chronology of the various styles from the archaic Perigordian cycle at the dawn of the Upper Palaeolithic (i.e. in the Aurignacian or Gravettian culture phase) to the great polychromes in the Magdalenian.[18]

Among very early examples of parietal art—the art *mobilier* of the French prehistorians—are the sculptured and engraved female figurines, commonly called 'Venuses', which have the maternal organs grossly emphasized. These began to make their appearance in the Gravettian culture, having come into Europe from Western Asia at the beginning of the Upper Palaeolithic. Although more widely distributed than the decorated caves, these figurines have been found in several of the cavern sanctuaries (e.g. at PecheMerle at Cabrerets, Lot; at Laussel in the Dordogne; and at AnglessurAnglin in Vienne). At PecheMerle three female silhouettes traced with the fingers on the clay ceiling of the large hall, which is also decorated with mammoth designs, are thought to be the oldest figures in the cave. The breasts are pendulous, and in an extension of the cave discovered in 1949 on one ceiling a collection of stalagmites have been shaped like female breasts and smeared with black. In the sculptured Venuses the breasts are nearly always given great prominence, together with the other sexual organs, buttocks and abdomen, while the face, if portrayed at all, usually is featureless. In the basrelief discovered by Dr Lalanne at Laussel the body of a nude woman holding a horn in her right hand was painted red, the colour and surrogate of blood. In association with it was a relief depicting either an accouchement or a copulation.[19]

These representations were the emblems of a cultus having for its main purpose the giving of life through the symbols of maternal fecundity. It was not, however, only to make the human species fruitful and replenish the earth that this fertility ritual was employed in Palaeolithic times. Thus, incised on the wall of a recess in the cave known as Les Combarelles near Les Eyzies are a series of anthropomorphic figures which appear to be masked. Among them is the engraving of an obese man following a woman in an erotic attitude, possibly clothed in a skin with tails: there is the silhouette of a human figure appa rently with a mammoth mask, while other figures have also the heads of animals engraved on them.[20] These would seem to represent dancers engaged in a mimetic ritual to promote the fertility of the beasts they depicted, like the engraving of three masked figures on stag-horn at Abri Mège, Dordogne, masquerading in the skin of a chamois. Similar designs occur in the cave at Marsoulas in Haute Garonne, and on a schist plaque found at Lourdes a man with a long beard, the tail of a horse, and perhaps the antlers of a stag is portrayed.

That dances were held to promote fecundity in Palaeolithic cavern sanctuaries is clear from the heel-marks found in a recess in the Tuc d'Audoubert, St Girons, Ariège. They are at the end of a long gallery near the figures of a female and male bison which had been modelled in clay. These imprints almost certainly were made by young people engaged in a fertility dance round a small hillock; perhaps associated with the clay phallus also found in this alcove.[21] In the neighbouring cave discovered by the three sons of the Count Begouen in 1918, and now appropriately called Les Trois Frères, the much-discussed masked figure, known as 'the Sorcerer', is engraved and painted in black four metres above the floor on the wall of a small chamber at the end of a winding corridor. There, beside a sort of window overlooking an alcove and surrounded with a tangled mass of animal engravings which are exceedingly difficult to decipher, is the representation of a composite figure 75 cm. high and 50 cm. wide. Its face has round eyes like an owl, with between them a line for a nose, while the ears are those of a wolf and there are two stag antlers above the forehead. The claws might belong to a lion and the tail is that of a horse or wolf. The feet and toes indicate an attitude of dancing and the legs are bent.

Whether or not it represented a sorcerer, or shaman, embodying the attributes and functions of the animals portrayed, or, as Breuil now suggests, the Spirit controlling the multiplication of game and hunting expeditions,[22] a cult was practised here in which human beings and animals were brought together in a mystic communion with the god or spirit controlling

the food supply in order to conserve and promote the abun/
dance of the species on which the community depended. If
the hybrid figure is that of a sorcerer, or ritual expert, he has
arrayed himself in the skin and antlers of a stag, the tail of a
horse and the ears of a wolf, thus acquiring their attributes and
establishing what may be described as sacramental relations
with the source of providential bounty through a dance in
which no doubt the behaviour of the animal species personi/
fied were imitated.

To obtain communion in this beneficent abundance it is
necessary to become *en rapport* with the sacred species vener/
ated, so that for the time being the human agent (i.e. the
shaman or dancer) in all probability believed and felt himself
to be the creatures he represented. From the analogy of those
who act in this capacity in primitive states of culture today, the
ritual expert did what he set out to do in the performance of
the prescribed cultus. He caught and killed his prey; he made the
copulation of male and female to be productive of offspring;
he controlled the fortunes of the chase by depicting wounded
animals, and uttered incantations over his designs to secure the
catching and killing of the quarry; and he established a mystic
relationship between his human group and the spiritual powers
responsible for the maintenance of the food supply. Through a
series of rhythmical muscular movements strong emotional
urges and desires were given efficacious expression which under
Palaeolithic conditions and requirements were centred in fe/
cundity and fertility, birth and generation, especially at critical
junctures in the life of nature (e.g. mating seasons), or of man.

The will to live being the primary emotion, it was dis/
charged by rites anticipatory of a successful hunt, or of the
propagation of the species, thereby giving vent to pent/up
emotions and longings. As the artist externalizes a feeling and
mood, an emotional impulse and interpretation of reality as he
conceives it in paint or stone, so the ritual expert gives visible
and dramatic expression to the vital urge and rhythmic rela/
tions to life in response to concrete situations and current needs.
It is not surprising, therefore, that ritual, dance and art should

have conjoined in their earliest manifestations; and from this conjunction have emerged the fundamental concepts and prin´ ciple, centred in nutrition and propagation and their respective ritual techniques, which lie at the base of sacrifice and sacra´ mental communion.

It was not so much because 'like produces like' that these sacred actions were sacrificially and sacramentally efficacious, but because a ritual that involved a more or less realistic reproduc´ tion of some practical activity based on an urgent requirement established the *ex post facto* idea of 'sympathetic causation'. In the first instance the rites were performed to procure food by abundance of the supply and successful hunting, the urge to act discharging itself on the symbol and made effective by the technique employed. The symbol as the prototype of the sacri´ ficial victim, or the sacramental sign, was regarded and treated in the same way as the spiritual entity it symbolized, be it god, spirit, totem, ancestor or undefined numinous power, by virtue of the supernatural quality it acquired. Hence the efficacy of the designs, disguises, masks, mimetic dances, and the various adjuncts of the cultus as it was executed by the ritual experts for the common good of the community in the remote and eerie recesses of their sanctuaries.

The Gift Theory

Inherent in this *communio*, however, is the idea, fundamental in the institution of sacrifice, of giving and of the exchange of gifts. In primitive society, offerings in the form of presents are a regu´ lar occurrence both in social intercourse and in approach to gods and spirits. Therefore, in the ordinary course of events gifts are made to a divinity as if he were a chief or a deceased ancestor, to gratify, appease or propitiate him, to obtain favours from him, or eucharistically as an act of gratitude for benefits received. When such offerings are made sacrificially they are normally immolated, as the destruction of the victim is an integral element in any holocaust. It is, in fact, that which makes it a sacrifice. The pouring out of the blood, or whatever may be the vital essence, constitutes the essential gift because it is the symbol of the life consecrated and liberated to effect the union with the divine. Intercourse with divinity may be brought about, it is true, through presents whole and entire, sometimes on a *do-ut-des* bargain basis, so familiar in piacular sacrifices, but usually the life of the victim is required, actually or by symbolic ritual representation. The gift then is the offer-ing of the inherent vital principle, the death or destruction of the victim being incidental to the process of the liberation of its life by the pouring out of its blood.[23]

Indeed, this is a fundamental conception in the institution of sacrifice in all stages of its development from the crude anthro-pomorphic interpretations of deity to those of a highly spiritual evaluation. As Loisy says, 'to die is but to live again; life issues from death, and death is the condition and means of life. To destroy in order to create, to liberate through death, the power that lies latent in a living being.'[24] Therefore, the primary pur-pose of the sacrificial gift is to establish and maintain a vital bond of union between the worshipper and the object of wor-ship rather than ward off evil by bribes, or to remove it as a substantive miasma by cathartic agents, such as blood or water.

The Offering of the First-fruits

As the gift must be a life, actual or symbolical, immolated in order that life may be acquired in greater abundance, it readily becomes associated with the sacramental meal when the sacred flesh and blood of the victim is consumed by the offerers. Thus, in agricultural society the first-fruits of the soil often have been regarded as sacrificial food either because, having been dedi-cated to the god controlling the harvest, they were set apart and tabu, or because they were thought to embody the soul-substance, or life principle, of the vegetation spirit. Therefore, they have assumed the nature of a sacrificial victim and until they have undergone a process of desacralization the crops as a whole may not be eaten as ordinary food.

Vegetation being the offspring of Mother Earth and ani-mated by a sacral soul-substance analogous to that which animals share with man, the situation in an agricultural society is not very different from that which obtains among hunting tribes who have resorted to seasonal ceremonies of the Intichium type to secure an adequate food supply. The crops being the staple diet, their growth and harvesting call forth the same emotional reaction. Therefore, when the soil is prepared and later when the harvest is gathered the malevolent forces of evil equated with famine and pestilence must be overcome with those of good, identified with plenty and beneficence. This is achieved by vegetation rites having as their purpose the estab' lishment of a bond of union with the benevolent powers in order to secure their good offices, and to expel the malign influences by a fresh outpouring of vital potency.

Since blood is the life-giving agent *par excellence* it has played the principle role in this seasonal ritual, and, as in the Cain and Abel story in Hebrew tradition (Gen. iv, 1-5), it has generally been regarded as more efficacious than the bloodless oblation. Thus, among the Matabele of Southern Rhodesia the new crops were tabu until many oxen had been sacrificed during the desacralization ceremonies and the king had partaken of them; then, on the fourth day, they were distributed among the people.[25] In Northern Rhodesia the Yombe to the west of Lake Tanganyika forbade the first-fruits to be eaten until the chief had offered a bull before the tomb of his grandfather on the top of the Kalanga mountain, and had deposited in front of the shrine pots of freshly brewed beer and porridge made from the first-fruits. Then the ground around the tomb was care' fully weeded, and the blood of the bull was sprinkled on the soil. After the ghost of the grandfather had been thanked for the harvest and he had been asked to accept the gift of the first' fruits, the chief returned to the village where a feast was held on the carcass of the bull, the beer and porridge, followed by dancing.[26]

The Desacralization of the New Crops

In the south and west of Africa it has been a common custom for the chief or king alone to eat of the new crops in order to desacralize them, a ritual frequently accompanied by an animal, and sometimes a human, sacrifice.[27] This can be paralleled in Japan where among the Ainu the new millet had first to be ceremonially eaten by the old men in the form of cereal cakes. These they addressed as the cereal divinity and after thanking him for the fine crop of millet, they beseeched him to nourish the people. They then solemnly partook of the cakes in much the same manner as they killed with profuse apology and ate the bear cub at their bear-festival at the end of the winter.[28] A similar sacred meal is held by the Caffras of Natal and Zululand at the beginning of the new year in January when the king feeds each of his assembled people with some of the new fruits which have been boiled in large pots. This has a sanctifying effect for the rest of the year on those who partake of it.

In Mexico, among the Aztecs during the May festival in honour of Uitzilopochtli, the virgins fashioned an image of this war god in dough in which a quantity of beet seed and roasted maize were mingled and moulded with honey. It was next covered with a rich garment by noblemen and placed in a chair on a litter. Accompanied by maidens in white and young men in red robes, both crowned with garlands of maize, they then carried it in procession to the foot of a pyramid-shaped temple. In the court below the flight of steps up which they conveyed the image amid strains of music of flutes, trumpets, cornets and drums, to a shrine filled with roses, the people stood in reverence and awe. The virgins brought innumerable pieces of paste compounded with beets and roasted maize made in the shape of large bones. These, which represented the flesh and bones of Uitzilopochtli, were given to the young men, who laid them at the feet of the image. From the other temples priests and attendants adorned with garlands in like manner, and veils of diverse colours, each according to his rank, joined the procession and were followed by their gods and goddesses attired in the same livery. All having assembled themselves round the dough figure, the consecration rites to transform the pieces of paste into the flesh and bones of the deity began.

A number of human victims were then sacrificed and the youths and maids came forth from the temple in order of rank. A dance accompanied by drums began in which the nobles joined with them in an outer circle. Then the image was broken into very small fragments and given to the people who received the sacred food 'with such tears, fears and reverence as it was an admirable thing, saying that they did eat the flesh and bones of the god, wherewith they were grieved'. A strict fast was observed until after the ceremonies had ended, and the sick had also been communicated by a portion of the sacred food carried to them in their houses by their relatives.[29]

In December at the winter solstice an effigy of the same god was made in the likeness of man out of seeds of various kinds kneaded into dough and fortified with the blood of children, very much as in the May rites a large number of human sacri/ fices were offered when the image was consecrated. The bones of the deity were represented by pieces of acacia, and the figure thus constructed was placed upon the principal altar in the temple on the day of the festival to be censed by the king. The next day it was taken down and stood on its feet in a great hall to be pierced through with a flint/tipped dart by a priest impersonating the Toltec culture hero Quetzalcoatl. The heart was cut out by one of the priests and eaten by the king, while the rest of the effigy was broken into small fragments and con/ sumed by all the male members of the community including infants in the cradle. Women, however, were forbidden to par/ take of it or have any part in the teoqualo (i.e. the 'god is eaten') ceremony.[30] Similar smaller images of a paste of various seeds dressed in paper ornaments were venerated in houses at another festival at this season in Mexico; after food offerings had been made to these models at intervals during the night they were stabbed by priests at the break of day, their heads cut off and their hearts extracted to be presented to the head of the household on a green saucer. The bodies of the images were then eaten by the family and their servants ostensibly to ward off certain diseases.[31]

The main purpose of these sacrificial communions in which

gifts to the indwelling god were involved was that of securing the well-being of the maize, with the secondary aim of obtaining good health and a renewal of strength for those who partook of the food charged with the potency of the deity.

In North America the Natchez of Louisiana held a 'feast of grain' in the seventh moon, when the chief known as the Great Sun was seated in his royal estate on a litter upon the shoulders of warriors like the Aztec cereal image, and carried to a round granary outside the village. There he alighted, having first saluted the new corn thrice, and sat on his throne. New fire was made by friction and when everything was prepared for dressing the corn, it was solemnly cooked and distributed to the female Suns, and then to all the women who took it with haste to their huts to prepare it. This done, the Great Sun presented a plate of it to the four quarters of the earth, and ordered first the warriors and then the boys and women to eat it in their huts. Throughout the night a torchlight dance was held, and the following day two troops led by the Great Sun and the Chief of War respectively engaged in a violent contest with a ball of deer-skin. The proceedings concluded with the Great Sun being carried back on his litter, and the return of the people to their village.[32]

The great sanctity with which the new crops were regarded in the Mississippi valley and the desert to the east of the river, is shown by the drastic preparations for the observance in the Creek country in July and August when the corn was ripe. In addition to the extinguishing of all the fires in the village, the scouring of the cooking-vessels, and the sweeping of the public square by warriors, a strict fast was observed for two nights and a day which involved purging with emetics. New fire was then kindled by the high-priest and placed on the altar in the temple, and a basket of new fruits was offered to 'the bountiful holy spirit of fire, as a first-fruit offering and an animal oblation for sin'. The purifications completed, the new crops were dressed on the new fires and eaten with bear's oil, the men rubbing the corn between their hands and on their faces and breasts. For eight days the ceremonies continued and towards

the end of the festival the warriors fought a mock battle. Continence was strictly observed throughout the rites, and not until
the end did men and women dance together—a survival perhaps of the proceedings concluding with a sacred marriage.
Finally, having smeared themselves with white clay, they
bathed in running water to complete their purification and
regeneration.[33]

Since the permission of the chief was sought before the new
crops were eaten, it is not improbable that the act of desacralization was a precaution against their being gathered too soon;
nevertheless, it was their inherent sacredness that rendered them
tabu and gave them their sacramental character. Sometimes, as
among the Ainu and the Thompson River Indians, the mysterious vitality was interpreted in terms of a cereal divinity or a
corn spirit. In other cases it was more in the nature of an impersonal soul-substance capable of transference through a ritual
meal, and, like the Polynesian kava, the Vedic Soma, the
Avestan Haoma, and the Greek ambrosia, it was endowed
with supernatural properties as a life-giving agent. Thus, the
eating of this sacred food and the drinking of these sacred
beverages, which originally seem to have been confined to
chiefs and kings in their sacral capacity, bestowed health,
wisdom and immortality by virtue of the qualities imparted to
the recipients of them at their consecration.

Similarly, the effigies composed of newly cut seedlings, or
the last sheaf of corn in which the vegetation spirit was thought
to reside, often in the form of a maiden or an old woman, imparted the supernatural powers and properties inherent in the
first-fruits. When the corn spirit was regarded as a 'mother',
originally personifying the goddess, the image might be made
by one of the elder women in the village, as in Styria, its first
ears being plucked out to be made into a wreath carried by the
prettiest girl. The effigy was placed on the top of a pile of wood
during the harvest supper and dance, and then hung up in the
barn till the threshing was over, and the wreath was dedicated
in the church. At Christmas the image was placed in the crib
to make the cattle thrive, and on Holy Saturday the grain was

rubbed out of it and scattered among the young corn by a seventeen-year-old girl.[34]

Behind rites of this nature, which are of common occurrence in the peasant cultures of Central Europe and elsewhere, is the idea of ensuring the continued prosperity of the crops through the transmission of the potency inherent in either the first-fruits or the last sheaf, symbolized by the figure of the Great Mother as the source of fertility. Thus, in Westphalia, the last sheaf is frequently designated the 'Great Mother' or 'Grandmother', and is adorned with flowers, ribbons and an apron.[35] In Peru it was thought to conceive and give birth to the maize and so was venerated with sacred dances before it was burnt sacrificially to obtain an abundant crop of the cereal during the forthcoming season.[36]

But the cutting and ingathering of the crops involves what is virtually the sacrifice of the indwelling vegetation spirit so that the harvest becomes intimately associated with the ancient theme of the dying and reviving year-god who personified the seasonal sequence in agricultural communities. Consequently, there is always the fear of incurring the revenge of the slain divinity who might cause the failure of the crops by the withdrawal of her fertilizing powers, or mete out some form of vengeance upon those responsible for her death. Thus, in the Highlands of Scotland there was a struggle to escape from being the last to cut corn and so having to feed until the next harvest the 'famine of the farm' in the shape of an old woman called Cailleach.[37] Furthermore, she was supposed to bring disaster upon the crops of the unfortunate last reaper. It was not, however, only at the ingathering of harvest that the Cailleach was to be feared. At Christmas the head of the house often went to a wood on Christmas Eve, cut down a tree stump, carved it into the resemblance of an old woman, the Cailleach Nollich, carried it home and placed it on a peat fire as the Yule log sacrificed to propitiate the angel of death, in the hope that he would refrain from visiting the house during the year. Therefore, the vegetation spirit has become associated with death as well as with the renewal and revivification of the crops. In this dual capacity it was virtually a sacrificial victim.

Expiation and Atonement

Since the slaying of the Corn-mother involves also the renewal of the evil impeding the stream of life, the negative side of the institution of sacrifice inheres within the twofold purpose of these vegetation rites. On the one hand, the vitality embodied in the first-fruits or the last sheaf is regarded as having quick-ening and fertilizing power. On the other hand, the symbol has a sinister significance connected with famine and death. This, however, is only the expression of the age-long dual endeavour to expel evil in order to secure good—'out with famine, in with health and wealth'—in order to drive forth death and to gain life. The demonic power residing in the soil and its products has to be rendered harmless by an expulsion and expiation ritual regarded as an atoning sacrifice. Death is met with an outpouring of life on behalf of the person making the oblation, and an atonement for evil or misfortune incurred is made by way of expiation in order to re-establish right relations with the sacred order and the gods on whom well-being de-pends.

As for the primitive mind the good is primarily life, health, abundance and prosperity, and evil is death, sickness, barren-ness and famine, each under the control of transcendental forces, everything that prevents or impedes providential beneficence has to be removed and counteracted by ritual devices, tech-niques and institutions: of these the piaculum is the most out-standing example by reason of its efficacy and potency, often involving a human victim. But any disaster or misfortune is always liable to be regarded as a manifestation of divine dis-pleasure requiring propitiation by way of atonement, to remove the cause and occasion of the evil manifestations. Since the anger of the gods, however incurred, finds expression in the failure of the crops, outbreaks of plague and sickness, and similar calamities, it is appeased and reconciliation effected by the offering of a sacrificial oblation, or by some expulsion or cathartic means, such as a 'scapegoat' or sin-carrier, ablutions, and other purifying agents.

Although this ritual removal of sin and error may be little more than a mechanical 'wiping away' or 'covering' of pollution, expiatory offerings entailing the death of a victim involve the idea of substitution of its life for that of the sacrificer with whom it is identified at its consecration. As Emerson recognized, a gift to be true must be the flowing of the giver to the receiver, and of the recipient to the donor,[38] a principle which finds its highest expression in altruistic self-giving whereby a life is laid down voluntarily in order to give life in greater abundance and to eliminate harmful and evil forces and influences. The animal victim can only assume this role by being set apart as a substitute for and a symbol of the offerer with whom it thereby becomes identified.

At a higher level the sacral king or chief invested with divine power may be called upon either to renew his royal potency by a ritual act of some kind, or by sacrificing himself (in person or in a substitute) for the good of his people in order that his power may be passed on to his more vigorous and virile successor. By offering himself vicariously in a representative capacity to renew at its dynamic centre the life of the community over which he reigns he becomes at once priest and victim. Like the rising sun from which in Egypt and elsewhere he so often claimed descent, he may rise and set, but the throne remains unshaken because as the source of potency its occupant is for ever young and virile, crowned with honour and glory. Actually he has been regarded as the substitute of the god dying for his people so that royal divine power may be preserved and a rich harvest ensue. But a pseudo-temporary king invested with his potency for a given period has been immolated in his stead very much as the real king has himself been a substitute for the god and the divine representative of the tribe or nation. It has been the vicarious sacrifice that has mattered. Therefore, when the offering was transferred to the ritual sphere the priesthood responsible for the oblation, as the masters of sacrifice, notably in Vedic India, took the place of the king who then receded into the background leaving the Brahmins in supreme control of the ritual technique upon which the existence of the universe and the gods depended.

By the act of consecration the victim, be it a human being, an animal, or its vegetation equivalent, is identified with the sacri, ficer so that the life of the one is usually inseparable from that of the other; the king, for instance, being at once priest and victim, sacrifices his life in his representative capacity or by consecrating an animal to make it an integral part of himself. In the case of the piaculum, by virtue of the principle of sub, stitution the evil or pollution is eliminated, expelled or pro, pitiated through a process of transference of the sin or guilt or defilement to the victim. Therefore, when the sin,receiver is destroyed or driven forth the evil is destroyed or expelled because the victim is identified with the sinner and his sin, and by his death his life is liberated as an expiation to remove the guilt or pollution contracted by the sacrificer.

CHAPTER II

Priesthood and Sacrifice

ANCIENT EGYPT

No preliminary survey of the institution of sacrifice and of the sacramental principle would be complete without an examination of the place and function of priesthood since at all times and everywhere the priest is the master of sacrifice. This always has been his first responsibility, the *raison d'être* of the sacerdotal office, existing for the express purpose of effecting and maintaining the vital bond of communion between man and his god or gods upon which not only his own well-being depends but that of the whole creative process. Sacrifice is the dynamic centre of this relationship. Thus in the hieratic type of society that characterized the rise of civilization in the Fertile Crescent, notably in Egypt, from the fourth millennium B.C. and onwards, the interrelation between the priesthood and the sacral kingship found its fullest expression.

The Royal Priesthood in Egypt

Since in the Nile valley the Pharaoh was regarded as a god incarnate he was at once the mediator between the divinities he embodied and the priest *par excellence* by virtue of his divine nature. At first he was identified with Horus, who may have been either one of the falcon gods in predynastic Egypt, or the local god of Buto who early became associated with Re, the Sun-god of Heliopolis. After the conquest of Upper Egypt by the Lower Kingdom the cult of Horus was established at Edfu (Behdet), and with the union of the country as a single nation Horus the Behdetite became the predominant figure in the kingship. However, at the time of the Fifth Dynasty (*c.* 2580 B.C.) the powerful Heliopolitan priesthood in order to enhance its own prestige made the reigning Pharaoh the son of Re, the Sun-god, of whom they were the official representatives. In due course, under the influence of the Osiris myth, the reigning king became Horus, the posthumous son of Osiris, the popular predynastic deity of the Eastern Delta. Osiris combined the roles of a human king or chief, a culture hero and lord of the realms of the dead after his resurrection achieved by his devoted wife Isis. Having surrounded the throne with all the glamour and prestige of a solar significance and descent and incorporated Osiris in the Heliopolitan Ennead, thereby adding universal sovereignty to the Pharaoh in his Horus capacity, the priesthood secured preeminence and consolidated the nation on a hieratic basis. The divinity of the king was firmly established, both by his descent from the gods and as the heir of Osiris whose claims had been vindicated by the gods of Heliopolis against those of his rival Seth.[1]

For cult purposes, as every god was in theory an Osiris so every living king was a Horus and the high priest of every god. In all important ceremonies he alone was depicted in the temple scenes as the officiant, and the performance of the funerary ritual at first was his sole privilege. At the death of a Pharaoh, who then became Osiris and was reunited with his heavenly father Re, in the celestial realms, his successor was duly installed in the divine office in accordance with the hereditary principle inherent in the sacred monarchy and the prescribed rites. To avoid any possible complications with regard to the succession, the heirapparent acted as a coregent during the lifetime of the reigning sovereign, and was described as 'Horus appearing in the arms of his father Osiris'. So he automatically acceded to the throne at dawn on the day of the death of the old Pharaoh. Then all that was required was the transfer of the royal office and its prerogatives to the new king, by coronation and investiture with the insignia at the beginning of one of the three seasons, the kingship being so intimately connected with the renewal of nature and growth of the crops.[2]

Exactly what took place on these occasions can only be conjectured from the daily 'Toilet Ceremonies' performed by the reigning Pharaoh which seem to have been a reproduction of the coronation ritual and the Mystery Play of the Succession

of Senusert', the second king of the Twelfth Dynasty.[3] From
these sources, it is very likely that he was first asperged and
then censed to unite him with Horus, and given balls of
natron to chew to complete his daily rebirth and renewal. He
then ascended the stairs to the great window to behold his
celestial father, the Sun-god, was vested, anointed and crowned
with the royal diadem of Upper and Lower Egypt, and was
presented with the flail and crook or sceptre.[4] These installation rites were preceded apparently by visits to a number of
towns in the royal barge; at each of these the new sovereign
played the role of Horus in the portrayal of his victory over
Seth and the dismemberment of Osiris in a vegetation setting,
and his revival by his son. The proceedings concluded with investiture scenes, censings, the distribution of bread, the singing
of dirges by women personifying Isis and Nephthys lamenting
over the mutilated body of Osiris, followed by his restoration,
ascent to the sky and a banquet.

Sacramental Regeneration

Thus, it appears to have been the drama of the death and
resurrection of Osiris, coupled with the daily solar renewal
ritual, that were enacted at the coronation installation. These
accession rites were repeated in the temple liturgy when at
dawn the cult-image was treated in the same manner by the
priests as the official deputies of the Pharaoh. In this capacity
they impersonated the king in the daily worship in the temples
in his role of the son of the Sun-god, and of that of Horus. The
Toilet Ceremonies were a sacramental ritual of rebirth derived
from that celebrated on behalf of Re at Heliopolis. As it was
based on the coronation installation, it had a re-creative significance shown in the preliminary purification of the priest in
the water of the sacred pool—identified with the primeval
ocean (Nun) that gave birth to Re. The solemn opening of the
doors of the shrine and the censing of the image, the renewal of
its garments and ornaments and its re-investiture with royal
apparel and insignia, completed the regeneration. The process
concluded with the presentation of food and drink offerings

typifying a sacramental meal of which the dead were also sup/ posed to partake.[5] On the anniversaries of the birthday of the god, and on certain other occasions, the offerings were in/ creased and were shared among the worshippers in a common feast. Thus, the sacramental banquet remained an essential feature in the daily temple liturgy, having been incorporated in the Heliopolitan rite.

Lustration, again, had a sacramental significance, as water was regarded as the principal regenerative agent—the life/ giving essence of the primeval ocean, the matrix of the Sun/ god, out of which his incarnate son on earth was reborn each morning. Water, therefore, became the medium of regenera/ tion and, as such, it was a vital element in the daily worship: each temple was equipped with a sacred pool in which the priest purified himself on his arrival before proceeding to the shrine to asperge the cult/image and make lustrations before it in the mask of the god he impersonated.[6]

The Temple Ritual

The Osirianization of the temple liturgy in the Fifth Dynasty did not materially affect the solar Heliopolitan sacramental ritual because the inundation of the Nile was equated with the fluid that issued from the corpse of Osiris, which was alleged to have been concealed in a tomb at Elephantine, the First Cataract. At the approach of the annual flood, Geb, the Earth/god, was represented in the Pyramid Texts as saying to Osiris, 'the divine fluid that is in thee cries out, thy heart lives, thy divine limbs move, thy joints are loosed'. In other words, the waters that bring life to the soil proceed from the resurrec/ tion of Osiris. Similarly, in the hymns of the New Kingdom he is identified with Hapi, the fertilizing god of the Nile, and gods and men are said to live by the moisture that is in him.[7] In short, Osiris was the imperishable principle of life bringing forth abundance every year as 'the Water of Renewal' rises, and Isis, 'the wife of the Lord of the Inundation' and 'Creatrix of the Nile flood', was the fruitful land irrigated and fertilized by her brother/spouse the begetter. As the power of the Nile, she was identified with Satis, the goddess of the Cataract; as the producer of fecundity by her waters, she was called Anget; as the giver of life, she was Ankhet; and as the lady of the Under, world, Amant, she shared with Osiris the attribute of 'giver of life' and became the female counterpart of the primeval watery abyss from which all life sprang.[8]

The cult of Isis, however, differed from that of Osiris in that it centred in the mystery of birth rather than of life issuing from death. The connecting link between the two aspects of the Osirian ritual was the Nile. Thus, a festival of Isis was held at the summer solstice when she was mourning for her husband and making the Nile swell and overflow by her tears.[9] The sign of the rising was the appearance in the sky of the star Sirius on June 15, and this was called 'Isis,Sothis'—'she who maketh the Nile to swell in his season at the beginning of the new year' —by whose benign influence the grain grew, gardens produced abundance and fruit ripened. As Osiris was Lord of the grain, so Isis was the Goddess of the crops, the personification of the tilled lands and the harvest fields; she represented the fertile earth fructified by the life,giver whose death and resurrection were celebrated in the autumn and the spring with all the wealth of symbolism, pageantry and ritual of the great Egyp, tian festivals, combining intense lamentation and exultant joy. But Isis had her daily worship, too, in which her votaries enjoyed communion with her sacramentally when her image was exposed by her priests, asperged with libations of Nile water, censed, vested, adorned and adored, like that of the Sun,god. But it was the Inundation with all its sacramental efficacy that was the common source of life and regenerative power in the cultus of the Osirian hero and heroine.

Behind this sacred drama of death and resurrection, its lustra, tions and banquets, lay the royal priesthood in all its com, plexity in which the sacrificial and sacramental elements were so deeply laid. In his solar and Osirian aspects the Pharaoh was the embodiment and representative of the nation, its dynamic centre, upon whose daily ministrations in his cere, monial office the well,being and prosperity of the Nile valley depended. He was, in short, the epitome of all that was divine, at once god, high-priest and sovereign ruler, bestowing his gifts upon the country by virtue of his mediatorial sacerdotal func/ tions, particularly in relation to the inundation so vital for the welfare of Egypt. In the daily temple liturgy and in the mor/ tuary ritual at the tombs, Isis deputies had to maintain the sacrificial routine of offerings to deities and for the benefit and use of the deceased beyond the grave. These often took the form of a banquet, or sacred meal, in which the living and departed shared; the priests, as in Israel in the days of Eli, claiming the largest and choicest portions. But even these sacrifices were made in the name of the king, designated as 'an offering which the king gives', he being in theory the only priest. Therefore all sacrifices, apart from simple mortuary gifts of food, ushabti figures, and other grave goods, were thought of in essence as royal oblations (*hip-di-nsw-t*) by virtue of the sacerdotal status of the Pharaoh.[10] As he was believed in fact to be the god he represented on a particular occasion and for a specific purpose, so the priest who deputized for him in the temples shared in his divinity and priesthood for the time being, though he was not actually himself divine in his own nature as was the king.

VEDIC INDIA

The Vedic Kingship and the Brahmanic Priesthood

In Vedic India on the other hand, the king became subordinate to the priesthood when the existence of the universe and all cosmic processes—even the gods—were made to depend upon the sacri/ ficial offering rather than on the divinely established throne as in Egypt. It is true that in the Code of Manu, variously dated from 300 B.C. to A.D. 150, the king is described as 'a great deity in human form' whom Brahman created for the protection of the world from the eternal particles of Indra, of Yama, of the Sun and of the Moon, of Fire, of Varuna, and of Kubera, thereby assigning to him divine status. 'He showers benefits upon his realm as Indra sends rain upon the earth; he must be as omnipresent as the wind; he must control all his subjects as does Yama; he must draw revenues from his kingdom as the sun draws water from the earth; he must be brilliant and blazing anger against crime like the radiance of fire; he must bind criminals as the fetters of Varuna enchain the wicked; he must be beautiful in the sight of his subjects as is the moon in the eyes of mankind; like the earth he must support all his subjects.'[11]

Much earlier in the *Rig-Veda*, dating from about 15,000 to 12,000 B.C., in a hymn attributed to Trasadasyu, the Puru king claimed to be the gods Indra and Varuna, and the recipient of the energies characteristic of the Asuras.[12] This association with the gods who gave life and birth suggests that originally he was the bestower of universal beneficence, as elsewhere in the Ancient World. As the Sun-god, he was the motive force and the fertilizing agent; as Mitra, he was Lord of justice; as Indra, he was the controller of storms and the giver of victory; as Varuna, he regulated the moral order and upheld the uni-verse; as Agni, he was equated with the sacred fire and sacri-ficial flame by which all creation was sustained. But as he was not himself invested with authority to offer sacrifice, the priests became responsible for upholding all things in heaven and on earth by their sacerdotal functions. Therefore, since it was they who virtually controlled the gods as well as the processes of creation, the Brahmanic priesthood usurped the position pre-viously occupied by the sacral kingship.

Every aspect of supernatural power fell within the domain of the Brahmins, who were not only masters of the all-sustaining sacrifice but who also formed a particular caste of divine origin, said to have been brought forth from the mouth of Brahma. This caste, the first manifestation of the Absolute, was subsequently divided into three orders each with its own special sacrificial duties. Thus, the stage was set at a very early period for the ultimate predominance of the Brahmins. Al-though no attempt was made to establish a hieratic temple organization as in Egypt and Mesopotamia, by securing for themselves exclusively the knowledge of the Brahmanic texts and their ritual techniques, transmitted through the sacerdotal blood, they held the secret of the universe in their grasp. They alone knew precisely how the cosmic order could be sustained, and only they were qualified to perform the necessary rites effectively. This was facilitated by the prevailing Vedic conception of a single pantheistic divine principle, *Rta*, beyond the gods governing alike the mundane and the transcendental orders, and associated particularly with Varuna, the king of heaven, and with Agni the lord of sacrifice. It only required the Brahmanic ritual technology to be identified with *Rta*, and the altar to be regarded as 'the womb of *Rta*', to establish the supremacy of the priestly offering and to render the position of the Brahmins absolute.

The wielders of supreme power then became the agents of an impersonal dynamic process immanent in the cosmos, interpreted in sacrificial terms. In the *RigVeda* the world was represented as fashioned from the body of the Primal Man, Purusha, with his thousand heads, eyes and feet pervading the earth. In the *Brahmanas*, the ritual texts compiled between 800 and 500 B.C., when the priestly caste had come into being, 'the Lord of Creatures' Prajapati, the personification of the creative principle, who was at once creator and creation, pervaded pantheistically the universal cosmic and moral orders as the ruler of macrocosm and microcosm. By his primal sacrifice at the hands of the gods the universe was created as the several parts of his body, and the original cosmic unity was reconstituted by the repetition of the sacrifice by the Brahmins. 'As the sacrifice is the god Prajapati at his own sacrifice', so the priests became Prajapati and renewed the creative processes by the due performance of the sacrificial offering.[13]

The FireAltar

This was portrayed in the symbolism of the FireAltar described in very great detail in the *Satapatha Brahmana* (Books vi–x), where the Altar represented the structure of the universe, the sacred Vedas and the broken and restored body of the Creator. Composed of a quantity of bricks built up in seven layers in the form of a falcon, a firepan was carefully fashioned in its midst as a reproduction of the creation of the universe, for 'the sacrificer who makes the fire-pan thereby makes the world'. And as it is also the 'self' of Agni, the sacred sacrificial fire, the fire of the sun, the cosmic fire, and the priest of the gods, 'he who makes the fire-pan thereby makes Agni'.[14] Moreover, as Agni was also equated with the sun, he was born afresh every morning when the flame was kindled by the fire-sticks of the priests in order to re-create the life that pervaded and sustained the universe. Therefore, since Agni became identified with Prajapati as a cosmic sacrificial figure, the building of the Fire-Altar was a repetition of creation, and its restoration typified the bringing back of life to the dismembered body of the Lord of Creatures,[15] reminiscent of the re-animation of Osiris in the Egyptian renewal ritual.

Indeed, this remarkable Vedic rite and its symbolism was to all intents and purposes a repetition of its counterparts in the sacrificial cultus in the Fertile Crescent. The priests in a divine capacity played virtually the same role as the sacral king in the seasonal drama of regeneration, and for the same purpose; namely, to ensure the continuance of the cosmic order and the prosperity of the community. In the background of the Vedic Fire-Altar was a royal ritual in which the king as the embodi-ment of many gods doubtless made an offering to Agni with whom he became identified by sacrifice, thereby becoming the Fire-god.[16] The Brahmins usurping these royal prerogatives became the chief actors in the impersonal cosmic drama in which every part of the altar was equated with some part of the universe and the god who was responsible for it. The victim also represented the universe, and its parts were the parts of the universe. Thus, in the case of the cosmic sacrificial horse, the head was the dawn, the eyes the sun, the breath the wind, the back the sky, the belly the air, of the seasons.[17] The sacrificer in becoming the sacrifice was united with the universe in all its parts, resolved into a unity and sustained by a cosmic offering in which the body of the Creator (Prajapati) was broken anew and restored for the conservation of the world.

The Brahmanic Caste Organization

This represents the most extreme expression of the Brahmanic conception of priesthood and sacrifice arising within a rigidly established caste segmentation of *varnas* supposed to have sprung from the body of the Creator as fixed states of life. Although the foundations of this feature of Indian society and religious organization stereotyped in the Institutes of Manu lie deep in the Hindu social structure, it was superimposed on a much more fluid situation in its developed form in which the sacerdotal office was not hereditary. In the age of the *Rig-Veda* when the later aspect of sacrifice was beginning to emerge, it still existed side by side with the domestic cult of the household priest who often was in the employ of the king as 'chaplain'.

The offering was made to secure the favour and beneficence of the gods, and a common meal of a quasi-sacramental nature was held on the flesh of the sacrificial victim to establish closer relations with the god to whom it had been offered. Though the Brahmins came to be regarded as the head of the Creator, and the Kshatriyas, or warriors, his arms, all the several parts of the one divine body were a multiplicity in unity so that a Kshatriya could become a Brahmin, or vice versa. But as the more specialized conception of the cosmic sacrificial offering became established the complexity of the ritual was such that it was known only to the Brahmins and performed by four groups headed by four chief-priests, each of which was responsible for its own particular functions—invocation (*Hotri*), chanting, the ritual actions and utterances—under the guidance of the chief Brahmin. Symbolic significance then was attached to the minutiae of the ceremonies as a principle feature in the Brahmana texts in which magic and religion were so intermingled as to be indistinguishable.

It was against this mechanical magical sacerdotalism and its caste organization that, about 600 B.C., the Upanishadic reaction introduced a mystical reinterpretation of the sacrifice. Even in the Brahmanas there are indications that knowledge rather than sacrificial gifts is the ultimate goal,[18] but it remained for the *Brhadaranyaka Upanishad* to interpret the horse sacrifice as a meditative act in which the contemplative mystic rather than the sacrificial priest offers up the universe in place of the horse, and by a supreme act of renunciation attains the identification of the individual self (*atman*) with the cosmic divine Reality (*Brahman*)—*tat tvam tsi*, 'That thou art'.[19]

This opened the way for the rejection of the exclusive claims of the Brahmins to be the masters of sacrifice and the inter-preters of the Veda, the significance of which was discounted in favour of mystical insight and knowledge. With the rise of Jainism and Buddhism the hereditary claims of Brahmin superiority were rejected together with the caste system. In Hinduism, however, in due course, sacrifice and the study of the Veda were rehabilitated and brought into relation with the Upanishadic tradition with the establishment of four *asramas*, or stages of life, the highest of which is the Brahmin who brings a spiritual rule into life. Radhakrishnan, in fact, maintained that 'the true Brahmin is one who has sensed the deepest self and acts out of that consciousness.' Having found knowledge he communicates it to others giving moral guidance, but they reveal without enforcing, practical administration not being their task. 'They lay down the science of values, draw out the blue-prints for social reconstruction, and persuade the world to accept the high ends of life.'[20]

Although this is an idealized conception of the Brahmanic priesthood it is true that 'a class of disinterested seekers after truth supported by society, influencing it and placed above the corrupting tendency of power', in spite of the anomalies of the caste system, has been a potent element in social stability in Hindu India.[21] Therefore, the priestly offering as the all-sustaining rite which gave the Brahmins their unique position in the cosmic order and in the social structure, supplemented by the Upanishadic, Vedantic and Mimamsa sublimations, has produced a consolidating hieratic organization in the sub-continent firmly established on a transcendental basis detached from the vagaries of the transient and the temporal. Being the masters of the sacrifice that sustains the universe, their function, as a sacerdotal caste in a closely integrated hierarchy, has been to control this transcendental divine principle pervading the phenomenal world.

But the absence of a Deity with whom personal relations are possible has placed the emphasis on the institution of priest/ hood as the means by which impersonal divine power (*Brah/ man*) is manipulated and dispensed rather than on the sacer/ dotal instrumentality of a living God whose priests are his servants and representatives. In Hinduism the sacrifice became a world process executed with automatic precision by those who had the requisite equipment, before it was transformed into an intuitive identification of the Atman with the Brahman. Then ritual technology underwent a profound change, the Brahmin becoming a mystic and an ascetic, and in Jainism and Buddhism he dropped out of the picture altogether.

Jain and Buddhist Orders

Nevertheless, in both these non/theistic sectarian movements a monastic system was evolved which to some extent carried on the Brahmanic tradition, even though the Veda, caste and sacrifice were abandoned together with Upanishadic mysti/ cism. The Jain monks and nuns were primarily ascetics devoted to the quest of perfection by absolute abstinence from the taking of life in any state or form, and to the pursuit of chastity and truthfulness. Their beliefs involved complete detachment from any person, property or possessions, and the adoption of a mendicant life of meditation and spiritual exercises, which included the confession of sin. In the Digambara and Svetam/ bara sects a temple cultus centred round the veneration of a divine being Tirthankara.

In the case of Buddhism many of the earliest converts were Brahmins, and although the ascetic element was very con/ siderably modified and relinquished, a monastic organization was adopted with prescribed robes, a daily routine of offices, which included the collection of alms, and the study, exposi/ tion and translation of the sacred texts and theological works. The principal object of the members of these congregations being to attain self/perfection, the goal of the *bhikku*, they were

open to all healthy free men over twenty years of age, and later—
with some reluctance—to women. Through a graded system
of progression towards Arahanship, beginning with the novitiate, the monks endeavoured to reach the final state of enlightenment and the attainment of the passionless peace of Nib-
bana. Their public administrations at births, marriages, times
of sickness, and occasions requiring incantations, were usually
performed in private houses rather than temples. As priestly
functions were not required in the absence of sacrificial worship, their offices were chiefly restricted to invocations and the
recitation of the texts, and were attended only by the resident
members of the Order. They did not admit of lay participation.
Only in Tantric Buddhism in Tibet is there a Lamistic
hierarchy with the Dalai Lama as the vice-regent of the Buddha
officiating as a priest in a quasi-liturgical cultus in which
Western elements have been incorporated.

Nevertheless, in the Mahayana northern school of Buddhism, the spiritual assistance of the deified Buddha and the grace-
bestowing power of the bodhisattvas have acquired some of the
characteristics of sacerdotalism. In this tradition are the pro-
phylactic and incantational recitations of the sacred texts by the
monks, and the shrines erected in the temples to the honour of
the Buddha where the image of the Blessed One seated on a
lotus bedecked with floral offerings is honoured. The more
sophisticated bonzes, it is true, regard these invocations as a
subjective spiritual discipline, the Buddha being unconscious,
but in popular devotion it is believed to be a method of acquiring merit, like the repetition of a sacred formula such as *Namu-
O-mi-to*, or *Amida-Butzu*, or the recitation of a Sutra. Nevertheless, as these exercises do not require the presence of a priest and
have no sacrificial significance, they can hardly be described as
sacerdotal.

Indeed, Buddhism apart from Tantric magic has never
developed a hierarchic segmentation and a genuine priesthood
because it has interpreted unity in terms of Becoming instead of
in those of Being, and replaced the Atman by its negation
Anatta, the unreality of the Self. Enlightenment can be gained

only by man's own insight and efforts, and no human interme-diary can be of any avail in this quest. If any assistance is to be obtained to this end, as Mahayana at length conceded, it could only come from divine sources in which human mediation had no part.

The Theistic Conception of Priesthood

In the West, on the other hand, the concepts of 'mediation' and 'representation' in the establishment and maintenance of a right and beneficial relationship between man and the living God are fundamental. Standing between the two extremes of a wholly transcendent extramundane unconditioned Absolute, and an intramundane immanental principle in which God and the world are merged in a monistic or pantheistic unity, the great Western theisms regard the Creator as the sovereign ruler of all things and yet at work in the universe which he has created, ordering the course of events in accordance with his will and purpose.

As the most real Being and the centre and essence of all that is other than himself, the Creator is distinct from the pheno-menal order: as the intelligent self-conscious omniscient will and the highest good, he is the living unity of existence and values in a vital relationship with his creation. An Abso-lute monistically or pantheistically conceived involves the absence of external relations, leaving the All either as a deistic Creator completely dissociated from the universe, or as the sole Reality of which man and nature are partial manifestations and emanations, lacking permanence and individuality, or even independent existence when the phenomenal order is regarded as illusory (Maya). Such a conception of divinity finds ex-pression in a mystical experience of impersonal unity with the Absolute, everything proceeding from the One and leading back to the ultimate Source of all Reality in a cyclic process of emancipation, absorption and identity. This precludes a per-sonal relationship with a living active God whose sovereign will has called the entire created universe into being, transcend-ing the cosmic process and its ritual control.

It is in this theistic context that priesthood normally has exercised its sacrificial functions. Enormous as was the power of priesthood as the master of sacrifice in Brahmanism, it so completely overshadowed that of the gods that they became merely names or symbols for certain powers and principles liberated by the sacerdotal ritual. Apart from the sacrificial rite, the gods in fact had no independent existence or function as personal beings. All individuality was submerged in the priestly office and its offering until it was reduced to one event —the universal sacrifice of the Primal Man, Purusha, from which everything emanated. The Western affirmation of the individual personality stands in striking contrast to the oriental quest for perfection in uniting the self with the Abso-lute, for losing the Atman in Brahman as a river loses itself in the sea.

Once this was accomplished, however, in Upanishadic my-sticism, the ritual order become an anachronism and both sacri-fice and the priesthood lost their vital significance. A theistic interpretation in terms of the concept of a personal Deity at once transcendent and immanent results in a very different situation.

Then the intervention of a human agent, often like the vic-tim, in a mediatorial capacity, becomes increasingly apparent because when Deity is thought of as a Person disclosing him-self and dispensing his divine power to persons for specific purposes, the relationship between God and man and the universe must be maintained. As the accredited and spiritually endowed representatives on earth of the God or gods under whom they serve, the priests are set apart by their ordination or consecration to establish, maintain and restore intercourse and adjustment between the sacred and the secular orders.

As this equilibrium is always liable to be disturbed either deliberately through human frailty and perverseness, or in-advertently by accident or ignorance, the balance has to be con-stantly restored by the prescribed ritual techniques and devices of which sacrifice is the most important and significant institu-tion.

JUDAISM

The Priesthood and the Levites in Judaism

As the master of sacrifice and ritual science the priest in his capacity of mediator is the stabilizing influence in the religious organization, the social structure, and the personal adjustment of the individual in his relations with the supernatural world. At the theistic level mediation involves a more spiritual bond which finds expression in a covenant organization transcending the interactions within the community. Thus, in Judaism the hierarchy and the temple sacrificial cultus became the unifying theocratic centre after the Exile. This may have begun during the reforms of Hezekiah and Josiah in the seventh century B.C.[22] when the focus of worship was concentrated at Jerusalem, and the way was opened for the priestly office to be restricted to the Levitical house of Aaron, segregated ritualistically like the Brahmins. Prior to this sacerdotal movement in the seventh century in Israel the priests were drawn from several lines of descent—those of Zadok, Nathan, Micah and Abinadab, as well as the royal line of David and the Asaronite Levitical succession.[23] Whether in fact the Levites ever were a sacerdotal tribe is open to question, but in any case neither Joshua nor Samuel were members of it.[24]

Without having a monopoly of the service of the altar the Levites were the guardians of the sanctuary and like Moses, Aaron and Samuel they were seers as well as priests, having knowledge of the commandments of Yahweh and engaging in oracular and prophetic functions, often of an ecstatic nature as *Nebi'im*. Their claims, however, were not unchallenged as were those of the Brahmins in India, judging from the stories of the alleged rivalries in the desert between Moses and his allies and the non-Aaronite Levites, of whom Dathan, Korah and Abiram, Miriam the prophetess and the enigmatic Aaron, were the centres of disaffection. These rivalries doubtless were reflections of profound jealousies and antagonisms among rival priestly confraternities and their respective sanctuaries (e.g. Dan, Shilo, Bethel and Jerusalem).[25] It was not until after the Exile that the distinction between priests and Levites became absolute, and the priesthood was assigned exclusively to the Aaronite succession in spite of the descent of the Zado׳ kites from Eleazer.[26]

The centralization of worship at Jerusalem, and the reaction against the local shrines stimulated by the Josiah reformation, had given the sons of Zadok precedence in the temple sacrificial ritual. After the fall of the capital in 538 B.C. in the post׳exilic temple only the faithful Zadokites, duly arrayed in their sacer׳ dotal vestments, were permitted to make the oblation of the blood poured out at the altar, and the defaulting Levites, who had gone astray at the local shrines, were relegated to menial service as doorkeepers and slayers of the burnt offerings.[27] With the promulgation of the Priestly Code towards the end of the fifth century B.C. the Aaronic succession was re׳established, the descendants of Aaron being alone permitted to offer sacri׳ fice, though the privilege was also granted to those tracing their descent from Ithamar as well as by Eleazer; the latter were none other than the sons of Zadok. The Levites were assigned their subordinate duties as servants of the sanctuary, and the cultic functionaries subsequently were merged with them to form the personnel of the choirs (*Nethinion*) under Levitical direction.[28] Thus, Levites and cultic prophets were brought under the dominion of the Aaronite priesthood with its sacerdotal status and prerogatives.

The Temple Cultus in Post׳exilic Judaism

Therefore, when the nation was restored to its own land after the Exile the ritual tradition and the Priestly school became pre׳ dominant, with the temple and its cultus as the consolidating centre. Prophecy had fulfilled its function, and although its influence was still felt in the re׳establishment of the exiles the temple worship was the principal force. Haggai and Zechariah, in their efforts to restore the temple, endeavoured to combine ethics and ritualism and to bring the people back to their god through an elaborate prescribed order of sacrifice. Already Ezekiel had prepared the way by his emphasis on a meticulous observance of ceremonial minutiae and regulations. These concerned the age, kind and sex of the victims to be offered on different days in the sequence of fast and festival, and extended to details of priestly vestures and behaviour interpreted as divine revelations.[29] Moreover, the Law, canonized as the verbally inspired Word of God to Moses, made prophecy of secondary importance, and the whole body of tradition, ordinances and rules of conduct embodied in the Levitical Torah gave the Levites increasing prominence and prestige, as they had authoritative knowledge of the divine prescriptions.

The observance of the Sabbath and the rest of the ritual order centred in the sacrificial temple cultus produced a reaction against visionary experience and oracular divinatory exercises. As the earliest visions were detached from their origin and given an eschatological significance, prophecy became apocalyptic. The prosperity of the nation depended upon the regular offering of the prescribed sacrifices without blemish to Yahweh and their acceptance by him. But while immoral and unjust practices were not condoned, ethical conduct was subordinated to ritual requirements.[30] It is clear, however, from the Psalms of the period that the temple and its worship were held in great veneration in Jerusalem and among Jews of the Dispersion far and wide. Much as they loved the stately processions and sacrificial offerings, they realized the deeper spiritual realities behind them and their ceremonial called forth genuine expressions of penitence, piety and thanksgiving.[31]

The Effects of the Fall of Jerusalem

It was because the institution of sacrifice and the temple worship as a whole had acquired this spiritual content that when the sacrificial system and the priesthood collapsed as a result of the destruction of the temple on Mount Zion by Titus in A.D. 70, the Torah, and all that this had come to signify in Judaism, survived. The priestly blessing (*Kirkath kohanim* or *Duchan*) continued to be given in the synagogues by kohens claiming descent from Aaron, and they retained the right to be the first called upon to read the Torah in the services, followed by a Levite. On the thirteenth day after the birth of the first-born son in a family they were entitled to receive five shekels for his redemption although these privileges have been questioned by some Rabbinical authorities. In Rabbinic Judaism, however, while the end of the sacrificial system gave greater emphasis to subjective repentance and the forgiveness of sin, priestly media' tion was exercised in the making of atonement. Such parts of the Day of Atonement ceremonial as could be observed have been set down in Rabbinic legislation.[32] Those claiming priestly descent were subject to the rules of Levitical ritual parity, and in a modified form these so far as they are practicable have remained a condition for giving the priestly blessing or reading the Torah. In the Talmud the sacrificial worship con' tinued to be discussed in great detail and represented as merely in abeyance until the temple would be rebuilt and its cultus restored. But even before the collapse of the capital in A.D. 70 the Torah had begun to replace temple worship for the Dias' pora, and the atoning efficacy of repentance, prayer, almsgiving and fasting were recognized as the essential requirements, together with the recitation of the appropriate lessons in the daily services.

CHRISTIANITY

The Sacrifice and Priesthood of Christ

It was at this critical juncture in the history of Judaism that Christianity, with its own particular conception of sacrifice and priesthood centred in the vicarious self'offering of its Founder, was launched in Palestine and the surrounding region of the Graeco'Roman world. The Gospel narratives show that al' though Christ predicted the imminent destruction of the temple and its worship,[33] and contrasted his own doctrine of mercy with that of sacrifice,[34] he nevertheless condoned the prescribed Jewish ordinances, and took part in the festivals. The sacrificial significance of the Paschal oblation and the Covenant sacri' fice was perpetuated by instituting the Eucharist in a setting connected with his own death.[35]

In an age saturated with sacrificial ideas, and against the background of the highly developed Levitical conception of priesthood, the death, resurrection and ascension of Christ were interpreted as a priestly oblation to reconcile God and man and a fulfilment of what had been foreshadowed by the sacrifices of the Old Dispensation. In the Fourth Gospel his own realization of priesthood is summed up in what is called his 'High-Priestly Prayer' (St John vii). In Christian theology he became the victorious ascended King exalted as a Prince and a Saviour, living on High to offer his eternal sacrifice as 'the Lamb slain from the foundation of the world' and in his priestly mediatorial capacity to make intercession for those who come unto God through him.[36]

The Aaronic priesthood and its ritual were the shadows, in a Platonic sense, of the archetypal order of the eternal sacrifice, according to the author of the Epistle to the Hebrews, and therefore failed to make perfect those who drew near to it. Christ 'beyond the veil' alone was able to save those who came unto God through him because he had removed for those who were in a state of grace the barrier of sin that separated man and God.[37]

The offering of Christ in the heavenly tabernacle was interpreted in terms of that of the Jewish high-priest in the Day of Atonement ceremonial. In this very ancient and primitive symbolism, to be considered later (cf. Chapter IV), an annual expiation was made for the high-priest, the priesthood and the congregation of Israel by a piacular sin-offering accompanied by censings and the manipulation of the blood. Then followed the transference of the guilt of the nation to a sin-receiver, or 'scapegoat', assigned to Azazel, a goat demon whose abode was in the desert. In its post-exilic observance the uncleanness of the temple and the sins and pollutions of the priests and the people contracted during the year were removed by these ritual means in which the high-priest occupied a special position as the successor of the king and stood in a particular sacerdotal relationship with Yahweh. The temple was the dynamic centre of the spiritual life of the restored nation and so its holiness and that of its servants had to be carefully maintained by an annual atonement and renewal.

The Levitical priesthood and the Jewish sacrificial system, however, according to the author of the Epistle to the Hebrews, belonged essentially to this world and the present age, and were only copies of eternal realities in the heavens.[38] The sacrifice of Christ, on the other hand, as that of the eternal high-priest after the order of Melchizedek, belonged to the 'age to come' in the heavenly sphere. By his incarnate life, resurrection and ascension he had opened a new and living way to God, so that those who were united to him by faith and sacrament partook of this future life while still pursuing their earthly pilgrimage.[39] That which was dimly foreshadowed by the entry of the Levitical transitory high-priest into the Holy of Holies on the Day of Atonement became through the perfect priesthood and sacrifice of Christ an accomplished fact and a timeless reality with a moral significance: the New Israel as God's people were cleansed and reconciled to him in a relationship which rested on the apprehension of the unseen world and achieved what the animal sacrifices of the Old Dispensation had failed to secure.[40] Thus, the Jewish sacrificial oblation and the Levitical priesthood were represented as the shadow of the plan of redemption finally revealed in the fullness of the New Covenant and the offering of Christ. In this way the people were brought into relation with Christ in the role of victim and priest. What had been anticipated in the cultus of the Hebrew covenant now acquired its full analogical meaning in and for the New Israel.

The Christian Priesthood

The analogy between the sacrificial functions of the Jewish high-priest in the Holy of Holies on the Day of Atonement and those of Christ in the heavenly tabernacle had its counterpart in the Eucharist as the sacrificial memorial before God of the death of Christ who 'by his own blood entered in once into the holy place, having obtained eternal redemption.'[41] Thus, in the Early Church the Eucharist was connected with the heavenly session of Christ, and in Western Christendom the offering of the gifts on the altar on earth symbolized their heavenly presentation by the eternal high-priest at the altar on

High. This necessitated a sacerdotal hierarchy in line with that of the Hebrew priesthood but tracing its descent not from Aaronic and Levitical sources, but from Christ and his Apostles who had developed a synagogue form of ecclesiastical organization with 'elders' (πρεσβύτεροι) and 'Overseers' (επίσχοποι) from the Jewish background.[42]

At first it would seem these two offices were identical, but from the second century A.D., the term 'episcopos' was reserved for those who presided over the presbyterate. By the end of the century the presbyters were called *sacerdotes* by St Cyprian because they shared in the episcopal *sacerdotium*, which included offering the Eucharistic sacrifice. In the pre-Nicene period the principal function of the episcopate seems to have been that of 'offering gifts', assisted by the deacons who 'brought up', or presented, that which was offered.[43] Although until the prac-tice was forbidden at the Council of Arles in 314, deacons appeared to have celebrated the Holy Mysteries in some local churches, this duty was normally confined to the *sacerdotes*, be they bishops or presbyters. Except in the case of concelebra-tion, when the Elements were consecrated jointly as at an Ordination, the offering of the Eucharist was originally an episcopal prerogative which could be and frequently was a delegated duty in the absence of the bishop. With the spread of localized parish churches served by presbyters exercising a sacerdotal ministry, the right to consecrate the sacred Elements was bestowed upon them as the official deputies of the bishop under whom they served. This occurred without the bishop relinquishing his episcopal rights as the normal celebrant in theory, very much as in Ancient Egypt the priests deputized for the Pharaoh.[44] He was, in fact, the heir of the divine king reserving to himself the fullness of priesthood but compelled by force of circumstances arising from the developing ecclesias-tical organization and the expansion of the Church to delegate his functions to his subordinates.[45]

Moreover, in the West the absolute supremacy and the uni-versal jurisdiction claimed by the occupants of the Holy See as the successors of the Prince of the Apostles, and the use of the imperial title of *Pontifex Maximus* conferred on Augustus in 13 B.C., and adopted by the Papacy in A.D. 375 in its capacity of *Pastor Pastorum*, gave a new emphasis to the ancient prin-ciple of the royal priesthood. This supremacy did not become established until after the Christianization of the Empire in the fourth century, whether or not it was inherent in the Apostolic or sub-Apostolic constitution. But once it was acclaimed and accepted in Western Christendom, its effects on the Christian interpretation of priesthood were considerable. In an age of intermittent persecution and heresy, like that in which St Cyprian (*c.* 200–258) lived in Carthage, coupled with rapid expansion, the Church required a unifying dynamic com-parable to the divine kingship in ancient society. This the Papacy supplied, and as Harnack says, the Bishop of Rome, even in the eyes of Eastern Christians, had 'something special attaching to him which no other bishop had, a halo which gave him a quite peculiar authority.'[46] But until the Christian Empire came into being it was manifestly impossible to organ-ize ecclesiastical jurisdiction on an oecumenical basis. Once this was accomplished, the Holy See with all the prestige of Rome behind it, and claiming to be in possession of the relics of St Peter and St Paul, the Princes of the Apostles, occupied a unique position in Christendom. Moreover, the removal of Constantine to the new capital on the Bosphorus left the Bishop of Rome the most imposing figure in the ancient and venerable city, long regarded as the mistress of the world.

Thus, from presiding at the Eucharist the bishop as the heir of the sacral kingship assumed the fullness of priesthood when the occupant of the Holy See attained Petrine supremacy and universal jurisdiction. Gaining precedence and priority over the patriarchal Sees, Carthage, Alexandria, Antioch and Constantinople, disputes between local provinces and prelates were referred to the judgment of Rome, and it only remained for Leo the Great (440–461) to unify ecclesiastical control through legatine metropolitans to complete the universal juris-diction of the Papacy. To establish the position on a divine foundation when the secular Empire and its capital were threatened with dissolution, he boldly proclaimed himself the successor of St Peter, the vicegerent on earth of Christ, and so asserted the spiritual authority of the office, independent of its imperial precedents and prestige.

Thus, from the conception of Christ reconciling God and man by His sacrificial death as priest and victim, the Christian priesthood was established in the Church especially for the perpetuation of the Eucharistic memorial of his self-offering. As the idea of priesthood developed in relation to the episcopal *sacerdotium* it acquired an ecclesiastical jurisdiction with the growth of the Church and eventually became a rallying force and consolidating centre in an age of imperial disruption.

CHAPTER III

The Blood-offering

THE SACRIFICIAL SIGNIFICANCE OF BLOOD

THE fundamental importance and significance of blood in the institution of sacrifice has been such that the subject demands detailed consideration at this stage. As we have seen, the recognition that it is the life principle in man and beast alike goes back at any rate to the beginning of the Upper Palaeolithic,[1] and ever since it has been regarded as the seat of vitality *par excellence*. Therefore, at a very early period it was equated with the animating principle, or soul-substance, associated with certain essential parts of the body and its secretions: among these the liver is prominent, doubtless because it contains an abnormal amount of blood.

Blood as the Soul-substance

It was not, however, until the circulatory system had been discovered and demonstrated by Harvey in 1628 that its physiological functions were understood. Early man judged things as he saw them, and as loss of blood produced loss of vitality he concluded that it must be the vital essence. Therefore, as its potency was transmissible from one person or animal to another, the restoration and renewal of life could be secured by a ritual transference of this sanguinary soul-substance. This is the principle underlying the blood-offering, the possession of a common vitality establishing a mystic bond between all who shared the same life-essence.

Nowhere is this more clearly shown than in the Hebrew conception of the *nephesh*, or principle of life, the extinguishing of which constitutes death.[2] Thus the *nephesh* of the flesh is said to reside in the blood, which is sacrificed upon the altar 'to make atonement for your *nephashoth* (souls); for it is the blood that makes atonement by reason of the *nephesh*'.[3] Therefore, its intermingling establishes a vital alliance between those united in a blood bond, and it has been a potent agent in consolidating tribal relationships and effecting intercommunion between the human and the sacred orders. This is apparent in the totemic blood rites performed by the men of the Undiaro kangaroo totem in Central Australia,[4] and it explains the ratification of the Mosaic covenant by the sprinkling on the altar of the blood of the oxen slain as a peace-offering and on the congregation of Israel in the Hebrew ritual.[5] The application of the life-giving essence brought together Yahweh and his chosen nation in a sacred bond of a common life uniting the contracting parties in a vital relationship like that of the common meal, or eating salt together.[6]

The Blood Covenant and Kinship

From this notion of blood as a soul-substance responsible for the phenomenon of life, a notion so prominent and widespread in primitive society and in Semitic religion, a sense of kinship appears to have developed at a very early period between man and between the human group and the animals upon which subsistence depended. The possession of a common vital principle gave rise to the idea of a blood-brotherhood, and this found expression in the complex system of ritual and belief that was centred in the tribal kinship organization and eventually in the institution of sacrifice and of sacramental communion. From an artificial brotherhood came the blood covenant established by the union of one life with another by the exchange of blood which was extended to allied human and animal groups, and to the sacred order as the ultimate source of all life. In the absence of any clear-cut distinction between the sacred and the profane, the natural and the supernatural, and animal and man, the entire universe, its inhabitants and institutions are conceived by the primitive mind to belong to one great system of interrelated and inherent life—probably the unconscious expression of the religious emotion itself.[7]

Thus animals, which are the sources and agents of man's food supply, belong to the human domain. Moreover, they may possess powers in which man is deficient—muscular strength, keenness of sight and smell, a remarkable sense of direction, ability in tracking, flying and running at great speed. There-fore they are regarded as superior to man and may be assigned an ancestral status in the human group as in a totemic com-munity. They are held in veneration and surrounded with tabus because they belong to the sacred order and stand in the most intimate relation to the human group, whether it be in the capacity of a supernatural ally, to totem or tutelary spirit like the *nagual* and *manitu* among the North American Indian tribes.[8] All conduct themselves in much the same way and man merely feels himself to be at best *primus inter pares*, rather than above the animals.[9] The vital bond between them is rati-fied and sealed in a collective ritual by means of which a sacramental union is established with the ultimate source of life in the sacred world. The union is achieved by the human group participating in the spiritual nature of the divinity or sacred species with whom it is identified so that the twain become one through the life principle. Man and animal are distinct entities but share a common soul-substance in relation to the divine. Similarly, when the sacramental relationship is represented by a material symbol, the symbol is regarded and treated in the same way as the spiritual entity it symbolizes because it has acquired a spiritual quality which cannot belong to it without changing its outward and visible characteristic form. It is this conception of kinship which lies behind the blood covenant and its mystic sacramental relationships, sym-bolism and participation. It does not, however, contravene either 'the law of contradiction' or that of logic, as Lévy-Bruhl has argued.[10] If the primitive mind identifies organisms and objects which to us seem to be mutually exclusive, and asserts connexions and affinities between things we regard as having nothing to do with each other, it is because it has little or no conception of the universality and continuity of natural causa-tion, and of contradictions and differentiation. It does not dis-tinguish clearly between cause and effect, agent and act, the symbol and the thing symbolized, because they all belong to one integrated undifferentiated whole pervaded by an inherent vitality.

This, however, is not conceived pantheistically as in later Hindu speculation because it presupposes the existence of an extramundane sacred order standing over and against, and in a particular relation with, this world over which it exercises spiritual control, determining the course of events and human destinies, and supplying man's fundamental needs. It is this interpretation of the universe rooted and grounded in supra/mundane power and causation that gives the blood covenant and the kinship organization their cohesion, welding to/gether the divine, human and animal creations as a composite whole and establishing a sacramental relationship between them.

THE SACRIFICIAL VICTIM

Therefore, since animals and men in these conditions of men/tality are believed to share a common life principle the bond between them is not unnaturally thought to be strengthened and conditioned by the vital essence. This is most apparent in totemic society where the human group may imbibe the soul/substance of the totem for this purpose, even though such rites do not represent an act of sacramental communion with a slain god, as Robertson Smith supposed. Nevertheless, the one life running through the group, human and animal, opened the way, when the practice of substitution became a recognized principle, for the use of animals for sacrifice in place of human victims.

The Sacral King

In the ancient civilizations in the Near East, however, as in primitive agricultural tribal society in Africa and elsewhere where the sacral kingship was an established institution, the occupant of the throne himself often appears to have been the vicarious victim who either at the end of an allotted period of sovereignty, or when his virility showed signs of diminishing, had to be put to death to make way for a vigorous successor.

This custom arose from the king being regarded as the embodiment of the vegetation principle in nature so that the succession
of the seasons, the growth of the crops and fecundity in general
were dependent upon his vitality. In the absence of any clearly
defined distinction between the secular and the sacred, the king
was a cosmic dynamic figure whose function it was to maintain the prosperity and well-being of an integrated community
in which he was the focal point and unifying centre, and
ensure its harmony with the supernatural order. Consequently,
when he was no longer able to fulfil his proper functions his
reign had to be summarily ended.

Many examples of this practice have been recorded among
the native tribes of the Nilotic Sudan, the classical instance
being that of the Shilluk king who reigned as the incarnation
of the ancestral ruler and culture hero Nyikang. Whether or
not he was eventually walled up in a hut or killed in mortal
combat with an adversary as Seligman believed[11]—a conjecture regarded by Professor Evans-Pritchard as a fiction arising
from the dual personality of the king who is both himself and
Nyikang[12]—it is not disputed that Shilluk rulers usually met
a violent death. And regicide has been too widespread a custom in Africa, generally connected with the renewal of
vegetation and rain-making, to be dismissed altogether.

Moreover, among the Shilluk the *reth* (king), by virtue of his
descent from Nyikang whom he embodied, occupies the
central position in the ritual order as the royal high-priest and
the symbol of the politico-religious structure of the nation.
Therefore, he assists at the sacrifice for rain at the shrines of his
divine ancestor, invoking him to send refreshing showers to
renew the earth, and acts as the mediator in the settlement of
feuds.[13] Indeed, as Professor Evans-Pritchard says, 'we can
only understand the place of the kingship in Shilluk society
when we realize that it is not the individual at any time reigning who is king, but Nyikang who is the medium between man
and the god (Juok), and is believed in some way to participate
in God as he does in the king.'[14] It is this relationship which
gives the *reth* his sacerdotal status, invoking his ancestor for

rain as the royal high-priest at the sacrifices held at the shrine of Nyikang. It doubtless also lies behind whatever may have happened in former times about the killing of kings when they became sick or senile, or by a more powerful aspirant to the 'sacred stool'. Being the official representative of Nyikang he becomes responsible for the maintenance of the food supply, the right ordering and consolidation of society, and the control of the weather on which the harvests depend. All this requires a potent sacral king to maintain the bond between the human and divine orders, and to exercise his mediatorial functions.

To endow him with these heavenly gifts and consecrate him to his office and status, the accession ceremonies are held about a year after his election. The images of Nyikang and of his son Dak are brought by the priests, accompanied by warriors and an army, from the cult centre of Akurwa in the north of Fashoda. Outside the capital they engage in a mock battle with the forces of the king-elect from the south and having conquered them they take the *reth* to Fashoda. The image of Nyikang is placed on the sacred stool, and after a bullock has been sacrificed and eaten sacramentally by the descendants of the third of the Shilluk kings called *ororo*, the image is removed and the new king is seated in its place so that the spirit of Nyikang may enter into him. The royal bride is then seized by Nyikang and a second combat is fought between the two opposed forces, in the course of which the girl is captured for the king. Peace is restored, the newly enthroned monarch receives the homage of the chiefs and undertakes to rule well by virtue of the spirit and power of Nyikang with which he has been endowed, and of the relationship in which he stands to Juok, the High God.[15]

In this type of sacral kinship in which priesthood and sovereignty are combined, the occupant of the throne is primarily a ceremonial figure responsible for the control of the weather, the productivity of the crops, and the integration and welfare of society. It is through him, as the intermediary with the transcendental world, that the supernatural potency flows to the body politic and the processes of nature. Therefore the throne always must have a virile, alert and strong occupant. This may be secured in some measure by a succession of periodic ritual renewals, but at length the time arrives when his natural forces show signs of waning, and then unless some form of abdication is devised he must pay the supreme penalty of his office, sacrificing himself on behalf of his people.

Ritual Renewal

Thus, the sacral king not infrequently became at once the priest and victim engaged in sacerdotal functions in his royal capacity during his lifetime for the well-being of his people, eventually surrendering his life in what amounts to an act of self-sacrifice on their behalf. Throughout his sacrosanct career he lived a dedicated life consecrated to the service of the community over which he ruled in a divine capacity knowing full well what the destined end was to be. But this altruism had its limitations, and although it represents one of the roots of the institution of sacrifice as the supreme blood-offering, it is hardly surprising that it tended to give place to various devices to enable the royal victim to escape his appointed doom. Annual or periodic ritual renewals such as were adopted in Mesopotamia and Egypt met the situation to some extent, if in fact in either of these ancient civilizations regicide ever had been practised. But in any case, ritual renewals were only temporary expedients when the earlier more drastic custom was in process of decline and modification.

In Babylon on the fifth day of the Annual Festival in the spring the king relinquished his regalia, placing his sceptre, ring, scimitar and crown before the statue of Marduk, the chief god of the city and head of the pantheon. He was then struck on the face by the high-priest, forced to his knees to declare his innocence, and reinstated in his office for the forthcoming year.[16] The powers of death were defeated by the arrival of Nabu, the son of Marduk, at the end of the five days of sacrifice, atonement, lamentation and purification culminating in the king's humiliation, abdication and reinstatement. Marduk having been released from the mountain, typifying the underworld, the gods were next assembled and led forth in procession to the Festival House (*Bit Akitu*) on the outskirts of the city, where the victory of Marduk over Tiamat was celebrated at a great banquet before the return to the city for the fixing of the destinies of the new year, and the connubium, or sacred mar, riage of the king and the queen, or a royal priestess, in the Esagila (Marduk's temple in Babylon).[17]

In Egypt the rejuvenation of the Pharaoh was effected either thirty years after the accession, or at shorter intervals, at the very ancient Sed-festival, which probably goes back to the time of Menes, the traditional founder of the Dynasty, and which was held on the first day of the first month of 'the Season of Coming Forth' (Tybi).[18] That it was a survival of the killing of kings when they became senile, or after a number of years, as has been suggested,[19] is a plausible conjecture for which, however, there is no evidence apart from the nature of the observance. But the details and precise significance of the event unfortu, nately are very obscure and uncertain. It seems to have coin, cided with the date of the coronation and to have been a reinvestiture involving the rejuvenescence of the Pharaoh to confirm his reign and renew his powers as the mediator be, tween heaven and earth.

Accompanied by the leading officials, princes and royal kins, men, he visited the shrines of the gods erected in the Festival court of the Temple in which, after purification, the solemni, ties were held, and made offerings to them. For several days he walked in the processions with the statues of the gods and their priesthoods, the standard of the royal placenta, fan-bearers and attendants, and seated upon his throne, received pledges of loyalty. Afterwards his feet were ceremonially washed before he entered 'the palace', as the robing-room was called, to re, invest. He then sat alternately on two thrones to symbolize his rule over Upper and Lower Egypt, and crossed ceremonially the area of the temple court known as 'the field', which repre, sented Egypt as a whole. Finally he was carried on a litter preceded by the standard of the jackal-god Upuaut of Siut to the chapel of Horus of Libya to receive the sceptre, flail and crook. Wrapped in a cloak he was proclaimed four times and received the homage of his subjects and the blessing of the gods. In return he made appropriate offerings to them, and taking off his cloak he ran four courses clad only in a kilt with the tail of an animal, wearing the crown of Upper Egypt and carrying a short sceptre and whisk which he offered to Upuaut. The proceedings concluded with a visit to the chapels of Horus of Edfu and of Seth of Ombos, where he shot arrows of victory towards the four cardinal points, just as he was enthroned four times facing the four quarters of the earth.[20]

Until recently it has been generally thought that the Pharaoh impersonated Osiris in his vestures and insignia at the Sed-festival, which was celebrated in close association with the raising of the Djed-column at the Feast of Khoiak when the inundation was subsiding.[21] This has now been denied by Griffiths on the grounds that the purpose of the Sed-festival was the renewal of the existing kingship of the occupant of the throne rather than to establish the succession as in the corona-tion rite.[22] But whether or not Osiris was impersonated in a death and resurrection ritual, or in his Horus role as the reign-ing Pharaoh maintaining a right relationship between heaven and earth, and the union of Upper and Lower Egypt re-enacted, he was in any case re-established and strengthened in his divine office. Investiture with a bull's tail (closely connected apparently with the name of the festival, Sed) may have been part of the sacramental renewal,[23] as the king is said 'to be reborn by renewing his festival of Sed', flourishing again 'like the infant god of the Moon and Nun at the beginning of the ages'.[24] But there is no evidence that the Sed-festival was an amelioration of the sacrifice of ageing kings as elsewhere in tribal Africa. If such a custom ever existed, as is by no means impossible, it had ceased before the predynastic Egyptians became established in the Nile valley.

Substitute Kings

Ritual renewal, however, had its limitations as sooner or later the king, though he might contrive to escape a premature violent end, must grow old and die from natural causes. Such devices as the Sed-festival, if they had any connexion with the practice, could be but modifications of regicide to stave off decease. An alternative procedure was for either a member of the royal family (e.g. the son of the king) or a commoner im-personating the king for a given period to be put to death instead of the reigning monarch. If the victim was a blood rela-tive of the real king this had the advantage that to some extent he was already in possession of the royal soul-substance which gave him the right status for the office, and a sacramental installation could be made to invest him with the powers required for the exercise of his functions. This, of course, was particularly essential in the case of the prisoner of war or slave selected to be the mock king for a year or a day, or whatever might be the determined period, since to be effective he had to be raised to the royal sacral status before he could be sacri-ficed.

The eldest son as the first-born has generally been regarded as well endowed with parental potency and therefore he has seemed to be the most efficacious offering. Thus, in Greek mythology when Athamas, a legendary Thessalian king, just escaped being sacrificed himself during a severe famine, it was decreed by an oracle that the eldest son of the royal family hence should be offered to Laphystian Zeus by a member of his household if he ever returned to his country. When any of the descendants of Athamas did appear and attempted to enter the town-hall they were sacrificed.[25] On Mount Lykaion in Arcadio King Tantalus fed the gods with the flesh of his son, very much as human victims were torn to pieces and devoured in Dionysian cannibal feasts.[26] Behind these traditions may lie the ancient practice, especially in Thessaly and Boeotia, of kings sacrificing their sons instead of themselves to Laphystian Zeus for the well-being of the country.

In due course, however, the practice was mitigated by the substitution of a ram for the royal victim, as in Israel the first-born of man eventually was redeemed by an animal, and later by a fixed sum of money per head.[27] The various accounts of

the Paschal observances have been overlaid with later interpretations of the Exodus story and allied incidents, themes, and
festivals; but, as Frazer says, 'the one thing that looms clear
through the haze of this weird tradition is the memory of a
great massacre of firstborn'.[28] Long after this offering had been
abandoned it was still maintained that all firstlings—'whatever
openeth the matrix both of man and beast'—belonged to Yahweh,[29] and therefore the ancient injunction could be surmounted only by a process of substitution and redemption, as
in the case of the redemption of Jonathan from death at the
hand of his father by the people.[30] But, even so, the conviction
that the god of Israel demanded the sacrifice of their first-born
male offspring was so deeply laid that it was always liable to
recur, and it found expression as a perfectly natural and
accepted practice in the story of the vow of Jephthah.[31] That
Ahaz and Manasseh offered their sons was regarded as repre-
hensible,[32] and the revival of child-sacrifice at Topheth, a
sanctuary in the valley of Hinnom near Jerusalem, about 600
B.C., was deplored. But it still persisted and Ezekiel lamented
that, despite the efforts of Josiah and the Deuteronomic Law,[33]
the people combined the worship of Yahweh with passing
their children through the fire to Moloch in the valley of
Hinnom.[34]

No doubt the story of the offerings of Isaac[35] in the eighth-
century prophetic Midrash was based on a legend of a sanctuary where at one time human victims were sacrificed before
rams took their place on the altar. But, notwithstanding the
literary skill of the Hebrew writer in retelling the story in the
light of the Deuteronomic attitude to human sacrifice, the action
of the traditional founder of the nation is taken for granted, the
substitution of the ram being represented merely as a reward of
the 'faith' of Abraham. It was not until after the Exile when
the first-born rite was replaced by a tribute, that the custom was
permanently eliminated in Judaism. Whereupon to offer the
prescribed oblations, to observe the Torah, and to do the will
of Yahweh became the undisputed duty of the faithful Israelite, the kingship having been transformed into a Messianic

hope and expectation which eventually found expression in an apocalyptic eschatology.

But the covenant in Israel had a wider significance than the Hebrew monarchy and was independent of the earthly throne since behind it lay that of Yahweh with Abraham and, later, Moses representing the nation as a whole. The Hebrew king was a sacred person, the anointed servant of Yahweh, who exercised sacerdotal functions but was never the dynamic centre of the social structure and religious organization, or the con-troller of the processes of vegetation and of the cosmic order. The emphasis in Israel was on the theocratic state in which the king ruled by divine permission and the will of the people, not as in Egypt by divine descent and decree as the earthly em-bodiment of the gods he incarnated, or as in Mesopotamia as the deified bridegroom of the Mother-goddess. Therefore, when the monarchy finally came to an end in the sixth century B.C., its place was taken in the post-exilic community by the governor and high-priest without any dislocation in the social structure. At the restoration by Cyrus the Persian, to whom the title of 'Messiah' had been attached by the Deutero-Isaiah, the governor of Jerusalem, Zerubbabel, was hailed as a descendant of David and deputy of Yahweh, occupying a posi-tion in the cultus comparable to that of the 'Prince' in Eze-kiel.[36] He ruled in conjunction with the high-priest, and when his mission came to an end the high-priest alone remained as the consolidating centre so that around him the hierarchic organization and its sacrificial system were established. But the office never bore an organic relationship to nature or the nation, or anything approaching a divine status, as elsewhere in the Fertile Crescent. Therefore, the vitality and demise of its holder had no reciprocal consequences in Jewry.

It was not until the Messiahship was developed around the figures of the Davidic King, the Son of Man and eventually the Suffering Servant, that it acquired a new sacrificial sig-nificance in an eschatological setting. Although beneath the figures there was an underlying unity of conception,[37] the anointed of Yahweh, or 'Messiah' (*mashiakh*), does not appear to have been expected to fulfil his office and vocation through suffering and death, the Isaianic Servant at the time of the Exile being the stricken nation.[38] Indeed, if such a conception had been generally recognized when the Gospel tradition was in process of formulation the disciples of Jesus would hardly have been represented as bewildered by his predictions of the Passion and death as a prelude to the Parousia.[39] Neither the figure of the Davidic King nor that of the Son of Man could have been equated in their minds, it would seem, with the Suffering Servant, especially as his death when it occurred was for the time being the end of their hopes and aspirations.

Nevertheless, the figure of the *Ecce Homo* as portrayed in the Passion narratives was that of a mock king clad in a scarlet robe, with a reed in his right hand and a crown of thorns on his brow, subjected to brutal and ignominious veneration and mockery,[40] like so many victims in this role in the long history of the sacral kingship.[41] Whether or not the Roman soldiers had the Saturnalian mock king in mind when they meted out this treatment to Jesus,[42] his recorded answer to Pilate's question, 'Art thou a king then?' was 'Thou sayest that I am a king. To this end have I been born, and to this end came I into the world.'[43] And it was as 'The King of the Jews' that he was crucified.[44]

However the account of what took place is interpreted, the fact remains that the Passion and death of Christ introduced into the Jewish Messiah tradition the ancient conception of the divine Saviour King suffering and dying for the salvation of mankind. Henceforth the Messianic office was conceived by those who accepted the Christian evaluation of Calvary as the central event in the redemptive process. The Davidic King was transformed into the Saviour of the world, at once priest and victim in an eternal sacrificial self-offering, fulfilling in one supreme oblation all the prototypes and archetypes of the office; defeated yet victorious and invested with apocalyptic glory. In the background lay the figure of the virile Young God triumphing over death and the powers of evil, and restored to the land of the living to give new life in the rhythm of nature. In Christian tradition this theme of the dying and reviving Year-god was brought into relation with that of the conquering Christ under the apocalyptic symbolism of the lamb slain sacrificially from the foundation of the world to ensure the final triumph of good over evil and of life over death.[45]

The Christian and Rabbinic Conceptions of the Blood-offering

That the sacrifice of Christ was regarded as a blood-offering is clear from the institution of the Eucharist in the sacrificial context of the Passover, and the reference to the shedding of his blood as a New Covenant 'for the remission of sins'.[46] As the Lamb of God he was represented as a sacrificial victim voluntarily giving his life in self-oblation on behalf rather than instead of mankind.[47] Various interpretations, which will be considered later,[48] have been given to this imagery by theologians, but for the author of the Epistle to the Hebrews the traditional conception of the atoning efficacy of sacrificial blood was axiomatic. Communion with God, he maintained, required the outpouring of the vital essence of the victim exemplified in the Judaic sin-offering. He recognized, however, that it was not possible for the blood of bulls and goats to take away sin. This only could be done by the perfect self-offering of the dedicated life of Christ immolated on the Cross. Therefore Calvary, as he contended, was the true sacrifice of supreme and complete validity effecting what hitherto has been foreshadowed partially and symbolically in the cultus of the Jewish covenant.[49]

The sacrificial immolation was renewed perpetually in a ritual commemoration, the priest offering himself at his own sacrifice not as a substitute but as a royal victim restored after humiliation like the sacral king. The blood-shedding was once and for all and did not require to be repeated year by year, or at fixed periods, as in the ritual renewals of the kingship. In the Christian interpretation of the institution of sacrifice there is but one oblation offered in a bloody manner on the Cross. The Eucharist is the unbloody commemoration and continuation of this sole redemptive offering for the sins of the world, instituted and commanded by Christ at the Last Supper on the night of the betrayal. Once the victim had been slain, his liberated life could be immolated in a ritual sacrifice and made accessible and available for all mankind and for all time under the sacramental signs of his broken body and poured-out blood. The Eucharistic offering, however, is unbloody because it is made by means of the sacramental elements as the symbols of the all-sufficient sacrifice. Since it is not the death of the victim that is the essence of the sacrificial oblation but the surrender of its life, in the dual capacity of priest and victim the risen and ascended Christ is represented as laying down his life in order to take it again and bestow it in all its fullness in and through the appointed channels in his mystical body, the Church.

Although it was within the context of Judaism that this conception arose, it constituted a new departure in the spiritual and symbolic significance of the blood-offering. Thus, after the destruction of the temple in A.D. 70 a very different attitude was adopted by the Rabbis, who, though earnestly desiring the restoration of the temple worship, affirmed that prayer was better than sacrifice.[50] The position is explained in the additional *'Amidah* for sabbaths and festivals:

> Sovereign of the universe! thou didst command us to offer the daily sacrifice in its appointed time that the priests should officiate in their service and the Levites at their stand and the Israelites by their delegates. But, at the present, on account of our sins, the temple is laid waste, and the daily sacrifice hath ceased; for we have neither an officiating priest nor a Levite at his stand nor an Israelite delegate. But thou hast said that the prayers of our lips shall be as the offerings of bulls (Hos. xiv, 2). Therefore, let it be thy will, O Lord our God, and the God of our fathers, that the prayers of our lips may be accounted, accepted and esteemed before thee, as if we had offered the daily sacrifice at its appointed time and had been represented by our delegation.[51]

Originally in the Rabbinic period (though the situation may be found today in Israel) it was only in the 'present distress' that the substitution of synagogue prayers, the reading of appropriate portions of the Torah and fasting were considered to be temporary expedients for the prescribed sacrificial worship and its blood-offerings. Thus, in the Prayer of the Rabbi Sheshet it is stated:

Lord of the world, when the Temple was standing one who sinned offered a sacrifice of which only the fat and blood were taken, and thereby his sins were forgiven. I have fasted today, and through this fasting my blood and my fat have been decreased. Deign to look upon the part of my blood and my fat which I have lost through my fasting as if I had offered it to Thee, and forgive my sins in return.'[52]

It was, however, definitely a substitute for the blood-offering, and in the *'Amidah* repeated three times daily by the devout the petition is made, 'mayest Thou bring back the sacrifices of the holy house, and the fire-offerings, as well as their prayers receive with favour'.

The position in Judaism in the Tannaitic period, therefore, was not very different from the attitude adopted by Ezekiel during the Exile. The people then were looking for the return of the former worship, but the prophetic movement had made it possible to adopt non-sacrificial substitutes, such as prayer and fasting and the reading of the Law, for the prescribed offerings. As a result, by so doing the ancient blood ritual underwent a fundamental change in character so that the con-cept of life-giving became that of self-oblation, the sacrifice of the lips instead of that of the calves.[53]

In Christianity the ethical and spiritual interpretation of the sacrificial approach to a righteous God as a means of advance in the way of personal holiness underwent a further change. Christ appears to have accepted the Levitical sacrificial sys-tem though he subordinated it to 'mercy'[54] and predicted the imminent destruction of the temple and its worship.[55] Before the close of the first century A.D., as we have seen, his death was proclaimed by the Church as the supreme sacrifice, the offering of his blood being connected with the sin-offering in the Old Dispensation,[56] and he himself represented as the Paschal Victim and the eternal high-priest of the human race.[57] The introduction of the doctrine of mediation gave a new significance to the idea of the blood covenant. While the blood of bulls and goats could not effect a true expiation in terms of ethical righteousness, the death of Christ became an atoning sacrifice analogous to the post-exilic piacular through a perfect act of self-surrender, as will be considered in greater detail later.[58] Therefore, as St Paul maintained, 'God sent forth his Son to be an expiation, through faith, by his blood because of the passing over of the sins done aforetime.'[59]

This went very much further than the Rabbinic substitution of prayer, fasting and the Torah for the temple worship, and gave the ancient blood ritual a new lease of life by incorporation in an ethical and spiritual theological context. In this, as Hocart says, 'the Lamb of God became a symbol expressing a sum of innocence, purity, gentleness, self-sacrifice, redemption and divinity which no form of words could express with such forceful appeal.'[60] But the sacrificial interpretation of the death of Christ involved the oblation of the blood which normally would be poured out partly on the altar and partly on the worshipper to reunite him with his god in a covenant relationship. Subjectively this could be spiritualized in the guise of a heavenly offering made accessible by faith instead of by ritual. Nevertheless, the institution of the Eucharist in the context of the Passover and the Covenant sacrifice bestowed a sacrificial significance on the blood-shedding on Calvary which has remained in some form or other the focus of Christian worship throughout the ages, and has given a new permanence to the ancient blood-offering.

CHAPTER IV

Human Sacrifice

AMERICA

OF all blood-offerings the most efficacious have been those connected with the killing of sacral kings either after a fixed number of years or when their powers have begun to wane, with reciprocal effects upon fertility in general.[1] This practice, as we have seen, has often led to one of the sons of the reigning monarch, or someone assigned to assume the royal divine status for a given period, being put to death in the guise and on behalf of the real king. It is in this context that human sacrifice must be set, its occurrence being most prevalent among the relatively higher grades of agricultural peoples, and associated with the calendrical sequence.

The Rite in Mexico

Ritual sacrifice reached its zenith in Central America, where it has been estimated that twenty thousand human victims perished annually on Aztec and Nahua altars in the maize ritual in the fourteenth century A.D., just before the Spanish conquest. The practice arose from the belief that only with this grim aid could the sun, on which the nation depended for its survival, continue its life-giving functions. This, however, appears to have been a somewhat late introduction into the region, no reference having been made to it in connexion with the worship of the sun by the Maya when they first penetrated into the Mexican valley about A.D. 300. Hearts of animals, it is true, were torn out in March and cast into the flames during a fire-ceremony, and in May a dog was treated in the same manner to make the soil fertile and the new crops abundant. But it does not seem to have been extended to human beings.

According to the *Popol Vuh*, a heroic saga of the Quiche Indians of Guatemala, when the Quiche ancestors set out from

Tulan, the ancient capital, where each of the tribes began its migration under the leadership of its god, the sun had not been created. Their Thunder-god Tohil supplied them with fire by striking it from his sandal. When the other tribes begged it from them they consented only on condition that in return they would be united with Tohil 'beneath the girdles and beneath the armpits'.[2] This was a carefully concealed demand for the offering of their hearts, and all but the Kokchiquel fell into the trap. Henceforth human sacrifice was practised; at first this was done secretly, but soon it became generally recog-nized that the sun and the maize crops required perpetual regeneration, which could be obtained only by the offering of the hearts of human victims in the prime of their vigour as re-vitalizing agents, who, before death, had been raised to divine status. This led to endless wars that the altars might be supplied with a constant stream of virile victims, and it may have been one of the causes of the break-up of the Toltec Empire in the middle of the eleventh century A.D. before the incursions of Chichimec hordes. Others followed, and finally about the fourteenth century the last of the invading Nahua tribes, the Aztecs, became dominant.

The culture hero, Quetzalcoatl, 'Feathered Serpent', the 'Father of the Toltecs', who is alleged to have introduced civilization into Mexico, is represented as opposing the practice in his struggle with the war- and sky-gods of the later Aztec polytheism. This suggests that human sacrifice was already established among the pre-Aztec nomads, and, while it was not adopted by the priests and worshippers of Quetzalcoatl in centres such as Cholula, where his cult flourished, it was restored after the overthrow of the Toltec Empire. When the Aztec warrior-god Huitzilopochtli was transformed into the solar divinity, he was thought to require a colossal supply of human hearts to enable him to perform his vegetation func-tions, demanding an extensive campaign into northern Oaxaca to obtain no fewer than seventeen to eighteen thousand captives as victims[3] at the height of the holocaust. In course of time these sanguinary rites on a less prodigious scale became associated with even the worship of Quetzalcoatl when he was given a place in the sun, and in Oaxaca the Zapotecs believed that it was he who first taught men to offer their own blood.[4] But among the Aztecs he was always regarded as a foreign god of alien character, and his priests were a separate caste.

The Aztec Calendrical Rites

But it was essentially in connexion with the agricultural calen/ drical sequence rather than in a nomadic pastoral setting that human sacrifice attained its hideous prominence and propor/ tions in Mexico, featuring not only in the cult of Huitzilo/ pochtli but also in that of Tlazolteotl, the goddess of maize and of the earth, being a synonym of the Earth/mother Teteo/ innan. In February, children were sacrificed to the rain/gods, and before the sowing in the second twentieth, a virile prisoner of war was shot with arrows in an extended position as an offering to Totec, a form of the Moon/god, to fertilize the earth. After a succession of similar oblations the festival concluded with a dance in which the priests clad in the skins of the vic/ tims were disguised as maize/ears and stalks.[5]

In the third twentieth (Tocoztli: 'awakening'), the month of the first/fruits, children were sacrificed in the temple of Xipe, 'the Flayed god of planting and seedtime, the patron of sowing'. The skins of the victims in the previous festival were now dis/ carded by those who had worn them, and buried solemnly. On April 23, Toxcatl, the principal feast of the year, was held in honour of Tezcatlipoca, the Aztec Zeus or Jupiter, at which the most handsome, brave and attractive prisoner of war was put to death after he had impersonated the god for a year and been given divine honours and homage. Twenty days before the fatal festival he consorted with four beautiful young brides representing respectively the goddess of flowers, the goddess of the young maize, the goddess of 'Our Mother among the waters', and the goddess of salt. When the destined day arrived he bade a tender farewell to his wives and led a triumphal pro/ cession, accompanied by his eight attendants and eight priests, to a lonely pyramidal temple. He ascended the steps and at the top he was seized and turned over the sacrificial block; then his heart was extracted in the customary manner.⁶ His successor was installed immediately in the office; *Le roi est mort, vive le roi.*

In the rainy season in the sixth twentieth, human victims were offered to the figure of Tlaloc, the rain-god, and on June 2, in the seventh month, a woman was sacrificed in the guise of Huixtocihuatl, the goddess of salt and sister of the rain-gods. When the maize was ripe on June 22, a young woman was dressed as Xiulonen, the goddess of the young maize, with the upper part of her face painted red, the lower part yellow, and her arms and legs covered with red feathers. Holding a shield in her left hand and a crimson baton in her right hand, she danced all night before the temple of Centeotl, the goddess of maize; whereafter she was seized by a priest and decapitated, and her heart was extracted. Then the green ears of maize might be eaten.⁷

In the tenth twentieth commencing on August 1, the most revolting rite was performed in honour of Xiuhtecuhtli, the god of fire. After a dance round a huge fire, prisoners of war were bound hand and feet and thrown into the flames. They were then dragged out by the priests with hooks, and while yet alive their hearts were wrenched from their charred bodies to be offered to the god to renew his energy. A figure of Xocotl, the god of Otomi, 'the soul of the dead warrior', was erected on the top of a pole in the form of a bird, a butterfly or a mummy bundle. Virile young men vied with one another in reaching it and bringing it down to add to the holocaust.⁸

After this feast of the dead there was a great expiation on August 21, the eleventh month of the Aztec year, on the occasion of the harvest festival. A woman representing Teteo-innan, the Mother of the gods, was decapitated at midnight and flayed, the skin being worn by the priest who played the role of the goddess during the ensuing ceremonies. One of the thighs of the victim was flayed separately and a mask made from the skin was worn by a priest impersonating the son of the Mother of the gods. The chief purpose of the observance was the im-pregnation of the goddess by Huitzilopochtli, and in the procession to meet him Teteoinnan was accompanied by phallic deities and warriors (Cuexteca). At the end of the rite the man impersonating the goddess was decorated in her apparel on the highest point of her temple where at the break of day he sacri/ ficed four captives, and the priests completed the slaughter of the rest who remained alive. In the concluding dances Teteo/ innan was replaced by Centeotl, the maize/goddess, with whom she was virtually synonymous. After the warriors had run races, the priest wearing the skin of the victim impersona/ ting the goddess was driven out of the town and the skin was hung on a framework in her sanctuary near a hostile frontier of the tribe.[9]

Amid universal rejoicing in the twelfth twentieth (Septem/ ber 10), a feast of all the gods was held to celebrate the return of the fire divinities at the end of the rainy season. At its con/ clusion living human victims were thrown into the flames of a ceremonial fire, as in the harvest rites which were continued at the end of the month with more offerings to the rain/gods. The fourteenth feast (Quetchotli), associated with Mixcoatl, the god of hunting and war, required the sacrifice of a repre/ sentative of Tezcatlipoca, the chief god of the pantheon, together with a number of slaves bound like captive deer.[10] In November at the fifteenth feast (Panquetzaliztli) in honour of the birth and victory of Huitzilopochtli, the warriors and the prisoners engaged in a combat at the end of which the victims were burnt alive on a great cylindrical stone at the foot of the staircase of the temple of the god. Later in the month more sacrifices were offered to Tlaloc, and in December a woman impersonating the goddess Ilamtecuhtli, the Old Goddess related to corn and the earth, was decapitated at sundown and her head given to a priest wearing her costume and mask. He then led a dance round the platform on which the sacrifice had been offered, followed by priests similarly attired.[11]

The year with its succession of human immolations came to an end on January 8, the eighteenth twentieth, with a feast called Izcalli, dedicated to Xiuhtecuhtli, the god of fire, sometimes known as Huehuetcotl, the Old God, who was represented as a vegetation deity clothed in green quetzal-feathers and wearing a mask of turquoises and green stones, and alter-natively as a fire-god clad in red macaw feathers and having a mask of red and black stones. Every fourth year, men and their wives were arrayed in the attire of the fire-god and thrown into the flames only to be raked out and their hearts extracted, as in the harvest rite.[12] The purpose of this barbarous observance may have been to consecrate the victims by passing them through the fire before making the life-giving oblation of their hearts at the end of the year in the Aztec solar calendar.

Throughout these rites the underlying purpose was to enable the sun to continue its beneficent functions upon which the means of subsistence depended. As three suns were believed to have been destroyed, representing a succession of world-ages, causing universal destruction and the transformation of men into animals, the present epoch was in a precarious position under the control of the Sun-god Tonatiuh, being destined to be destroyed by earthquakes.[13] Therefore, every effort had to be made to prevent a recurrence of the catastrophe, or to delay the ultimate destiny as long as possible. The Aztecs, however, were not so vicious a people as their rites would suggest, or oblivious of human suffering. They were rather themselves the victims of their mythology as recorded on their Calendar Stone in Tenochtitlan. This belief put into practice entailed constant wars to keep up the supply of victims from outside, and so the sun was the god of warriors as well as the lord of the vegetation deities who controlled the forces of nature and promoted the growth of the maize, the principal cereal of Mexico. Without the requisite number of captives as sacrificial victims the crops would fail. Therefore, the calendrical rites were solar in origin and significance, military in practice. It was not, however, until the pastoral Aztec civilization developed and became pre-dominant that the indigenous vegetation cults took over this military characteristic, though warlike qualities always have been displayed by the Great Mother. And in Central America this aspect of her cultus was particularly prominent, and was linked with the mode of obtaining the steady flow of human victims on the grand scale required to keep the sun in being.

It is true that the entire pantheon, male and female, became incorporated in the calendrical ritual, assuming various inde/ pendent roles; nevertheless, it was the solar theory that lay behind the ritual in the first instance. Thus, the sun was *Tonatiuh*, the god *par excellence*, and if hearts were plucked out for the benefit of other deities, usually they were offered to him as well because he was the ultimate source of life. Therefore, behind the ghastly solar seasonal sequence lay the fundamental belief in the nourishment required by the sun to enable him to continue to supply the kindly fruits of the earth through the good offices of the several departmental gods and goddesses, notably the Mexican Mother of the gods. But since the king no longer sacrificed himself on behalf of his nation, as so fre/ quently was the case in regions where the sacral kingship was established,[14] it became necessary to secure efficacious sub/ stitutes. This requirement was met by the selection of the cour/ ageous, well-born virile young warrior elected to play the role of Tezcatlipoca for a year and in that capacity to be slain sacrificially at the Annual Festival, Toxcatl, when the sun was at its zenith on April 23.

Vestiges of it in agricultural communities in other parts of the continent suggest that the practice was not confined to the Aztecs or to Central America in the New World. Thus, in the North, among the Hurons, a confederation of four Iro/ quoian tribes in Ontario, prisoners of war, were tortured to death as an offering to the War-god, who seems to have been another form of the Sun-god, after they had impersonated him for a given period, and then were duly venerated after their death.[15] Elsewhere human sacrifice has recurred sporadically among the Iroquois,[16] the Skidi Pawnee,[17] and the Natchez of Louisiana.[18]

Human Sacrifice in Peru

In Peru human victims were offered to maintain the vigour of the Sun-god, though the custom was modified under Inca rule, being confined to the death of a ruler and the accession of his successor 'to give health and preserve his kingdom in peace', and that he might reach a great age, and 'pass his time without illness'.[19] So great was the ardour of the wives of the ruler and his attendants to accompany him to the tomb, however, that many of those who clamoured to be buried alive with him had to be restrained.[20] Only one or two were offered from each village and clan, together with cattle and sheep; sometimes their hearts were extracted and their blood smeared on a statue of the god to whom the oblation was made, be he the Sun, the Creator, the Moon, or Thunder.[21] The bodies were then buried with the rest of the offerings. That the victims, in addi-tion to children, included the wives and other women is indicated by a cemetery in the precincts of the temple of Pacha-camac, the Great Spirit, containing sumptuously dressed fe-males evidently sacrificed to the sun.[22]

It would seem, therefore, that however much human sacri-fice may have been mitigated in the Inca Empire the welfare of the ruler and of the community was thought to be dependent upon it to some extent. Resort was made to it at the festival at Huanacauri in honour of a *huaca*, or divine being, who was turned to stone there, and on such occasions as the beginning of wars or the celebration of notable victories. Since children also were offered to sacred stones 'that the sun might not lose its power', and on a hill called Mantocalla, where the sun was supposed to descend to sleep when the grain was removed from the maize-cobs,[23] the practice appears to have had a solar sig-nificance. It is said, in fact, that the native tribes of Ecuador were in the habit of sacrificing over a hundred children annually at the harvest to maintain the maize-crops.[24] More-over, so deeply engrained was the practice that it survived not only in the Inca Empire but after the Spanish occupation of Peru.

Pawnee Survivals

In the Pawnee confederacy in the Mississippi basin as late as 1817 a Comanche girl who had been taken prisoner by the

Skidi was rescued from being offered to the Morning Star by a Chanti warrior who dashed into the assembly, seized the victim and carried her off to her tribe on his horse. This daring deed was followed by other attempts at rescue, but it did not prevent a Sioux girl in her early teens being dedicated to the Morning Star for six months in 1838 and treated as sacred in the manner of the Aztec young divine victim. Two days before she was due to be sacrificed she was led from wigwam to wigwam accompanied by the chiefs and warriors. At each she received wood and paint, and on April 22 she was painted half red and half black, tied to a sort of ladder, slowly roasted over a slow fire, and then shot with arrows. The chief sacrificer tore out her heart and devoured it while the rest of her body was cut into small pieces and placed in baskets to be taken to a neighbouring cornfield. There the blood was squeezed on the new grains of corn to vitalize them. The flesh was made into a kind of paste which was rubbed on the potatoes, beans and seeds to fertilize them. The implements were burnt in the fire and the ashes strewn on the fields for the same purpose.[25] As the Skidi came from the south it is possible that they retained earlier influences derived from Mexican sources unʹ like the rest of the confederacy in which the rite was obsolete.

The Khond Sacrifice of the Meriah in India

In India a very similar custom prevailed among the Khonds, a Dravidian people in Bengal. To ensure good crops and imʹ munity from disease, a victim called the Meriah was purʹ chased—unless he was the son of a Meriah or had been devoted to the altar from childhood. Having attained the status in one or other of these ways, he was treated with great reverence as a consecrated person until, when the destined day arrived, his hair was cut off and he was arrayed in a new garment before being led in solemn procession amid music and dancing to a sacred grove set apart for the purpose. There he was tied to a post, anointed with oil, ghee and turmeric, adorned with flowers and reverenced throughout the day and night. Having exonerated themselves from any guilt in making the sacrifice, and asking the Earth-goddess to give them 'good crops, seasons, and health', after anointing him again they either strangled or squeezed the Meriah to death, or cut him to pieces. The flesh was distributed among the villages and divided into two portions by the priest. One was offered to the Earth-goddess by burying it in a hole in the ground, the other given to the heads of the houses to be buried in their best fields, or hung on a pole at the stream which watered them. The head, bones and intestines were burned in a pyre together with a sheep on the following day, and the ashes scattered over the fields and granaries or mixed with new corn.[26]

While there may have been a propitiatory intention in the rite to appease the Earth-goddess,[27] Frazer is probably right when he says that the treatment of the body of the victim implies that to it was ascribed 'a direct or intrinsic power of making the crops grow, quite independent of the indirect goodwill of the deity.'[28] The flesh and the ashes were regarded as endowed with fertilizing power like the blood of the Skidi girl employed to give life to the new corn, and, as in Mexico, to promote the growth of the crops. It was for this reason that they were performed at the sowing of the fields, at the in-gathering of harvest, or at the beginning of the rainy or the dry season in the sequence of the agricultural year. The Meriah was set apart by descent or consecration as a sacred person, as in the Aztec and Pawnee counterparts of the ritual. In all these cases, the victims were treated with great reverence and respect, sometimes with divine honours, and it is not im-probable that in the background of this type of human sacri-fice lay the widespread custom of securing substitutes for sacral kings to maintain the processes of vegetation.

Head-hunting Expeditions in Indonesia

At a lower cultural level the practice of head-hunting among the Dravidian Indian tribes in the Naga Hills, in Indonesia, and the Pacific is closely related to that of human sacrifice as its purpose has been primarily to fertilize the crops or to pro-mote the well-being of the cattle. The head was regarded as particularly rich in soul-substance.[29] Thus, in Burma and Borneo human heads are thought to contain the *toh* (life principle or ghost) which, if conveyed to the soil, stimulates the growth of the crops and brings prosperity to the person responsible for securing them.[30] Therefore, head-hunting expeditions have been rife at the times of planting and reaping the crops to secure trophies to make the rice grow green, the maize ripen, and the poppy fields flourish.[31] In the Philippine Islands every Bantoc farm requires at least one new head at the time of the planting and sowing of the rice, necessitating raiding expeditions at these seasons. On the raiders' return to their village amid rejoicing the skulls are exposed on trees around which dances are held. When the flesh has decayed the head is taken home by the man who captured it, and is preserved at his farm, while those who assisted him do the same with the hands and the feet.[32]

In Borneo head-hunting is regarded as a tradition bequeathed by the tribal ancestors to give plentiful harvests and prevent sickness. So essential are the trophies that should they get destroyed fragments of skulls have to be procured from somewhere to prevent the loss of vitality.[33] Dr Hose explains the practice as a desire to supply the dead with slaves to continue their service beyond the grave,[34] but this seems to be a later interpretation of the earlier and more widespread fertility motive. Thus, head-hunting is certainly not confined to funerary ritual, being mainly an adjunct to spring and autumn festivals to which have been added a mortuary extension in association with a combat on the return from a funeral.[35] Hutton in fact thinks that placing heads on graves on the mainland is the result of a people practising human sacrifice in their funeral ceremonies, having had contact with head-hunters.[36] Similarly, Rivers maintained that in Melanesia the offering of the head of an enemy arose directly out of the practice of human sacrifice and the cult of the dead, head-hunting being originally the outcome of the idea of the head as the seat of potency.[37]

Since the head has been regarded as the source of vital power it has become a revivifying agent alike for the crops and for a corpse. This explains the custom of preserving the skull for a period for use in connexion with spring and harvest rites, as, for instance, among the Ao who desiccate the corpse in the smoke of a fire to keep it until the eating of the first-fruits at the next harvest.[38] In Indonesia the Cham of Annam bury pieces of the frontal bone of the skull of the deceased in a metal box at the foot of a tree for seven years, and then deposit it near the best of the family fields, surrounded with trees and marked by a tombstone.[39] In Upper Burma the Wild Wa set forth in March on head-hunting expeditions to find victims among strangers in their mountain ranges. Their heads are brought back to the village, and after wild dances in a drunken orgy the trophies are taken to the spirit-house on the highest point of the local hills. There wrapped in grass or leaves they are hung up in a basket to dry and bleach before they are deposited in the golgotha where all the skulls are set on posts in an avenue of trees to make the rice grow in the valley, the maize on the mountain-sides, and the poppies on the hill-tops.[40] Similarly, in southern Melanesia the heads of old women are set on poles as charms for good crops in New Caledonia,[41] and the Maoris take the dried heads of those decapitated in war from their graves to the fields where sweet potatoes are to be sown to fertilize the soil.[42]

Heads, then, have been preserved not merely as trophies but chiefly for purposes connected with fertilization, often brought into conjunction with the cult of the dead, and sometimes with the veneration of ancestors and heroes whose potency has been in proportion to their eminence. As an adjunct of human sacrifice the ritual treatment of the head of the victim has been due to its vitality, like the outpouring of the life-giving blood. The special treatment reserved for it in the Hebrew sacrificial system—where it had to be laid on the altar and burnt, or in the case of the sin-offering of ignorance, taken outside the camp and burnt[43]—in all probability was a survival of the special sanctity which was assigned to the head in the earlier ritual transferred to the animal victim in the post-exilic temple worship.

The Cult of Skulls and Sacramental Anthropophagy

The very ancient practice of eating the brain sacramentally has been prevalent in the cult of skulls and their preservation going back to Palaeolithic times. Thus, the cutting off of the head and the preservation of the skullcap after the brain had been eaten in a sacred meal was a prominent feature apparently in the caves near Chou Kon T'ien in North China in the Lower Pleistocene, and the custom continued in the Upper Palaeolithic in Europe at Placard, Charente in France, at Krapina in Croatia, and at Ofnet in the Jura. Where it has been adopted among primitive peoples today it has generally been for the purpose of imbibing the strength, courage, wisdom or other mental qualities of the deceased. The same intention also underlies the use of the skull as a drinking vessel, to which sometimes was added the hope of becoming possessed by the spirit of a dead chief, warrior or magician, as, for example, among the ancient Arabs,[44] as well as in Uganda,[45] the Congo and Fiji.[46]

But this sacramental consumption of a sacrificial victim or sacred person in order to obtain his qualities was not confined to the head. Among the Aztecs, as we have seen, the bodies of the victims in the calendrical ritual were given to the warriors who captured them so that they could hold a banquet on their flesh with their friends. Furthermore, twice a year, in May and December, a dough image of Huitzilopochtli was eaten sacramentally to secure health and strength. At the winter festival the blood of children was kneaded into maize paste, and the heart of the image was cut out by a priest and eaten by the king, the rest being distributed among the men,[47] very much as the body of the virile young representative of Tezcatlipoca was consumed by the priests and nobles as 'blessed food'. The Sioux in North America were in the habit of reducing to powder the heart of a valiant foe and swallowing it to appropriate his valour, and Chippewa women fed their children with the flesh and blood of English prisoners to make them warriors.[48] For the same reason the Nahua ate the hearts of the Spaniards during the wars of the conquest of Central

America, while more recently the Ashanti chiefs devoured the heart of Sir C. J. McCarthy to obtain his courage.[49]

In addition to the idea of gaining renewal of strength and vigour from a sacred meal on food charged with supernatural or divine potency, the notion of establishing a blood covenant with the source of bounty and beneficence, as well as with the illustrious dead, was an integral feature in sacramental anthro, pophagous ritual. By sharing in the life, or soul, substance, a new kinship was effected between the living and the dead, calculated to make for the well, being and stability of the indi, viduals concerned and of the community at large. Conversely, the custom of the slayer eating a portion of the man he has slain may have arisen from a desire to form a sacred bond with the victim as a means of escaping his revenge by making him his kinsman. Thus, he absorbs his vitality and at the same time prevents the ghost from doing him harm. It was only at a later stage in the development of the practice, in all probability, that anthropophagy lost its ritual significance and degenerated into acts of revenge, fear of the dead and gluttony, or into a means of obtaining food, as when Samaria was besieged by the Syrians.[50] Originally, however, it seems to have been primar, ily a sacramental aspect of the institution of sacrifice.

THE FERTILE CRESCENT

Human Sacrifice in Ancient Egypt

Precisely to what extent human sacrifice and anthropophagy were practised in the Ancient Near East is not very easy to determine. In the Fertile Crescent prisoners of war were taken in considerable numbers and slain on a grand scale, but it does not follow that they were necessarily sacrificial victims, as Budge has contended.[51] Certainly, in some of the predynastic graves in Ancient Egypt there are signs that the flesh was removed and the bodies dismembered, the head having been wrapped in a cloth after decapitation. The normal procedure, however, was for the corpse to be covered with skins below the neck or wrapped in matting in the Amratian burials, though this custom tended to be abandoned in due course. When the head was removed sometimes a pot or an ostrich eye was substituted for it; which hardly suggests that the bodies were those of sacrificial victims. Neither the scene depicted on an ivory plaque at Abydos wherein a First Dynasty king holds an enemy by his hair and is about to smash his skull with a mace, nor the representation of ten decapitated captives before the emblems of the gods, on the slate palette of King Narmer,[52] often quoted as evidence of human sacrifice, necessarily implies anything more than the slaughter of enemies by the victorious king after a battle; these may be compared to the slaying of Agag by Samuel,[53] which may or may not have had a sacrificial intention. The same applies to the other similar scenes reproduced by Budge in this connexion,[54] of which a considerable number occur throughout the Dynastic period. The strangling of two Nubian slaves brought on a sledge by a 'sem' priest to the grave-pit and subsequently burned, illustrated on a tomb of the New Kingdom,[55] could indicate a holocaust at the funeral of a magnate, but it is not a direct proof that such human sacrifices were offered to Osiris under the New Empire, as has been suggested.

Nevertheless, it would not be surprising to find that the classical writers were correct in their repeated references to the immolation of human beings in Egypt. For example, Diodorus Siculus affirms that the Pharaohs formerly sacrificed men of the colour of Sethor Typhon (i.e. red-headed foreigners) on the tomb of Osiris.[56] Porphyry says that Amosis modified the sacrifices to Hera at Heliopolis by substituting wax images for the human victims.[57] Procopius mentions the offering of human victims to the Sun-god at Philae,[58] Ovid refers to foreigners having been sacrificed during a famine caused by a low Nile for nine years,[59] and Ruffinus deplores the fact that heads of children were preserved in the temple of Serapis at Alexandria.[60] Herodotus, on the other hand, dismisses the evidence on the subject in general as 'dragomans' tales' to tourists.[61] But the statements taken collectively suggest that the rite was known in the Nile valley even though it was never an established institution as in the New World. This is confirmed by the burial of servants with the rest of her funerary equipment at the interment of a princess in the First Dynasty, and the inclusion of several hundred Nubian slaves in the obsequies of 'the chief Headman of the South' in the Middle Kingdom. It is not improbable that they had been strangled, or, as at Ur in Mesopotamia, stupefied before they were laid on the floor with a few pots and pans, a sword and personal adornments, before the tumulus was filled in with earth.

The Royal Tombs at Ur

Both in the Nile valley and in Mesopotamia, royal tombs with grave goods of this nature appear to have been quite unique. Thus, those excavated by Sir Leonard Woolley at Ur, the traditional home of Abraham situated between Baghdad and the upper head of the Persian Gulf, and now dated at about 2250 B.C., are very different from the graves of the commoners in the cemetery outside the walls of the city. These enclose corpses in the flexed position in coffins of clay, wood and basket-work wrapped in matting, together with a few personal belongings, weapons, implements and the remains of food offerings.

The royal tombs, on the other hand, consist of domed chambers with a pit for offerings and additional burials. The quantities of furniture and goods brought to light in 1922 were immense; they included a fine head of a bull in gold with eyes of lapis lazuli and other animals in gold, clusters of pomegranates, trees and their fruits in gold and carnelian, silver bowls and tables, stone vessels, harps, lyres, an inlaid gaming board, the statue of a ram with its front legs bound to the branches of a tree with silver chains. Significantly, there were found, too, richly clad and ornamented bodies of courtiers, maids of honour and guards who, faithful to death, had been buried in order to continue the service to their ruler they had rendered so loyally and devotedly in their life. Besides these, there were soldiers in two ranks with copper spears by their sides, court ladies wearing a gala head-dress of lapis lazuli and carnelian beads, golden pendants, necklaces and ear-rings, on each of whose bodies had been laid a wooden harp, having the head of a bull in gold and copper respectively. Behind this chamber containing the body of the ruler, A,ber,gi, was a similar second chamber in which his queen, Shub,ad, had been buried on a wooden bier with a gold cup near her hand. On her skull were the remains of a head,dress, while a second one, ornamented with thousands of lapis lazuli beads and animal figures, lay by her side; the remains of two women attendants rested against the bier, one at the head and the other at the foot.

Around the interments were traces of a funeral feast and of fires. Thus arrayed in all their courtly attire and regalia, the attendants quite clearly must have accompanied the sovereign and his consort to the after,life. In the absence of any indications of a struggle or of a violent death, it is not improbable that as they walked to their appointed places in the chambers they drank some fatal potion such as hashish or opium from the little clay or metal cups each carried, and then, having lost consciousness, they were placed in position before the shaft was filled up.[62] So ended the sacrifice, doubtless gladly and volun, tarily made on behalf of the sacral Sumerian rulers by their entourage in the hope of continuing their service under new conditions beyond the grave.

This procedure, however, appears to have been unique in Mesopotamia, there being nothing in the Sumerian texts or the archaeological data to suggest that the practice of human sacri, fice was an established custom. It has been suggested that it represented the annual offering of a substitute for the divine king at the Spring Festival to renew the processes of vegetation as a fertility rite. But for such a purpose the sixteen graves at Ur seem to be quite inadequate, and there are no indications that they were part of the sacred marriage ceremonial with which these rites usually are associated. On the contrary, the names of the two royal occupants of the tomb have been discovered on cylinder seals, and all the circumstances of the elaborate inter, ment suggest the obsequies of a local sacral city,king and his queen at the rise of the Dynasty of Ur.

Babylonia and Assyria

There is no reason to suppose that the rite was perpetuated in Babylonia and Assyria. The few possible references to the practice are very obscure and open to question, though in one inscription the sacrifice of a slave with an ox or a sheep is mentioned.[63] In an Assyrian document belonging to the seventh century B.C., the eldest son or daughter is said to have been burnt in the fire in the service of a god,[64] reminiscent perhaps of the passing of children through the fire to Moloch in the valley of Hinnom in pre-exilic Israel before the Josiah re-formation.[65] But it seems to have been in the nature of a penalty for a breach of contract rather than an established institution.

The Offering of the First-born in Palestine

In Palestine, the numerous bodies of children discovered in the foundations of buildings leave no room for doubt that oblations of this character were of common occurrence among the Canaanites to strengthen the walls of houses and cities. Thus, in the whole area of the high place at Gezer skeletons of new-born infants were buried, deposited in jars with food-offerings in smaller vessels, two at least of the bodies showing marks of fire.[66] Similar jar-interments were found by Sellin at Taanach, while at Gezer two burnt skeletons of children of about six years of age were also unearthed inside the precincts. That the infants were an oblation of first-born devoted to the temple from birth may be deduced from the fact that they were less than a week old, and from the occurrence of similar offer-ings in the corners of houses or under the foundations.

This practice of first-born human sacrifice was, it seems, not confined to the Canaanites, for the eighth-century Hebrew prophetic Midrash records the impulse of Abraham to offer his son Isaac on the altar.[67] The story may be based on a legend of a sanctuary where at one time human victims of this nature were sacrificed before rams were substituted for them as an amelioration of the original rite. Similarly, the king of Moab offered his eldest son as a burnt-offering to Chemosh to induce him to turn his wrath upon Israel.[68] When Hiel rebuilt Jericho in the reign of Ahab (*c.* 880 B.C.) he laid the founda- tion in his first-born Abiram, and set up the gates in his young- est son, Segib.[69] Although there is no confirmation of these alleged foundation sacrifices in the occupation levels recently excavated by Miss Kenyon, the tradition shows that the curse upon the city was believed to require such offerings on the part of the Bethelite to prevent divine vengeance descending upon him. Even after the Exile when Nehemiah rebuilt the walls of Jericho 'great sacrifices' had to be made,[70] though there is no indication, of course, that they included human victims, the practice having long since been abandoned.

Human Sacrifice in Israel
Nevertheless, the belief that human offerings were acceptable to Yahweh was perpetuated in the story of the fulfilment of the vow of Jephthah in the sacrifice of his only daughter, especially as it appears to have become a cult-legend of a feast annually commemorating the event.[71] Indeed, in the days of the monarchy, after the offering of the first-born sons to Yahweh had been modified by the substitution of an animal or payment of a sum of money by way of compensation for the dark deed, it was continually reappearing in spite of the efforts to suppress it.[72] The passing of children through the fire to Moloch was for- bidden under pain of death,[73] but the indictment was ignored by Ahab and Manasseh;[74] and just before the Exile (*c.* 600 B.C.) there was a spate of child sacrifices at Topheth in the valley of Hinnom,[75] doubtless first-born victims dedicated mainly to Moloch and Baal, but often in conjunction with the worship of Yahweh[76] who was popularly felt to require this supreme form of sacrifice, following the example of Abraham, Jephthah, Hiel and Ahaz.

GREECE

The Funeral of Patroclus
Although in Greece the classical writers repudiated human sacrifice as a barbarous custom its memory persisted in heroic

tales such as the myth of Iphigenia, Andromeda and Hesione, Polyxena, and similar incidents in the legendary history of Troy and Athens, in the cult of Dionysus, and in the ritual of Zeus Lykaios.[77] In the account of the funeral of Patroclus in the *Iliad* (xxiii, 175), Homer records the slaying of twelve Trojan nobles before the pyre of Patroclus, together with four horses and two dogs. This was clearly not just an act of remorse by Achilles to avenge the death of his friend Patroclus, as Homer says. Rather was it a sacrificial slaughter of the retinue of the deceased, including his slaves, horses and dogs, to accompany him to the after-life, as in the case of the immo-lation of the victims in the royal tombs at Ur. That such an offering was out of keeping with the Homeric conception of the psyche becoming a witless shade (*eidolon*) in Hades sug-gests that Homer in fact was relating and reinterpreting a traditional tale handed down from an earlier age; an age when human sacrifice was a recognized practice in the obsequies of the illustrious dead, as in the funerary equipment of Scythian kings described by Herodotus, which included their cooks, butlers and other members of their household who were strangled and buried in their tombs.[78]

The Myth of Iphigenia

Similarly, the sacrifice of the daughter of Agamemnon by her father in the myth of Iphigenia recorded by Aeschylus,[79] was softened by Euripides when he made Artemis substitute a hind for her, and carry her away to the country of Tauri[80] where, instead of being offered upon the altar, she became the priestess of Artemis herself and sacrificed to the goddess all strangers found in the land. When in due course Orestes, her brother, arrived in Tauri with the image of Artemis, he and his companion Pylades were taken prisoner. When Iphigenia discovered their identity she contrived to get them to the sea-shore with the image, and with the help of Athena to secure their escape to Attica. There she continued to be the priestess of the goddess, now called Tauropolos. The last vestige of human sacrifice was the making of a small cut on the throat of

the man playing the role of the former victim in the performance of her rites at Halae.

The Cult of Dionysus

It is probable that the origin of the rites in Thrace and Phrygia,
during which a bull or a goat embodying the god Zagreus
(Dionysus) was torn to pieces and devoured, was a feast on
the raw flesh of a human victim treated in the same manner as
the animal substitute. Thus, on a red-figured vase in the British
Museum, probably belonging to the fourth century B.C.,[81] a
bearded man in Thracian attire is depicted with a child in his
left hand and holding part of its body to his mouth with his
right hand, apparently in the act of eating it. To the left stands
another bearded figure wreathed with ivy or a vine, and the
thyrsos in his right hand, representing unquestionably Dionysus. On the right is yet another bearded Thracian running
away, looking back, and extending his left hand as if in
horror or fear. Here the slaying and eating of an infant is shown
in a Dionysian context, though the barbaric rite in its original
Thracian form had been abandoned before the ritual reached
Greece; in the Athenian festival, either an animal or a rustic
song sung over a wine-press telling of the rending of Dionysus,[82] accompanied perhaps by a pantomimic performance of
the human omophagia, was the substitute.[83]

In Times of Stress

Moreover, this is not an isolated instance of the survival of
human sacrifice to Dionysus. Thus, before the battle of Salamis
in 480 B.C., three Persian nobles were sacrificed to him by
Themistocles at the command of Euphrantides the seer.[84] On
the island of Tenedos, between Thrace and Crete, infants were
offered to Palaimon, the son of the nurse of Dionysus, and on
Mount Lykaion in Arcadia at the sanctuary of Zeus Lykaios,
the entrails of a human victim were said to have been consumed
by the worshippers.[85] It is most improbable, however, that
such practices, or human sacrifices in any form to Zeus

Lykaios, could have survived in the time of Pausanias (*c.*
A.D. 150) in spite of his guarded references to 'secret sacrifices'
of this nature known to him, the details of which, he says, he
did not care to pry into.[86]

Nevertheless, the institution lingered on in Greek tradition,
but it was only under stress of intense emotional excitement, as
in the Dionysian rites, or of wars and serious calamities such
as the First Messenian War in the eighth century B.C., or the
battle of Salamis four hundred years later, that it was condoned, mitigated, or carefully veiled in classical times.[87] Then
the urge was too strong to be held in check. Domophoon, it is
alleged, could not resist sacrificing a maiden of noble birth to
Persephone in the face of an Argive invasion,[88] just as
the Athenians slew the daughters of Hyacinthus at the dic-
tates of an oracle when they were attacked by pestilence and
famine.[89] But when an Athenian Embaros had undertaken
to give his daughter as an offering to relieve a famine, he sacrificed a goat in her guise.[90]

The Thargelian Pharmakoi

Slaves were maintained in Athens at public expense to be
sacrificed whenever a plague or similar calamity befell the
city.[91] To drive away hunger and misfortune a condemned
criminal was thrown over a cliff into the sea annually at the
temple of Apollo in the island of Leucas, though the custom
later was ameliorated by making him slide down a rope into
the sea where he was rescued.[92] At the harvest festival of the
Thargelia in Athens two men called pharmakoi were led out
of the city, one representing the male section of the population,
the other the female, it may be for stoning, though the account
of the practice is very obscure on this score.[93] Nevertheless, the
Greeks in Asia Minor in the sixth century B.C. in the time of
plague, famine, or other disaster selected the ugliest man available to take upon himself the evils from which they were
suffering. He was then conveyed to a suitable place and cheese,
dried figs and cakes were put into his hand. Then he was
beaten with quills seven times on the genitals, burnt on a pyre,

and his ashes thrown into the sea.[94] Whether or not this persisted in Athens at the zenith of its civilization, that it represents the background of the Athenian Thargelia is supported
by later classical authorities who refer to an immolation and to
other instances of human sacrifice in Apolline ritual.[95]

ROME

Survivals in Roman Religion

Where Rome is concerned, whenever human sacrifice is mentioned in the literature it is referred to as a repulsive and
obsolete practice never tolerated in the State religion.[96] Nevertheless it was known.[97] Thus, as late as the second century A.D.
it is said that a man called a *bestiarus* was sacrificed to Jupiter
Latiaris on Mount Alban.[98] It is, however, an isolated
instance connected with a festival featuring gladiatorial shows
in which animal baiting and similar brutal and perilous
exploits were practised, doubtless involving a heavy toll of life.
This was, perhaps, subsequently interpreted as a ritual immolation. Another rather similar instance is the vow of the *ver
sacrum*, when in addition to animals and first-fruits of the
spring growth the male children born at a critical moment in
the Hannibalic War in 217 B.C. were dedicated to Mars. But
this, again, occurred only at a time of extreme stress, and also of
over-population when young men and women at the age of
twenty were sent beyond the boundaries of the state,[99] though
it is not clear whether they were actually slain.

The Rite of the Argei

On May 14 or 15, twenty-four or twenty-seven puppets made
of straw or rush to resemble human beings bound hand and
foot, and called *Argei*, were thrown into the Tiber from the
pons sublicius at Rome by the Vestal Virgins in the presence of
the Pontifex Maximus, the Pontifices, and the Flaminica
Dialis, who had laid aside her bridal dress in favour of mourning, probably because the ceremony was in the nature of a
purification rite at the beginning of the ingathering of the
crops.[100] The custom has been explained both by ancient and

modern writers as a survival of offerings of old men to the river, modified perhaps by the use of puppets as simulacra of the victims.[101] From the absence of any reference to the ceremony in the ancient calendars Wissowa conjectured that the sacrifice was of relatively recent origin (c. the third century B.C., be, tween the first and second Punic Wars) in response to an oracle obtained from the Sibylline books. After the drowning of the first victims the puppets were introduced and continued to be used. [102] But, as Warde Fowler has pointed out, if anything of this kind actually had occurred within living memory the custom would not have been ascribed to the ancient past (i.e. Numa), nor would it have given rise to such a crop of varied explanations.[103]

Mannhardt, on the other hand, regarded the puppets as the dying spirit of vegetation in the spring. At the beginning of summer they were thrown into the Tiber where they were revived by the water and so restored to fresh vigour to re, animate the fruits of the earth.[104] But the Ides of May were much too late in Rome for the performance of a spring rite, be it that of the vegetation spirit or the Jack,in,the,Green in modern May Day celebrations.[105] Neither of these interpreta, tions accounts for the figures being surrogates for human vic, tims, or for the presence of the Vestal Virgins and the cathartic setting of the rite in relation to their festivals for the purpose of averting evil influences at a critical juncture in the seasonal cycle. These associations seem to indicate an expulsion cere, mony in which in the distant past sin,receivers, probably human beings, played some part in the removal of pollution at an annual expiation held between March and June, and perhaps again in the autumn. A rite of this nature, combining propitiation, cleansing, mourning and rejoicing, would find its proper place in the agricultural sequence connected with the first,fruits and the harvest in order to avert evil influences always rampant on these occasions. In Rome they reached their climax in the Vestalia, which concluded with the sweeping of the *penus*, or temple storehouse of Vesta, in preparation for the new grain. Therefore, the presence of the Virgins at the

Argei rite would be very much in accord with their other functions in connexion with the grain (e.g. the *mola salsa*, the Consualia and the Opiconsivia, the Fordicidia and the Lupercalia), though much less so with the vegetation spirit with whom they had only very remote and indirect associations. This was also the case with regard to fertility ritual in general which lay outside their immediate province. But in the background of the *Argei* the puppets in all probability were substitutes for human beings even though it is doubtless true that human sacrifice was never an established institution in ancient Rome.

INDIA

Human Sacrifice in Vedic India

In Vedic India there are indications of a former prevalence of human sacrifice in spite of the efforts to suppress or ameliorate the practice when the Brahmanic literature was in process of compilation. Then the tendency was for either the victims to be released alive, or animals to be substituted for them. Nevertheless, prior to British rule in India, a male child was sacrificed to Kali, the sinister and terrible spouse of Shiva, every Friday evening in her shrine in the Saiva temple at Tanjore. In spite of the Hindu aversion to the shedding of blood, this was, in fact, a common recurrent feature of her cultus everywhere until it was strictly forbidden by British law in the last century. For example, human sacrifices were offered regularly at Kamakhya near Gauhati in Assam, the chief sanctuary of Saktism on the Brahmaputra, and it is admitted that only legal restrictions prevented the continuance of the custom. So deeply laid in the ritual texts are the prescriptions exacting one or more human victims, and the evil consequences thought to follow failure to comply with the injunctions, that they have never been entirely abolished or disposed of with the aid of symbolic representations.

Though the *Rig-Veda* contains no precise mention of human sacrifice, it cannot be dismissed as either the obsolete survival of a primitive barbarous institution or the aberration of a later morbid religious sense obsessed with the idea of a supreme sacrifice. It was far too widespread and firmly estab-lished in the sub-continent in the sixteenth century when Islam was introduced in Bengal to admit of these interpretations, and even the hideous Messiah rite continued to be practised among the Khonds until, under British rule, a goat or buffalo was substituted for the human victim. The more or less voluntary immolation of widows on the funeral pyres of their husbands, although not mentioned specifically in the Veda, was in vogue when the Greeks under Alexander the Great entered the Pun-jab.[106] Notwithstanding its prohibition in British territory in 1829, *Sati* has been regarded as a virtuous act on the part of a devoted wife, and it has never altogether ceased to be practised surreptitiously among the higher castes.

Vedic Texts and the Dravidian Cultus

Persistent allusions to the holocaust in the texts and tales leave no room for doubt that it was widely adopted. To some extent it may be regarded as a Dravidian heritage with an aboriginal background in north-east India and the Naga Hills where, as we have seen, head-hunting was particularly prevalent. The relative absence of evidence of the mention of human sacrifice in the early Vedic texts such as the Hymn of the Puruna and the *Rig-Veda*, in which sacrifice and its efficacy are discussed, suggests that this aspect of the institution did not come from Aryan sources in the first instance. We may perhaps detect in the mystical sacrifice of the Purusha, the Primal Male coeval with Brahman the Creator, for the purpose of producing the heavens and the earth,[107] traces of human sacrifice as a divinely appointed ordinance. But it is not certain whether the gigantic Vedic sacrifices, at which thousands of victims were supposed to have been immolated by hosts of priests extending over three generations, in fact included human victims. It was rather around the Mother-goddess in her manifold forms and modes of personification, especially in Bengal and Madras, that human blood flowed in torrents to avert evil, remove disease and other calamities. But the Goddess cult was pre-Aryan, in origin going back to the Harappa civilization, and not until it received Brahmanical sanction was it united with that of Purusha and Shiva. Then human sacrifice found a place in Vedic religion.

Thus, in the *Aitareya-Brahmana* to the *Rig-Veda* (vii, 13–18) a certain King Harischandra who had no son vowed that he would sacrifice to Varuna the first child born to him, but when in due course the child was begotten the king delayed fulfilling his vow until the boy was grown up. Knowing his fate, the lad fled and for six years wandered in the forest where he met a starving Brahman. He persuaded this man to sell him one of his sons for a hundred cows. This youth was then taken to the king who was suffering from dropsy as a punishment for not keeping his vow, but when the substitute was about to be sacrificed to appease Varuna, he was released by the other gods to whom the victim recited verses from the Veda. This ending to the episode would seem to suggest some Brahmanic uneasiness about the performance of the rite as foreign and repugnant to Aryan instincts, especially as in the same *Brahmana* is an account of the substitution of the sacrifice of horses, oxen, sheep and finally goats, for that of man. Later, in the *Satapatha Brahmana* it is stated that after human victims had been consecrated they were to be released,[108] but this is clearly a modification of an earlier rite in which they paid the supreme penalty of their dedication to the altar. It is evident, then, that in the background of Hinduism human sacrifice was by no means uncommon in the pre-Aryan tradition and that from this source it became gradually incorporated in the Vedic religion under Brahmanic influence, though it was permitted only with considerable hesitation and often with distaste as an excrescence derived from the Dravidian heritage and its aboriginal substratum. It was sufficiently endemic to be able to survive sporadically even in the later developments of Hinduism until ultimately it was forcibly suppressed under British rule in the last century.

CHAPTER V

Expiation and Atonement

SIN AND EXPIATION

THE deeply rooted and widespread belief that blood is the life of all organisms, human and animal, has given its sacrificial outpouring a piacular efficacy as an expiation for wrong-doing as well as making it a cathartic agent in removing uncleanness and ritual defilements. When a tabu has been broken, a pollu-tion incurred, or a god offended, wittingly or unwittingly, a life is required by way of propitiation in order that the evil and its consequences may be eliminated and divine favour and bene-ficence restored.

The Primitive Conception of Sin and Expiation

To the primitive mind good and evil, life and death, being in the nature of materialistic entities, are capable of expiation, expulsion or transference by ritual devices which have an aton-ing value. Divine displeasure is manifested in such disasters as the failure of the crops, outbreaks of plague and disease, and similar calamities attributed to some ritual defilement. This is quite distinct from moral wrong as understood in the higher religions and ethical systems. It follows that piacular sacrifices are offered primarily to expiate dangerous traits and harmful influences. For this purpose a human victim has often been selected because the offended god has been thought only to be appeased by the loss of the life of a man. Westermarck, in fact, based human sacrifice chiefly on the idea of substitution. The death of a human substitute, he maintained, was required to atone for the guilt. 'By sacrificing a man they hope to gratify the god's craving for human life, and thereby to avert the danger from themselves.'[1]

But why should human victims be offered to save the lives of those suffering from epidemics, famines, siege or similar misfortunes attributed to supernatural agencies? Dr Westermarck concludes that 'it is impossible to discover in every special case in what respect the worshippers believe the suffering of a fellow-creature to be gratifying to the deity.'[2] This may be true, but the worshippers never had definite views on the precise effect of the expiation achieved by the holocausts, as they are not restricted to any particular class or species of victims, or mode of offerings, as is evident in the Hebrew piaculum.[3] Nor is the operation of propitiatory sacrifices centred exclusively in one part of the ritual, though the blood-shedding invariably is the essential feature. The rite has atoning value because human life has always been regarded as having a peculiar potency, and men have offered their fellow-men to their gods to save themselves from divine anger and vengeance.

In the practice of offering life to preserve life the beginnings of the idea of substitution and propitiation may be detected in close association with the ritual removal of substantive pollution by quasi-mechanical means. When the sacrificer was himself in a condition of ritual impurity propitiatory offerings, ablutions, confessions and similar devices were required to purge the 'sin', or to transfer it to a human or animal victim or 'sin-carrier', to atone for, to cover or wipe out, or carry away the evil, and to re-establish the vital union with the supernatural order upon which the welfare of the individual and the community depends. The piacular victim combines the sacred and the profane, and the inherent potency, through its consecration and destruction, is transmitted either to or away from the sacrificer by a process of desacralization, thereby rendering harmful influences and dangerous conditions innocuous.

Sickness or death is met with a fresh outpouring of life, and atonement for the evil contracted or misfortune incurred is made by the act of expiation. If its source lies in an offended god whose hostility has been aroused by reason of an offence committed deliberately or inadvertently, a victim has to be offered to expiate the fault or error. If the evil is in the nature of a pollution contracted by the breach of a tabu or by contact with a defiling object (e.g. a corpse, a woman in childbirth, or the first-fruits), cathartic methods or expulsion may be sufficient but generally they are employed in conjunction with the sacrificial piaculum, the victim being set apart as a substitute for the offerer with whom he is identified by virtue of his consecration. He is actually giving part of himself.

Therefore, the piaculum has a dual purpose. It is an attempt to make a fresh start by driving away the accumulation of evil that hinders divine beneficence. It is also the means whereby vitality and energy, spiritual and physical, may be secured by the healing of the breach. In its primitive mode of expression it is devoid of any moral and ethical qualities in the modern sense, but, nevertheless, although sin is regarded as a ritual defilement, its expiation is a sacramental process of restoration of the state of religious purity and non-moral holiness on which the continuance of divine beneficence depends. Its purpose is to raise mankind either in an individual or corporate capacity to a higher spiritual status in which the transcendent exercises control over the physical and human, and the eternal over the temporal, but always through human agents and material instruments employed as the vehicle of purifying efficacy.

Good and evil have always been forces in perpetual conflict. This has given rise to elaborate systems of demonology as, for example, in Babylonia and Assyria where jinns, ghouls, vampires, disembodied ghosts of the dead (*edimmu*) and hordes of hostile spirits (*utukku, lilu, gallu,* etc.) abounded and required placation by piacular offerings and other expiatory rites of great complexity. Since sin was conceived as essentially demoniacal possession, the demons had to be expelled to regain the favour and protection of the gods, and the ban of the powers of evil loosened through such incantations as the Curse or Word of Power uttered by the priests in the name of their god Ea of Eridu, the Lord of Wisdom and Ruler of the healing waters. This magical rite not only exorcised the demons but conveyed mystic power to the persons or objects over which the Curse was pronounced by virtue of its institution by Ea investing Marduk with his own expiatory and consecrating powers.[4]

Thus, priests in uttering the Curse first proclaimed themselves as the duly commissioned agents of Ea to drive the demons into whatever substance (e.g. water, bread, grain or plants) might be selected for the purpose. This accomplished, the tainted article was then taken away to a 'clean place', or some-where where it was not likely to cause dangerous contamina-tions, and the ritual atonement was completed with the sacrifice of a goat or a lamb, presumably as a sin-offering.

The Babylonian sin-offering, which occupies a very promin-ent position in the texts, was always made to overcome some ritual error or offence, invariably committed unwittingly, so that the daily cry of the Sumerian penitent was the pathetic protest, 'I know not the sin which I have done; I know not the error which I have committed.'[5] Somehow he had brought down upon him the wrath of tyrannical deities who were always on the alert for the slightest infringement of the ritual order. The long list of possible misdemeanours enumerated in the incantational series called *Shurpu* covers, for example, ritual lapses, despising parents, insulting an elder sister, using false weights and shedding the blood of a neighbour.[6] Higher precepts of right and wrong are inserted perhaps by later redac-tors, as, for example, in the lofty prayers to Ishtar, where the Goddess is besought by the penitent to 'forgive my sin, my iniquity, my shameful deeds and my offences; overlook my transgressions, accept my prayer', ending with a rubric pre-scribing ceremonial lustrations with pure water and cleansings by means of aromatic woods and sacrificial offerings.[7] Nothing could sound more sublime than the prayer:

> The sin which I have done turn thou into goodness;
> The transgression which I have committed, let the wind carry it away;
> My many misdeeds I strip off like a garment;
> O my god, my transgressions are seven times seven; remove my trans-
> gressions.
> O my goddess, my transgressions are seven times seven; remove my transgressions.[8]

Yet the sins bewailed and expiated were for the most part ritual errors, often committed in ignorance; the general

outlook being that of the primitive conception of propitiation.

Similarly, in the royal public lamentation rituals, at a time
of calamity, purificatory rites had to be performed in conjunction with the magical lamentations uttered by the king on
behalf of the people. Here, again, moral faults were seldom
enumerated, and the cause of the misfortunes was unknown.
The ritual prescriptions, it is alleged, have been obeyed, the
feasts have been duly observed, and the images of the gods not
despised. The king, indeed, is represented in the Assyrian
bilingual texts as having suffered vicariously. The more he
gave himself to prayer and supplication, made 'sacrifice his
rule', 'the day of divine worship the pleasure of his heart', 'and
the procession of the goddess his riches and delight', the
more did he suffer and call in vain upon his god and 'entreated
the goddess but her head was not vouchsafed'. But when 'the
rust was wiped off' and 'the troubled' course became serene',
'the stain of slavery was cleansed away and the chain un-
bound' and the depth of despair was followed by a psalm of
thanksgiving. The ways of the gods were past finding out, and
all that could be done was to perform the prescribed incantations, the Curse of Ea and the other expiatory rites in the hope
of restoration, prosperity and protection from malevolent
influences in this life, the gods having denied the boon of
immortality to the human race.[9]

In Mesopotamia atonement was primarily a process of
removing evil (*gur*) by cathartic agents, among which blood
was not very conspicuous, and then casting away the objects
into which it had been projected. This act of expelling the
taint was called *kuppuru*, a word which implied a mechanical
act of atonement effecting the removal of the objects which had
absorbed the impurity, whether holy water, grain, or a sacrificial victim or sin-carrier. Although there is no evidence of
the transmission of evil to animals in Babylonia at all comparable to the Hebrew annual expiation in the seventh
month,[10] in a Sumerian incantation reference is made to a
horned wild goat taken by Marduk at the command of Ea, the

king bound by a curse, placing the goat's head against his head in order that his (the king's) 'poisonous venom into his mouth might be cast':

> May the king be pure, may he be clean.
> He who knows not the curse by which he is cured.
> From his body may he chase it away,
> May the demon of his device stand aside.[11]

On the reverse, according to Langdon's translation, mention is made of the kid 'unto the plain let loose', like the Hebrew Azazel. Atonement was made for the king described as the son of the god and the representative of the people. In this capacity he communicated their sins and the curse and ban of the demons to the sin-receiver, shooting it with an arrow. The role of the 'scapegoat' was not very different from that of a white goat dedicated to Tammuz whose heart had been extracted and placed near a man who had been seized upon by a demon to make atonement for him.[12] Here, evil was poured out on a goat which was then destroyed in order to dispose of the taint, very much as on the fifth day of the Annual Festival (Akitu) in Babylon the head of a sheep was cut off and, after an exorcist had recited spells and wiped the sanctuary of the chapel of Nebo with its carcass, the carcass was carried by the executioner to the river and thrown into the water facing west. The two men, having been contaminated by their contact with the sin-receiver, were required to retire to the country until the final reassembly of the gods in the chamber of Destinies on the twelfth day of the Festival.[13]

Piacular Atonement in Israel

There can be little doubt that the same attitude to piacular expiation and atonement was common both to the Babylonians and the Hebrews prior to the prophetic movement in the eighth century B.C. in Israel. Even after the Exile, when the Priestly Code was compiled, the infringements of the requirements of the cultus and the Torah (i.e. the Law) were punished with the same severity as moral offences.[14] The Hebrew priests and the sanctuaries in which they ministered were purged in the same ritual manner as their Babylonian counterparts,[15] and the original significance of the Hebrew cult-term *kipper*, translated 'atonement' in the A.V. and R.V. of the English Bible, seems to have been akin to that of the Babylonian *kup-puru*, meaning not only 'to cover' or 'wipe away' sin and appease divine wrath, but also to 'purge' and 'purify' persons and objects contaminated with uncleanness with the aid of a 'scapegoat' or sin-receiver, or with some other expiatory device,[16] normally sacrifice.

The conception of purgation in the post-exilic Jewish community is most apparent in the ceremonial of the annual expiation on the tenth day of the seventh month, Tishri. Although the observance as recorded in Leviticus xvi seems to have been relatively late, as no mention is made of it either in the book of Ezekiel or in that of Zechariah when the offerings and fasts in commemoration of national disasters were regu-lated,[17] its setting and ritual suggest that it had behind it a long history probably going back to a common source of Babylonian and Hebrew expiation. The earliest reference to a cleansing of the Temple is that in Ezekiel xlv, 18–20 where a dual purging of the sanctuary is mentioned, on the first day of the first month in the spring, and the other on the first day of the seventh month in the autumn. When in the fourth century B.C., after the return of the exiles from Babylon, the autumnal solemnity was instituted on the 10th of Tishri, it appears to have been a relatively simple expiation consisting of the sacri-fice of a bullock as a sin-offering for the priesthood and a ram for a burnt-offering. Two he-goats were then 'set before Yahweh', and lots were cast over them for the purpose of assigning one to Yahweh as a sin-offering and the other to Azazel, a divine being of the waste, as the sin-receiver. Yahweh's victim was then slain and Azazel's goat was despatched alive to a 'solitary land' laden with the unclean-ness of Israel and its sanctuary.[18]

Subsequently the ritual was elaborated with detailed regula-tions concerning the sprinkling of the blood of the bullock selected for the priesthood on and before the mercy-seat in the Holy of Holies. This is to be repeated with that of the goat as the sin-offering for the people 'to make atonement for the holy place and because of the uncleanness of the children of Israel'. The high-priest then sprinkled the blood on the altar, and con-fessed the sins of the nation over the live goat, laying his hands upon its head, and sending it away to the wilderness with its heavy burden. The sacrificed bullock and goat were taken 'out-side the camp' (i.e. the city),[19] and their carcasses, including their flesh, skins and dung, burnt in the fire. The man respon-sible for this had to undergo a thorough ablution before return-ing to the congregation of Israel.[20] Finally, a note was added ordering the Day of Atonement to be observed for ever as a 'high Sabbath' on which no kind of work was to be done and the people were to afflict their souls.[21]

This ceremonial clearly belongs to a very primitive concep-tion of expiation, despite its ethical and spiritual re-interpreta-tion in the Rabbinic literature. This is shown in the manipu-lation of the blood, the censings, lustrations and the transference of evil to a sin-carrier in the form of an animal. The blood made atonement 'by reason of the *nephesh*', or soul-substance, contained in it,[22] covering or wiping away the pollution and conferring sacredness on everything with which it came into direct contact by virtue of its atoning efficacy. The smoke of the life-giving incense and the cleansing potency of the holy water had the same effect, while the scapegoat, like the bird in the purification of the leper,[23] was the vehicle for carrying away the taints transferred to it.

Behind this conception of ritual expiation lay the covenant between Yahweh and Israel. Because any violation of the Law and the commandments was an affront to his holiness, the duly appointed acts of separation and ceremonial amendment were required when there had been any departure from the pre-scribed rules of conduct and worship, whether in ritual ob-servance or ethical behaviour, performed either intentionally or accidentally. Sin, being a failure to fulfil the requirements of Yahweh, produced an estrangement between the nation and its god, the creature and the Creator, resulting in a state of uncleanness. Men, animals, and inanimate objects equally were subject to the taint, and, therefore, required the same purifica/tion. Since it was the divine command that was at stake the expiation took the form of a piacular sin/offering by way of appeasement to secure release from the harmful supernatural influences and to restore again right relations with Yahweh. In post/exilic Judaism he alone was regarded as able to forgive sin and pardon iniquity, and he demanded a clean heart and a broken spirit as the first requirement.[24] Without these essential qualities the blood of bulls and the ashes of a heifer could not avail, and so in the later literature, while the daily sacrifice was held to expiate unintentional breaches of the Torah, the Day of Atonement piacular removed *ex opere operato* sins com/mitted with a 'high hand'; but, as the Rabbinic literature stressed, always on the condition that the offering was per/formed with sincerity of heart and true repentance.[25]

The book of Leviticus is a *rituale* rather than a manual of devotion (like the Psalms), or a work on moral theology. In an *Ordo* it is the things to be done set in the form of liturgical rubrics that are described, rather than their devotional or ethical significance. And before the destruction of the temple in A.D. 70 and the cessation of its sacrificial worship, the peni/tential aspects of the ritual were reproduced in the local syna/gogues as confessions of sin and absolutions, together with the observance of a strict fast, to enable Jews of the Diaspora, and those living too far from Mount Zion, to take part in the ritual performed by the high/priest in the Holy of Holies. In this way greater emphasis was given to the purification of the heart. In the Mishna, although the actual ceremonies of the Day of Atonement were represented as expiating sin,[26] the objective efficacy attributed to the rites was regarded as dependent upon the use made of them by God Himself. The Day was a Sab/bath of unique sanctity, and to neglect its duly appointed pre/scriptions and symbolism performed in the traditional manner would be equivalent to spurning the atonement offered to the sinner through the divinely ordained observance.[27] The loss of the 'scapegoat ritual' was keenly felt in Rabbinical circles because it was so intimately related to the need for the expiation of sin regulated by the deeply engrained belief in the covenant relationship between Yahweh and Israel.[28] It was not that an angry God had to be propitiated by gifts and offerings. That notion had been dispelled by Jeremiah and the rest of the Hebrew prophets immediately before the Exile. Evil, however, remained as a taint that had to be 'covered' or 'wiped out', and carried away, if the divine fellowship of the theocracy was to be maintained, until with the cessation of the temple worship and its sacrificial system, the manipulation of the blood of the victims and the offices of a 'scapegoat' were dispensed with because they were no longer available.

In later Judaism the Rabbinical penitential theory advanced spiritually to a much higher level. As Büchler says, 'acts of repentance, restitution, conciliation and confession preceding the sin-offering, and their religious and moral values, give insight into the Rabbinic concepts of sin and sacrificial atonement.'[29] The Mishnaic atonement, in fact, consisted in a complete act of repentance, and if 'good works' included almsgiving, fasting and other asceticisms, together with the appropriate sin-offering, the ultimate aim was the attainment of the ethical righteousness insisted on by the Hebrew prophets.[30]

Now that the blood of the sacrifices was no longer regarded as efficacious in a magico-religious manner because of the indwelling *nephesh* as a purifying element, the ultimate object of the expiatory rite was the forgiveness of the worshipper and the restoration of the favour of God without implying appeasement of an angry deity. As the earlier non-moral conception of sin as a substantive miasma and pollution gave place to the later ethical evaluation of holiness demanded by Yahweh in obedience to his will, the rites became the means of annulling the penal consequences of sin and effecting reconciliation with God through repentance and amendment of life coupled with affliction of the flesh and its lusts. Penitence and confession, humiliation and affliction, especially at the beginning of the New Year in the month of Tishri, were of the essence of the

Rabbinic interpretation of atonement, subsequently stressed and developed by Maimonides.[31] The sinner, moreover, had to abandon his sin and make peace not only with God but also with the person against whom he had offended on earth, before he could claim the forgiveness of heaven.

EXPIATORY SUFFERING

The vicarious principle inherent in the institution of sacrifice had also found expression in Israel in the idea of expiatory suffering, both in relation to the nation and the individual. Examples are the visitation of the sin of Achan on his household requiring their extermination to remove the guilt from the larger group,[32] and the slaughter of Saul's family by David to appease blood-guilt.[33] Behind these offerings, however, race solidarity rather than vicarious atonement was probably the primary motive, and it is only in the Servant Saga embedded in the later portion of the book of Isaiah[34] that the conception of expiatory sacrifice is clearly expressed. There the Servant, whether the martyr nation or some historical person, is represented as bearing the penalties which others should have borne because of their transgressions. As the officer of Yahweh this mysterious figure had been commissioned by God not only 'to raise up the tribes of Jacob and to restore the preserved of Israel, but also to be a light to the Gentiles that salvation might be to the ends of the earth.' This mission was accomplished by much suffering and, notwithstanding his innocence, it pleased Yahweh to bruise him and put him to grief in order that his soul might be 'an offering for sin'. He was led as a lamb to the slaughter that he might make an act of vicarious atonement—'He shall see the travail of his soul and shall be satisfied: by his knowledge shall my righteous servant justify many: and he shall bear their iniquities.'[35]

Again, why innocent suffering should expiate sin is not explained, but it is recognized that sin must be atoned for, and the sufferings of the righteous Servant are compared to the guilt-offering (*asham*), as the death of Miriam elsewhere is related to the expiatory ritual of the red heifer.[36] The death of

Aaron, again, appears in a similar context,[37] and a heifer was slain to atone for an undetected murder.[38] The underlying principle in these expiations was that a piacular was required to remove the death contagion. The idea of atonement being made by expiatory suffering and a vicarious self-offering in terms of the theology of the Epistle to the Hebrews[39] was, however, alien to Judaism.

The Suffering Messiah

The nearest approach to such a conception unquestionably occurs in the various interpretations of the Isaianic Servant in which suffering and death are assigned an atoning value. Nevertheless, it is unthinkable that any Israelite at the end of the Exile could have been of such a character as to justify the significance given to him by the Deutero-Isaiah,[40] and it has yet to be proved that the figure was identified with the Messiah before the Christian era.[41] There is undoubtedly a Messianic tone about such phrases as 'I have put my spirit upon him', and 'he shall bring forth judgment to the Gentiles',[42] but the Servant is not represented as a Davidic King destined to restore the former prosperity of Israel. He is essentially a suf-ferer,[43] 'a man of pains and known unto sickness, despised and rejected of men so that the people hid their faces from him, and esteemed him not.' This was very far removed from the idealized David as the prototype of the righteous King des-tined to rule in justice and peace for ever,[44] or of the Macca-baean conquerors or apocalyptic supernatural Son of Man in the centuries immediately preceding the Christian era. Some of the later Jewish interpreters in the Talmud and the Targums identified the Servant with the Messiah, but even so they explained away references to his death in Isaiah liii in terms of the 'sickness fallen upon Israel'.[45]

The idea of a suffering Messiah first appears in Rabbinic literature in the Messiah ben Ephraim, in the post-Christian Targum of pseudo-Jonathan, and in the Babylonian Targum. Later it recurs in the Targum of the Song of Songs. If it had been familiar when the Gospel tradition was in process of

formulation, the disciples of Jesus would hardly have been re/
presented as being confused and bewildered by his announce/
ment that in his Messianic role he must suffer.[46] The hero of the
Servant Saga is Israel as a nation, as is clearly shown in the
Septuagint rendering of Isaiah xlii, 1: 'Jacob is my servant, I will
help him; Israel is my chosen, my soul has accepted him; he
shall bring forth judgment to the Gentiles.' Its sufferings appear
to have been those endured by Jehoiachin and the exiles in
397 B.C., and by their predecessors in 586.[47] The tribulations
of the Jews during and after the fall of Jerusalem in A.D. 70 led
to the Rabbinic interpretation of self/inflicted suffering as an
atoning sacrifice in the expiation of national guilt, in prepara/
tion for the coming of the Messiah and the establishment of his
righteous reign.

THE CHRISTIAN CONCEPTION OF ATONEMENT

In Christian circles, once the significance of the Servant
prophecies was realized in relation to the Messiahship of Jesus,
it was the Passion, culminating in the Crucifixion and its
sequel, and all this involved and implied, which gave it its
central position in the theology and religious experience of
the Early Church. Calvary then became the event which was
destined to determine for Christianity the conception not only
of the Messianic office and its purposes, but also of the whole
redemptive process. The functions first attributed to the
Davidic King, and then invested with apocalyptic glory in
the supernatural Son of Man, became transfigured with suffer/
ing in the person of the defeated yet victorious Saviour of
mankind, who in his own Messianic consciousness applied
the Servant prophecies to himself.

When Roman rule in Palestine created nationalistic move/
ments during the Herodian dynasty, it was to a Davidic
Messiah that many were looking with hope and anticipation
of release from occupation. This precluded any idea of suffer/
ing and death as part of the Messianic office and vocation. In
the three figures, the Davidic King, the Son of Man and the
Suffering Servant, not only had a common underlying pattern

of thought emerged,[48] but there was also retained a common theme deeply laid in the myth and ritual of the sacral kingship, where the suffering Young god and the Mater dolorosa gave expression to the anxiety inherent in an unstable environment and uncertain destiny. In Mesopotamia the defeated hero was a virile figure combining weakness with strength, triumphing over death and the powers of evil, annually mourned and re, stored to newness of life, reflecting the ebb and flow in the seasonal sequence. In Christian tradition the theme of the dying and reviving god, combined with that of the Jewish Messianic categories, introduced a new and unique conception of the status and function of this fundamental figure.

In the complex Christological pattern that emerged, many strands, from Hebrew, Babylonian, Egyptian, Iranian and Graeco,Roman sources, can be detected, but it was the his, toric Jesus of Nazareth who in the first instance became con, scious of his Messianic vocation and destiny in the form in which he presented and fulfilled them in his teaching, life and death. It was he who gave rise to the conviction of his messiah, ship among his intimate followers, however bewildered and perplexed they may have been by the prediction of his passion, rejection and crucifixion at the hands of the Jewish hierarchy.[49] During his lifetime they failed to understand the nature of his mission and how it was to be accomplished. But once it was seen in the light of his sufferings and death interpreted in terms of the Servant prophecies, and subsequently of the apocalyptic Messianic figures and symbolism, the scheme of redemption emerged as a whole. The defeated, humiliated but conquering Christ then appeared as the lamb slain from the foundation of the world to ensure the final triumph of good over evil and of life over death. The malign forces personified in the dragon and his host had been overcome by the victory on the Cross, hell had been harrowed, and the tomb in the garden was empty because it could not imprison the Lord of life, while in heaven the triumph was celebrated by the sacred marriage of the Lamb as the prelude to the reign of universal peace, prosperity and righteousness.[50]

(a) *The New Testament.* The cult of the kingship, the ritual of the combat, the sacred marriage and the Heavenly Man, as well as the Hebrew Messianic prototypes and prophecies, exercised a formative influence on the development of the Christian doctrine of redemption and its symbolic setting. At the centre lay the atoning sacrifice which it was maintained had been offered once and for all by Christ in the capacity of the Redeemer of mankind. Through suffering he had entered into his glory, and because 'God was in Christ reconciling the world unto himself' a new divine relationship had been established. The status of humanity had been raised to that of sonship with God in a new creation.[51] The Pauline conception of the Atonement was that of a process of reconciliation involving justification in the sense of restoring right relations between God and man. In the formulation of his theological interpretation of the death of Christ in terms of a sacrificial expiation the Apostle was influenced by the sacrificial ideas in which he had been brought up at Tarsus and trained in the Rabbinical school at Jerusalem. Moreover, having undergone a profound spiritual experience himself on the Damascus road, and like St Augustine and Martin Luther, being the 'twice born' type, he was conscious of having become a 'new creature' 'dead unto sin but alive unto God in Christ Jesus'.[52]

The author of the Epistle to the Hebrews regarded the death of Christ as the fulfilment and abrogation of the Hebrew sacrificial system by the New Covenant effected by Christ as the High-priest after the order of Melchizedec in his eternal heavenly offering.[53] St Paul placed the emphasis on expiation through the vicarious suffering and death of an innocent Victim identifying himself with sinful humanity, and by his resurrection triumphing over sin and death. Indeed, he did not hesitate to affirm that he had been 'bought with a price' by the victorious Saviour of mankind whose sacrificial death had satisfied the justice of God and secured the 'justification' of sinful humanity.[54] Sin he regarded as a breach of the natural law written in the conscience of man everywhere, but since God is essentially righteous and just, atonement entailed the vicarious suffering of one who knew no sin whom he 'set forth to be a propitiation, through faith, by his blood, to shew his righteous' ness.' Therefore, he died sacrificially for the sins of mankind.[55]

In the first Epistle of St John, on the other hand, the new birth is described as a gift of eternal life bestowed through cleansing from sin, symbolized by water and blood represent' ing the removal of evil and the giving of life. Thus, it is affirmed that 'the blood of Jesus cleanseth us from all sin', but since the blood atones through the life which animates it, it was the life of Christ given in a sacrifice freely offered to God the Father that was set free by his death and made accessible for all time by his resurrection to those who live in union with him. As ritual purity has always been the condition of approach to the sacred, so the gradual and continuous removal of sin constitutes the first requirement for those who could here and now become partakers of eternal life in the New Dis' pensation. From the side of the crucified Redeemer flowed water and blood, which typified the two major sacraments of Baptism and the Eucharist as the divinely ordained channels of regeneration and life'giving power. To this was later added the sacrament of Penance wherein post'baptismal sin is absolved—the present tense used in 1 John i, 7, suggests con' tinuous cleansing rather than salvation wrought once and for all in an initial act of faith in the death of Christ, as was maintained by some of the Reformers in the sixteenth century.

The central theme of the author of the Epistle to the Hebrews is, as we have seen, that the Atonement is accomplished by the perpetuation in the eternal world of the perfect sacrifice once offered on the Cross in time and space. Nevertheless, he recog' nized that the poured'out blood symbolized the life of the sin' less Victim, who having passed into the heavens through death, continued to purge the consciences of the faithful by his blood in a manner that the Hebrew cathartic offerings could never accomplish, because they had not acquired atoning value in this measure.[56] However, it was recognized that without the shedding of blood there could be no remission of sin, and so the sacrificial blood of Christ was redemptive, because his risen and ascended life had a mystical efficacy in the eternal world where he exercised his priesthood on behalf of mankind. As the Church reflected upon salvation, particularly in its Pauline presentation, it became increasingly involved in the perplexing problem of how justification, sanctification, satis' faction, and communion with the risen and ascended Christ were made effective in heaven and earth. In short, if 'God was in Christ reconciling the world unto himself' how was this reconciliation made and maintained?

(b) *The Early Church.* The first theoretical interpretation of the doctrine of the Atonement assumed a forensic form which developed into the conception of a ransom paid to the devil to deliver the human race from the bondage of corruption. This received support from the recorded declaration of Jesus that he had come 'to give his life a ransom for many';[57] an alleged 'saying' that has long been a matter of debate.[58] Thus, in the third century, Irenaeus, Origen and Gregory of Nyssa adopted this view in one form or another, and although it was rejected by St Gregory of Nazianus, it was generally accepted with some modification by the Latin Fathers, including St Hilary of Poitiers, St Augustine, Gregory the Great, St Leo, and their successors (e.g. St Bernard of Clairvaux and Peter Lom' bard). The Greek theologians, on the other hand, tended to place the emphasis more on the power of the incarnate life of Christ to change human nature. Here his death was the result of his self'identification with sinful humanity rather than the supreme purpose of the Incarnation in a battle with Satan. In the words of St Athanasius, 'He became man that we might be made divine',[59] because only thus could man receive the new life indispensable for his salvation. He shared the suffer' ings of mankind even unto death that humanity might become partakers of his divine life and of a blessed immortality. In this redemptive process death was incidental as in the Fourth Gospel, and it was only in the speculative thought of Origen and Gregory of Nyssa that the idea of the payment of a debt developed into a ransom to free man from the dominion of sin, the manhood of Christ being represented as the bait for the devil, and his deity the hook by which Satan was caught.[60]

(c) *The Middle Ages.* In the skilful hands of Anselm in the eleventh century the emphasis was shifted from the idea of 'ransom' to that of 'satisfaction' by his making the vindication of God's honour the crucial issue, rather than a transaction with the devil. Already St Augustine in the formulation of his doctrine of original sin had represented the entire human race as the object of the wrath of an all-righteous Deity and as destined for perdition. Upon this assumption Anselm in his *Cur Deus Homo* argued that the two natures, divine and human, were united in the One Christ in order that he might render to God in his perfect humanity the satis-faction required for the redemption of man's sin. The death voluntarily borne by the sinless Saviour constituted the infinite satisfaction required for redemption without any question of a ransom to Satan, there being no reason to suppose that God owed any obligation to his adversary the devil. Man by his sin had violated the honour of the Creator and defiled his ruined creation. In his sinful condition he could not himself make adequate reparation to expiate his guilt by his own repentance and penitence, however sincere it might be. Only God him-self could do this. Therefore by becoming incarnate in time and space the God-man was able to make the satisfaction on behalf of humanity required to vindicate God's honour, and in order to obtain the forgiveness of man he voluntarily sur-rendered his perfect life in a sacrificial death as a *quid pro quo*, being himself exempt from the judicial consequences of sin. But ingenious as was this legalistic interpretation of the situa-tion, the Atonement still remained a vicarious offering of a substitute equivalent in value, differing from the ransom theory mainly in making the rights of God instead of those of Satan the object of the act of satisfaction. By offering satisfaction for human sin Christ, on this hypothesis, has given man a fresh start, but nothing is said about how in a fallen world this is to be sustained and carried to its ultimate goal in a state of perfection.

This legalistic interpretation remained, despite the fact that it gave the death of Christ a moral quality of obedience rather than a penal quality of endurance of infinite suffering. It provided a theoretical basis for the treasury of merits and the practice of indulgences. Against the contention that the death of Christ was a debt to God the Father rather than a ransom paid to the devil, Abelard, in his *Commentary on the Romans*, described it as the supreme demonstration and declaration of the love of God. It was effected primarily through its exemplary value because 'the loftiest love is inspired in us by the passion of Christ.' But this was repudiated alike by the Scholastics (e.g. St Bernard and St Thomas Aquinas), and subsequently by the Protestant Reformers (Calvin, Luther and the Puritans) who restated the penal theory in its crudest form, denying the Anselmic distinction between satisfaction and the infliction of penalty.[61]

St Thomas Aquinas, while accepting Anselm's doctrine of satisfaction, combined it with that of merit, sacrifice and redemption into a systematic construction with the doctrines of law and sacramental grace. Christ, having earned a store of merit by submission to an undeserved death outweighing that required to compensate for the guilt of original sin, bestows it as a gift of grace upon the soul through baptism and the sacrament of penance, thus ensuring forgiveness and the blotting out of past sins.[62] Against this the Scotists and Nominalists contended that the efficacy of the Atonement depended upon the 'extrinsic acceptance' by God rather than upon its own intrinsic value. But this robbed the death of Christ of its sacrificial significance since its worth rested solely upon God's will to accept it, and not upon its own efficacy. It was, unsurprisingly, rejected by the medieval Church, the Reformation, and the Council of Trent, all of which maintained in their several views an objective interpretation of the Atonement, in which the sacrifice and death of Christ were the essential facts in the purgative way of salvation.

(d) *The Reformation.* The Reformers repudiated the Counsels of Perfection and of monastic renunciation, and the Scholastic theory of satisfaction, and placed the emphasis on justification by faith and the penal doctrine of vicarious bearing of sin based on the absolute sovereignty of God in Augustinian terms. Thus for Calvin the rule and will of God were final, and sin was an act of disobedience meriting damnation. Luther regarded the Cross as the price of man's redemption paid once and for all and henceforth appropriated by the faith of the believer. Calvin went further in the penal direction, declaring that 'Christ was offered to the Father as a propitiatory victim; that, expiation being made by his sacrifice, we might cease to tremble at the divine wrath.' Christ, by becoming by divine decree the recipient of the sins of ruined human nature, experienced 'all the signs of an angry and punishing God', taking upon himself the penalty which by the just judgment of God threatened all sinners.[63]

The Socinians, in reaction against these exaggerated statements of the penal theory, adopted the theory that the death of Christ was primarily an example to his followers. Sin can be forgiven without any demand for satisfaction or punishment if God so willed. In the Old Testament repentance was the only condition required, while in the New Testament nothing is said about satisfaction. The only sense in which Christ could be said to expiate sin, it was concluded, was by his having saved man from the penalty of sin, namely death. Therefore, it was the resurrection and the eternal priesthood in heaven rather than the Cross that effected the expiation. 'He continually intercedes with God for us, and by the authority and power given to him by God he ever frees us from all ills, and so makes perpetual expiation for our sins.' He was represented as the Saviour because by his life, death and resurrection he had given eternal life to those who have faith in him.[64]

Although this subjective revival of Pelagianism and the Abelardian position has had its exponents (e.g. Jowett, Rashdall, Emmet) it was too far removed from the whole conception of expiatory redemption alike in Christian tradition and all that lay behind it to have been adopted except by eclectic

Idealists.[65] The trend has been increasingly towards re-
statements of the classical doctrine of the Atonement either in
its penal or Patristic form, involving in the Barthian theology
a Neo-Calvinistic attitude to sin, grace, reconciliation and substitution or in the attempt of the Swedish Bishop Aulen to
combine the Patristic, Anselmic and Lutheran interpretations
in a modified version of the ransom theory, against the background of the apocalyptic war in heaven.[66] Taking the doctrine of salvation as a whole, he maintains that in the life,
death and resurrection of Christ the victory over sin, death and
the devil has been won to rescue fallen humanity from the
clutches of Satan.[67]

In recent years there has been a trend towards an objective
approach to the doctrine of salvation. The emphasis has varied
according to the attitude and theory adopted towards the wider
issue. Thus, the liberal Abelardian subjective view as an
attempt to correct the Latin juridical theories failed to meet the
essential spiritual needs of a catastrophic age seeking means of
redemption and reconciliation with the transcendental forces
beyond human control. This, being a recurrent situation, has
led to much the same reactions as in former times, Christian
and pagan, historic and prehistoric. To be effective it has
required a doctrine implying that something has been done to
deal adequately with the prevailing urgent need, and the
Atonement is the Christian practical answer to the problem,
however it is interpreted theoretically and theologically. The
Gospels record the events in the Passion narratives with passing references to the Old Testament prototypes and prophecies,
but give little, if any, guidance in the precise interpretation of
their significance. St Paul, in the elaboration of his doctrine,
contrasted the failure of the Jewish Law and its sacrificial
system to supply what was required, with what had been
accomplished by the victorious death and recurrection of
Christ, producing a new status of sonship by securing justification and reconciliation. The author of the Epistle to the
Hebrews carried this a step further in laying the stress upon the
one all-sufficient sacrifice once offered in time and eternally re-

presented in the heavens, rather than on the oft-repeated sacrifices of the Old Covenant which never gave the satisfaction
required of them. Upon these foundations the theoretical construction of the doctrine was erected, with varying degrees of
success in accordance with the prevailing thought and practice
of the period in which it occurred.

The Doctrine of Justification

At the time of the Reformation the ideas of merit and satisfaction were predominant in the doctrine of justification, both
among Catholics and Protestant reformers. Calvin and Luther
and their followers maintained that man is acquitted of the
penalty of sin solely and entirely by faith (*sola fides*) in the
atoning sacrifice of Christ, independent of sanctification and
amendment of life as essential conditions, however much these
may have been inherent in the process. On this view justification was a judicial declaration involving the extrinsic imputation to the sinner of the merits of Christ who was punished and
died in place of man, and henceforth the saved sinner was
treated as though he was righteous. The Tridentine Decree on
the subject (Session vi, cap. 1 ff.), on the other hand, denied
that justification was confined to the remission of sins, and
required sanctification, baptismal regeneration to remove the
taint of original sin, and the assent of the will in turning from
sin to God, as against the Calvinistic doctrine of divine election and renewal of life involving the infusion of faith, hope
and charity and all Christian virtues by the Holy Ghost. In the
process of justification the Council of Trent assigned primacy of
place to faith, coupled with sanctifying grace, as inseparable
from sacrificial forgiveness; for, as St Thomas Aquinas had
affirmed, justification included the gift of sanctifying grace
requiring the absolution of post-baptismal mortal sin by resort
to the sacrament of penance to restore and maintain a state of
grace.

It is true the Reformers also recognized holiness as an essential quality of 'the saved', but for them salvation was an accomplished fact based on forgiveness acquired by faith in 'the

finished work of Christ' rather than a supernatural virtue in a continuous process in the quest of perfection and the practice of the sacramental way of life and belief. Their fear was that they should countenance any idea of man earning his own sal-vation by virtue of his good works, regarded by them as 'filthy rags'. Christ alone in his sinless perfection, they maintained, could do this. He had fought and won the battle against sin and death, and by his victory he had changed shame into glory and penalty into sacrifice. Vital as this interpretation of the Cross was for the Christian doctrine of the Atonement, it was only a part of the work of redemption, as the Tridentine Decree rightly stressed.

Too much emphasis was given by the Reformers to forgive-ness and acquittal, to expiation and satisfaction, substitution and imputation. These all have their place in justification and sanctification, but only in relation to one another and not as mutually exclusive terms and conceptions. Each of them started from his own 'private judgment' of the doctrine and its scriptural setting, and interpreted it accordingly regardless of the other implications, with justice, reward and punishment in the forefront of his mind. The 'scandal' of salvation was for them and their successors the essence of 'the saving work of Christ'. But shocking as have been some of these presentations, they have contained elements of truth, the process of justifica-tion and conciliation transcending as it does a strictly intellec-tual interpretation. In the Pietistic movements, where the cruder theories have been very firmly established, the institution of sacrifice and the sacramental principle have been as imper-fectly understood and as little practised as the ascetic theology of the Catholic Church.

The Sacrificial Death of Christ

The doctrine of the Atonement is essentially a sacrificial con-cept, and it can be evaluated rightly only in this context. Seen against the background of the long history of the institution of sacrifice, and in particular of the piaculum, it is clear that any interpretation of the doctrine must involve the immolation of the victim in order that its life may be liberated. First it has to be consecrated and dedicated to the service of the altar, then it has to be slain and its life-giving blood poured out sacrificially to expiate the evil or pollution that has upset right relations between God and man, individually and collectively. Finally, its sacred flesh may be consumed sacramentally to imbibe its life and supply a fresh outpouring of divine strength and power.

In the Christian conception of atonement Christ becomes the sinless sin-bearer who from the manger to the Cross was completely dedicated to the work of salvation for which he took the human flesh, uniting his humanity with his divine nature. Being tempted in all points like the rest of mankind, he was himself without sin, yet he was destined to endure the penalty of sin. This paradox constitutes the so-called 'scandal of the Cross', and has given rise to the penal, juridical and substitution theories of the Atonement as theoretical solutions of the problem. Their error lies in interpreting the death of Christ as a propitiation of an angry God to change this attitude to the sinner. As the sacrificial sin-bearer the sinless Christ shed his blood to expiate and take away sin because he was at once the priest and victim in an eternal self-offering of inestimable worth.

This, however, did not involve any transference of human guilt to him, as in the Jewish Day of Atonement 'scapegoat' rite. Indeed, in this annual expiation the goat who played the role of sin-receiver was not slain, and in the analogy in the Epistle to the Hebrews Christ is represented as the eternal high-priest, not as a substitutionary victim. He gave his sinless life as a voluntary sacrifice that through death he might become the eternal high-priest of the New Covenant, ever-living in the heavens to make intercession for his people. In this capacity as priest and victim he made a real expiation for sin, the act of atonement being completed in 'the holy place' in the sphere of its eternal operations.[68] The Cross is regarded as the path to the 'new and living way' by which the victorious Redeemer passed into the heavens. There he perpetually offers his perfect sacrifice in his boundless love for sinful humanity;

having freely laid down his life and taken it again to effect this reconciliation, and imparts to those living in union with him the infinite merits of his victory over sin and death. Hence-forth the remission of sin and the gift of eternal life were bestowed upon his new creation not by the propitiation of divine wrath towards sinful humanity, or by paying a ransom price to the devil to secure its freedom from his clutches, but by an act of redeeming love whereby the barrier set up by human transgression was removed, and as a result 'many sons were brought to glory'.[69]

The death and resurrection of Christ interpreted in terms of atoning sacrifice are thus in line with the fundamental theme in the institution of sacrifice in its various manifestations. The basic concept is the promotion and consecration of life. This entails the death or destruction of the victim, but is incidental in the process of the liberation of its life. It may be a far cry from the expiatory immolation of human or animal victims to a voluntary act of self-giving on the part of One whose whole being was animated by entire dedication to a sacred and noble purpose and inestimable love for sinful and suffering human-ity; yet there is a unity of principle in the desire for 'newness of life' which finds expression in the emergence of life from death and victory from defeat.

CHAPTER VI

Vegetation Offerings and Libations

THERE is a distinction between all types of blood-offerings and
piacular sacrifices, and the large class of bloodless oblations,
notably in the form of vegetation offerings and libations. Both
types are life-giving agents exercising their functions because of
their vitalizing qualities. Vegetation offerings belong essentially
to an agricultural state of culture, but have their counterparts
under Palaeolithic conditions in the so-called 'Venuses', or
female figurines, carved in bone, ivory or stone, with the face
often featureless or non-existent, and only the breasts, buttocks
and corpulent abdomen suggestive of pregnancy, being represented with prominence as the outward symbols of female
fecundity.

Palaeolithic Life-giving Agents

The Venus cult came into Europe from the East in the Gravettian culture in the Upper Palaeolithic, in all probability from
the southern Russian steppe. From Kostienki in the valley of
the Don and from Malta in Siberia, it made its way along the
Danube apparently to Unter Wisternitz in Moravia and
Willendorf near Vienna, then to the Apennines and to Menton on the Franco-Italian frontier, to Brassempouy in the
Landes, Lespugue in Haute Garonne and Laugerie-Basse in
the Dordogne. The figure of a nude woman holding the horn
of a bison in her right hand, carved in relief on a block of stone
in a rock-shelter at Laussel near Les Eyzies in the Beune
valley, was coloured with red pigment, widely used as a surrogate of blood for ritual purposes. Here, again, the face was
featureless. On the ground were fragments of two reliefs of
women, and a third may depict an accouchement, or possibly
a copulation.[1] The principal aim seems to have been to promote childbirth rather than conception; it seems that primitive

man was unclear about paternity and the generative process. The cult of birth, therefore, centred in the giving of life through the outward signs of the maternal organs.

Shells, again, were widely used as fertility charms and amulets in the Upper Palaeolithic. This applied particularly to the cowrie, shaped like the portal of birth, which may have come into Europe from the East in association with the Venuses, and from the Mediterranean. To give life to the dead they were scattered over the corpse as, for example, at Menton and at Laugerie-Basse. Thus, at the Grotte des Enfants at Grimaldi, four rows of pierced shells were arranged round the head of a youth whose skeleton had been stained red with peroxide of iron. In the adjoining Grotte du Cavillon were no less than 7,868 marine shells (*Nassa neritae*), of which 875 were pierced. At Barma Grande, the fifth cave of the series, the skeletons of a boy and of a young woman were adorned with Nissa shells, two large cowries, a necklace and a collar of teeth, in a grave lined with red ochre.[2] In the rock-shelter called Crô-Magnon at Les Eyzies in the Dordogne there were 300 sea-shells (*Littorina littorea*) and perforated pendants, and on the opposite bank of the Vézère at Laugerie-Basse cowries were carefully arranged in pairs on a corpse.[3]

As blood or red ochre was regarded as a potent vitalizing agent, so female figurines and bas-reliefs stressing maternal organs and functions, and certain shells such as cowries, appear to have been connected with the female principle and to have been employed as sacramental channels promoting and facilitating birth and revivifying the dead in a process of rebirth. Thus, in Palaeolithic times the cult of the female principle was established. Various amulets of this nature played a prominent part in the conservation of life among man, beast and the dead, and in the maintenance of the food supply.

Symbolism of the Goddess Cult in the Ancient Near East
With the discovery of agriculture and the practice of herding at the dawn of civilization, particularly in the Ancient Near East, very much the same symbolism persisted that had grown up

around the processes of birth and generation. Woman, being
the mother of the race, continued to be regarded as the life-
producer playing her essential role in the birth of offspring. The
transition from hunting, fishing and collecting edible roots and
fruits to the cultivation of the soil and its products, and the
keeping of flocks and herds, was very gradual. It was slowly
adopted and localized in certain places, generally in the form
of mixed farming often combined with the chase. Sir Mortimer
Wheeler may be right in thinking that settled communities
first arose in fertile oases like Jericho in Palestine (where a pre-
pottery Neolithic settlement has now been discovered dated
between 8000 and 6000 B.C.), rather than in the great river
valleys of the Nile and Euphrates, the Indus and the Huang
Ho, which were always liable to serious flooding.[4] In the
Jericho mound a spring has been found believed to have produced a thousand gallons of water a minute, which still supports the town and irrigates the luxuriant oasis.[5] Therefore, it
may well have been the symbol of the life it so lavishly bestows
in the midst of an arid plain, throwing into relief the mysterious forces of vegetation and stimulating the practice of
agriculture at a very early period.

With the establishment and development of agriculture,
Neolithic man became increasingly dependent upon the water
supply, the weather, and the seasonal sequence. Even after the
emergence of urban social and economic structures in the river
valleys in and after the fourth millennium B.C., the cultivation
of the surrounding soil was still a basic requirement. But this
was just as hazardous and beyond human control as the vagaries of the chase and of food-collection. Resort had still to be
made to magico-religious means and devices to supplement
human efforts. This found expression in a cultus in which the
two poles of creative energy were personified, the one female
and receptive, the other male and begettive, given their respective symbolic representation and sacramental significance. From
Neolithic times onwards phallic emblems became increasingly
prominent as the physiological functions of paternity were more
clearly understood and appreciated, but the maternal principle,

now becoming personified as the Mother-goddess, continued
to assume the leading role, especially in Western Asia, Crete
and the Aegean, where the Young god remained subordinate
to the Great Mother.

In the Mosul district of northern Iraq near the ancient city
of Nineveh on the Tigris, in the Chalcolithic mound Tell
Arpachiyah, going back to the fourth millennium B.C.,
numerous headless clay female figurines of the Venus type have
been found. The breasts are pendulous, the buttocks highly
developed, and the squatting posture is suggestive of child-
birth, though some appear to have been represented in an
advanced stage of pregnancy. The remarkable affinity with the
Palaeolithic examples indicates a very long and continuous
occurrence in this region of these magico-religious aids to
fecundity probably derived from the Gravettian prototypes
before the maternal principle had been personified in a single
Great Mother. Indeed, as Dr Mallowan says, there can be little
doubt that 'fertility worship connected with the Mother-
goddess cult must be one of the oldest and longest surviving
religions of the world.'[6] At first it would seem to have been
concentrated upon the mystery of birth, including all the major
aspects of fecundity and nutrition as the vital concern of man,
food and children being the two basic requirements at all
times.

In the Chalcolithic period it became the dominating influence from the Middle East to Anatolia and the Aegean, and
to Persia, Baluchistan and India. Apart from Tell Arpachiyah, however, it was not very prominent in Western Asia
prior to the Halafian age about 3800 B.C. when female figurines were very prevalent everywhere from the Syrian coast to the
Zagros mountains. At Tepe Gawra, north-west of Arpachiyah on the caravan route to Iran they are of common occurrence, and a highly stylized torso there may have been introduced
specifically to serve the purpose of safe and speedy delivery.[7]
At Tell Brak in the Khabur valley figures with large Eyes
found in abundance at a site called by Dr Mallowan 'the eye
Temple', dated about 3000 B.C., may represent the Meso-
potamian goddess Inanna-Ishtar, and a smaller male figure in

front of her, perhaps her son and consort Dumuzi-Tammuz.[8] In the earlier Chalcolithic levels of Yumuk Tepe, a mound near the small port of Mersin in Cicilia, on the southern Turkish coast situated on the direct route from east to west, a crude goddess-figure has been discovered among the remains of a village community engaged in agriculture and stock-breeding about 4000 B.C. when a more or less nomadic mode of life was giving place to that of the settled agriculturist. Above this horizon in the Bronze Age levels the statuettes suggest that the worship of the Mother-goddess had then become a permanent tradition in Anatolia.[9]

In Persia, when food production began to supplement and supplant food-gathering in the third millennium B.C., the cultus flourished apparently in the south-west, but no traces of it have come to light in the north-east.[10] At Anau in Trans-caspia on the fertile border of the plateau to the north of the Ezburg mountains extending from the Caspian Sea to the Pamirs, the widely diffused agricultural communities and the Goddess cult appear to have been a rather later intrusion into Turkestan and northern Iran by settlers from Sialk, Giyan and Hissa, on the edge of the Persian desert. Further to the east in the foothills of southern Baluchistan in Makran in the Zhob valley small farming groups were established before 3000 B.C. among whom grotesque clay figurines have been found which in spite of the maternal organs not being unduly prominent, Professor Piggott regards as 'a grim embodiment of the Mother-goddess who is the guardian of the dead—an under-world deity concerned alike with the crops and the seed-corn buried beneath the earth.'[11]

Similarly, in Sind and the Punjab in the Harappa civiliza-tion from 2500 to 1500 B.C., large quantities of terracotta female statuettes have been excavated by Sir John Marshall at Mohenjo-daro in the Indus valley, depicting as he says, 'a goddess with attributes very similar to those of the great Mother-goddess: Lady of Heaven, and a special patroness of women'.[12] This may explain why they were kept in the dwell-ings and in the streets in these ancient cities, and probably held in much the same veneration as are their successors today among the illiterate population faced with the problems: birth and nurturing of children. The Mother-goddess in India is the guardian of the house and of the village, and presides over child-birth and domestic affairs. Whether or not in the Harappa culture she had a male partner, as elsewhere in the Ancient Near East, is not established, but nude male figures associated with the sacred pipal-tree and cult animals frequently occur in the iconography, though not in juxtaposition with the God-dess. Nevertheless, limestone conical phallic emblems known as *linga* are frequently shown in conjunction with female *yoni* rings depicting vulva,[13] symbolizing the mystery of birth in which the Goddess was the most vital agent as the universal Mother, the author and giver of life. She was the sacramental source of fecundity and life-bestowing power in its various aspects, embodied in her images which were endowed with quickening and fertilizing potency, and made effective especially in vegetation ritual and that controlling the processes of generation.

It is uncertain whether the earliest emblems represented the Great Mother as a deity. They were certainly indicative of the recognition and veneration of maternity as a divine principle. This, as we have seen, appears to have become established on the southern Russian loess plain in the Upper Palaeolithic Gravettian culture, and from this diffusion-centre to have been extended through Western Asia to Baluchistan and north-west India as well as to Europe. Its importance in the develop-ment of the institution of sacrifice and of the sacramental prin-ciple lies in the status and attributes it accorded to the bloodless victim, which is comparable to that of the blood-offering, since both are in the same category of sacredness and animated by the same vital principle. Vegetation was regarded as the offspring of the fertile womb of Mother-earth, endowed with a quasi-divine soul-substance analogous to that which animals shared with man. So in agricultural communities the same symbolism recurred as among hunting tribes dependent upon the chase for their food supply.

VEGETATION RITUAL

The Corn-Mother

This has been particularly apparent in harvest rites, many of which have survived little changed throughout the ages. Effigies composed of newly cut seedlings of corn, rye, maize or rice have been made to represent the Corn-spirit, regarded either as an old woman or as a maiden. The growth of the crops has been likened to the maturing of the 'Mother'; the last sheaf is fashioned into the shape of a woman, sometimes by the oldest married woman in the village, sometimes by one from fifty to fifty-five years of age, when women tend to be in their prime and full of renewed vigour. In peasant Germany the finest ears are plucked out and made into a wreath twined with flowers and carried by the prettiest girl in procession. In some places two lads walking behind the girl have taken the Corn-mother to the house of the squire who, having received it, hung it in the hall. At the harvest supper it was placed on a pile of wood to preside over the feast, and around it dances were held. Until threshing was over it was kept in the barn and then dedi-cated in the church. On Holy Saturday the grain was rubbed out of it by a girl aged seven and scattered among the new corn, while at Christmas the straw of the wreath was placed in the manger to make the cattle thrive. The man who gave the last stroke in the threshing became the son of the Corn-mother, and was tied up in the effigy, beaten and carried through the village.[14]

Behind these folk customs lies the fertilizing power of the image, the Mother being regarded as the vitalizing influence extending from the newly sown corn to the cattle in the stall, ensuring the continuance of the crops through the potency of the mother symbol. The newly reaped cereals transmitted re-newed energy to the earth and the crops so that they might produce their fruits by virtue of the life-giving qualities be-stowed upon them in the rites. In the background is the shadowy form of the Great Mother whose image is the sacra-mental channel through which she dispenses her life-giving powers. Indeed, the last sheaf is often called 'Ceres', 'Great

Mother', or 'Grandmother',[15] and is treated accordingly, being preserved throughout the winter to ensure fertility, and its contents mingled with the food of the cattle and the new crops at Christmas and Easter.

In addition to these life-giving qualities, another sacrificial theme runs through the ritual. The crops are the means of subsistence, but their sacredness renders them tabu and danger-ous. Consequently, there is always the risk of encountering this sanctity and incurring the wrath and revenge of the slain Corn-spirit who may withdraw its beneficence from the pro-cesses of growth, or bring misfortune on the people most intimately involved. Thus, in the Highlands of Scotland, for example, there was a struggle to avoid being the last engaged in shearing and, when tillage in common existed, a ridge some-times was left which no one would claim because it was beyond the rest. The fear was of having 'the famine of the farm' in the form of an old woman known as *Cailleach* to feed till the next harvest.[16] Moreover, as we have seen, to have her on one's hands brought disaster, death and failure of the crops, so that every precaution was taken by the reapers to be well ahead with their work lest this misfortune should befall them. At Christmas a Yule log called *Cailleach Nollich* ('the Old Woman of Christmas') was cut from a tree stump in a wood by the head of the household at night on Christmas Eve, carved in resem-blance of an old woman, and then carried home to be placed in the middle of a peat fire in the centre of the living-room. As it blazed jokes were cracked, and festivities followed when the 'burnt-offering' was completely consumed as a propitiation of the angel of death, thereby freeing the house from his unwel-come visitations during the ensuing year.[17]

In these vegetation rites the promotion of fertility has often been combined with the expulsion of famine and death. These positive and negative attitudes are fundamental in the ritual expression of the will to live. The institution of sacrifice centres in the destruction of a life (i.e. a victim) of vital value and merit, concentrated especially in its blood, soul-substance, or vital essence. Strength and virility are given to the offerers or communicants; contradictory forces and ill luck are neutralized by gathering them into itself, or expelled or destroyed in the holo׳ caust. At the theistic level, when the victim becomes an inter׳ mediary between God and man, the more or less literal offering of food and drink, and tangible 'gifts', be they blood or blood׳ less, becomes an honorarium rather than a bribe, augmentation of vitality or expulsion of evil.

The Ritual of the First׳fruits

In agricultural society, so long as the cultivation of the crops has been the chief or only means of subsistence, their products have had to be treated with the utmost care and respect. This may involve an 'apology' for the painful necessity of being compelled to cut and consume them when they are ripe. Thus, among the Ainu of Japan the new millet was treated in the same way as the bear׳cub when he was killed after having been suckled by a woman, salaamed, and then eaten sacramentally.[18] Cakes of the cereal were carefully prepared, worshipped and addressed in endearing terms as the cereal deity. 'Thou hast grown very well', it was declared, 'and thy flavour will be sweet. Thou art good. The goddess of fire will be glad, and we also rejoice greatly. O thou god, O thou divine cereal, do thou nourish the people. I now partake of thee. I worship thee and give thee thanks.' A cake of it was then eaten and the tabu on the new millet was removed.[19] Similar desacralization rites are recorded among the Caffres of Zululand before the crops are gathered. The new fruits are boiled in a special pot reserved for the purpose, and a portion placed in the mouth of each man by the king. Anyone eating of them before this will die.[20] In the New World, as we have seen, the Natchez of Louisiana were accustomed to hold a 'Feast of Grain' in the seventh moon at which the new corn sown expressly for the purpose with appro׳ priate conditions and ceremonial was eaten solemnly. The ground in which it was grown had to be virgin soil dressed and prepared by warriors who were the only persons allowed to sow, tend and gather grain. When they had gathered it into a round granary the Great Sun was informed and he appointed the day of the festival. The entire nation then assembled at it, new fire was kindled by friction, the corn was solemnly pre-pared and cooked, and distributed sacramentally to the Female Suns and to all the women who prepared the grain in the huts. The Great Sun having offered a plate of it to the four quarters of the earth, gave commandment to the warriors to eat it. Next followed the boys and lastly the women.[21]

In the neighbouring Creek country a more elaborate festival known as *Busk* was held in July or August when the corn was ripe. All fires in the village and the temple had to be ex-tinguished, cooking-vessels scoured, houses and the public square swept, and a strict fast observed for two nights and a day involving purging with emetics. All traces of the food of the old year were thrown away. The high-priest then made new fire by friction on the altar in the main square after all the old embers had been swept away. All the people were silent. Next, a basket of new fruits was brought; the high-priest took a little of each sort, anointed them with bear's oil, and offered them with some flesh 'to the bountiful holy spirit of fire, as a first-fruit offering, and an annual oblation for sin'. He also conse-crated the sacred emetics (button-snake root and the cassina) by pouring a little of them into the fire. The people were exhorted to continue to observe the ancient rites and customs, and any who had contracted impurity were to depart 'lest the divine fire should spoil both them and the people'. The women carried the new fire with joy to their unpolluted hearths. The new fruits were now ready to be dressed on the new fires and eaten with bear's oil. For eight days the festival was continued, the warriors dancing round the fire in their martial array. Strict continence was observed throughout, and at the end of the festival all the people smeared themselves with white clay and bathed in running water to remove the last traces of evil incurred during the previous year.[22]

These elaborate preparations for the eating of the first-fruits show the sacredness with which they were regarded. Every possible precaution was taken to prevent contamination with ordinary food and the old crops and fires. Obtaining the permission of the chief before beginning the preparation of the new crop may have been a relic of a former precaution to prevent the gathering of the first-fruits too soon, but it was because of their inherent sanctity that a *rite de passage* was required to make the food supply accessible for the forthcoming year. Whether the indwelling mysterious vitality was regarded as a cereal deity or corn-spirit, or merely as an impersonal soul-substance, the ritual constituted an act of renewal of the process of vege-tation and the desacralization of its products. It was at once a sacrificial offering to the divinities primarily concerned with the growth of the crops and the fertility of the soil, removing dan-gerous conditions and malign influences liable to cause hunger and barrenness, sickness and death, and also a sacramental par-taking of and communion with divine beneficence. Before it was safe to eat freely it was necessary to eat ritually and sparingly with due acknowledgment of human dependence upon divine bounty.

The Sanctification of the Crops in Israel

In Israel fruit-trees remained untrimmed for three years after being planted. In the fourth year the fruit was 'a holiness of rejoicing before Yahweh'; only in the fifth year could it be eaten.[23] Before any harvest, the fields had to be sanctified and the god of the land given his share. In this token offering the harvest as a whole was represented because the first-fruits had been hallowed to Yahweh. They were able to impart their vitality to the entire field and stimulate productivity in general, be it grain or oil.[24]

There were three harvests in Palestine: those of barley, wheat and fruit. Each was assigned in Israel to its own festival; the Passover (*Pesach*) and the Feast of Unleavened Bread (*Mas-soth*) in the spring; the Feast of Weeks (*Shabuoth*) in the sum-mer; and the Feast of Ingathering (*Sukkoth*) in the autumn. Behind these, however, lay a combination of stock-breeding and agriculture, so that the Spring Festival was a composite observance which began at the full moon nearest to the vernal equinox (14th of Nisan) when the firstlings of the flocks were

offered as a pastoral lambing sacrifice, later interpreted in terms
of the Exodus from Egypt.[25] After the settlement of the
Hebrew tribes in Palestine it was brought into conjunction
with an agricultural rite celebrated at barley harvest (the
Massoth) as an offering of the first-fruits.[26] For seven days in
the month of Abib (Nisan), when according to tradition the
Exodus took place, only unleavened bread could be eaten,
while in the evening of the 14th of Nisan when the moon was
full and the barley ripening, the Paschal lamb had to be sacrificed, 'at the going down of the sun'.[27] The injunctions in the
books of Exodus and Deuteronomy represent a combination
of a solar and a lunar chronology brought into relation with
the agricultural year.[28]

Originally the Feast of Unleavened Bread was a first-fruit
ritual connected with the sanctification of the barley harvest.
It had a Canaanite background and history independent of
its later amalgamation with the pastoral *Pesach* and the commemoration of the escape from Egyptian bondage. As a result
of these syncretisms it lost its primary meaning and purpose
with regard to the ingathering of the barley, the emphasis being
on the offering of the first-born and the leaven tabu. That the
two aspects of the Spring Festival were formerly distinct is
indicated in the account of the supplementary Passover service
in the second month,[29] held for the benefit of those prevented
from taking part in the festival in Nisan by ceremonial uncleanness or absence from home. In both the J document in
Exodus and in the book of Deuteronomy the *Massoth* is given
precedence; yet no mention is made of it in the narrative in the
book of Numbers. There the offering of the first-born is represented as the earlier and the only genuine Paschal institution
with its lunar fertility affinities to ensure the increase of the
flocks and herds, in contrast with the more leisurely solar
agricultural festival connected with the barley harvest spread
over a week. On one of the days a sheaf made of the new crop
of barley (*omer*) was waved before Yahweh, as an act of sanctification and to promote fertility, the rites coming to an end on
the seventh day with a holy convocation.[30]

At first, no doubt, the crop was sanctified in the fields when it was ripe. When, however, the observance became a pil/ grimage feast performed at a particular sanctuary on behalf of the entire community, and incorporated in the Paschal Spring Festival, it was assigned to a particular date in the calendar. Sacrificial and sacramental elements derived from agricultural and pastoral sources were incorporated and made subservient to the Exodus cult legend. Eventually, after the Josiah re/ formation in 620 B.C., it was centralized in the temple at Jerusalem as the only place where Yahweh could be legiti/ mately worshipped.[31] But by this time it had lost its character as essentially a sanctification of the barley and an offering of the first/fruits of the crop.

The agricultural sequence was maintained in the celebration of the Feast of Weeks, or Pentecost, seven weeks after the Pass/ over, when the two 'wave loaves' made of fine flour of the new corn and baked with leaven were offered to Yahweh as the first/fruits of the wheat harvest.[32] This midsummer rite with its sacramental meal was probably observed independently as a family concern at the local sanctuaries all over the country as soon as the crop was ready to be gathered. Even after the Deuteronomic reforms in the seventh century Pentecost was still dated in relation to the barley harvest,[33] and until it was fixed by the temple ordinance it was probably a movable feast like sheep/shearing, determined by local conditions, cal/ culated from the reaping of the barley. In the Priestly calendar after the Exile this was reckoned at fifty days (Pentecost) from putting in the sickle to the standing crop. As the established national festival celebrating the first/fruits of the wheat harvest, it was celebrated in the temple with offerings of seven lambs without blemish of the first year, two of which were to be for a peace/offering, and one kid of the goats for a sin/offering; together with two cakes made of the new grain mixed with leaven which were waved before Yahweh before being given to the priests.[34]

The seven weeks of harvest from *Massoth* to Pentecost were the annual season of rejoicing when tribute was paid to Yah/

weh with a freewill offering according to the blessings that had
been given. From being a thank-offering it became in due
course an act of homage to the God of Israel as the 'Lord' of
the land, estimated by the value of the crops produced. Then
the community was allotted a fixed tithe to be paid on the
yield of the soil at the sanctuary,[35] which in the Priestly Code
included 'all the best of the soil, all the best of the vintage, and
of the corn', together with 'the first ripe fruits of all that is in
the land'.[36] Eventually, 'the first ripe fruits'—the prepared
corn, wine and oil known as *Ibikkurim*—were distinguished
from the payment in kind (*t'ruman*) for the priesthood which
was levied on all fruits.[37]

The Feast of Weeks, however, was obscured by the two great
ingathering festivals, the one in the spring and the other in the
autumn. Pentecost fell between these two significant events, at
the end of the corn-harvest when the wheat was ready to be
reaped. Then attention was directed more towards the fruits
of the vineyards and the orchards, much of the grain having
been already harvested. At the end of the agricultural year
when all the labour in the fields had been completed the oldest
and most important of the three festivals was held at full moon
in the month of Ethnaim, described after the Exile as 'the
seventh month [Tishri] between October and November
when the vintage had been completed.' Both its time and the
setting suggest a Canaanite origin connected with the grape
harvest at the autumnal equinox when the 'former rains' in
October were due to begin.[38]

When the Babylonian calendar was adopted in Israel after
the Exile, the earlier hilarious rites at 'the going out of the year'
continued to be observed for seven days as a pilgrimage viticulture feast, beginning on the fifteenth of Tishri with a holy
convocation. For a week all servile work ceased and booths
were made from the boughs of fruit-trees, branches of palm-
trees, of leaf-trees and of Atabah-trees from the river-beds, in
which the whole congregation of Israel dwelt during the Feast
of Tabernacles or Booths.[39] In its Canaanite background,
apparently, it included feasting and erotic dancing such as con-

tinued outside vineyards at this season of the year in the days of the Judges. In the story of Abimelech the people of Shechem are said to have gone into the field to gather their vineyards, tread the grapes, and keep festival (*hillulim*), going into their sanctuary and eating and drinking with their god in a sacra- mental meal.[40]

Similarly, from the much-glossed-over account of the rape of the maidens who danced ecstatically outside the vineyards of Shiloh,[41] it would seem that at the vintage feasts in Pales- tine ecstatic fertility rites occurred not very different from those of the maenads of Dionysus in Thrace and Phrygia. Moreover, since nuptial rites were often performed in booths of greenery at the Annual Festival in agricultural communities, it would not be surprising if behind the *Sukkoth*, or the Feast of Taber- nacles, lay the very ancient and widespread custom of resorting to bridal-chambers at the time of the autumnal ingathering to engage in a connubium as part of the riotous viticulture festival.

But if it was in this context that the practice arose, its earlier significance had been abandoned when it was revived after the Exile. Then it became 'the Feast'[42] because it repre- sented the climax of the agricultural year—the last and greatest of the three harvest festivals, and the inauguration of the new year that was about to open with the rainy season.

Essentially, however, it was the feast of the ingathering of 'the fruit of the land' spread over seven days from the fifteenth of the seventh month, with a holy convocation on the first and the last days.

But the presentation of the first-fruits in their several forms occurred from the Passover to the Feast of Tabernacles, and in the later period it was extended to the Hasmonaean Feast of the Dedication in the month of Kislev (December),[43] when the distinction was made between the first ripe raw fruits (i.e. *bikkurim*) and the corn, wine, oil and dough prepared from them (i.e. *reshith*), together with the meal offering consisting of parched corn in the ear with oil and frankincense, part of which was burnt.[44]

First-fruits and Tithes in Israel

The giving of tithe as part of the ritual of the first-fruits was in vogue in the time of Jeroboam II (*c.* 786–745 B.C.), as is shown by the prophet Amos when he ironically urged the people to go to Bethel to transgress, to Gilgal to multiply transgression, to bring their sacrifices every morning to these local sanctuaries, and pay their tithes every three days.[45] As Jacob is said to have vowed at Bethel to give a tenth of all that Yahweh would bestow upon him,[46] the custom would seem to have been long enough established to have acquired a place in the cult legend, though it may be a reflection of later practice. Similarly, Abraham is alleged to have paid tithes of all his possessions to Melchizedec, and in the ante-monarchist oration of Samuel reference is made to the fact that the king extracted a tenth of the flocks.[47]

Originally, however, it appears to have been a voluntary first-fruit offering of corn, wine and oil made at the local sanctuaries before it became a fixed charge on all the increase of seed grown in the fields.[48] After the Exile it was a sacerdotal tax due to the Levites as a compensation and salary extended to the yearly increase of the flocks and herds, and to the priesthood as a whole.[49] At this stage in the development of tithing it was a forced tribute to supply the wages of the servants of the sanc-tuary rather than a freewill offering of first-fruits of the sancti-fied crops as a gift to Yahweh, varying according to the annual yield. Both the first-fruits and tithes were extracted as dues,[50] and upon the regular payment of the tax the divine blessing on the nation depended.[51] Even the first-born of man, as we have seen, was not excluded from the law of firstlings in general, as they all belonged to Yahweh.[52]

Greece

In Greece tithes (δέκατη) and first-fruits (ἀπαρχή) were dependent one upon the other. A prescribed portion of the fruits of the earth was set apart for the gods, and this was extended to temple slaves and tribute-money.[53] When new land was first cultivated a part of it had to be left as an assignment to the guardian divinity, or a sacrifice had to be offered to him before taking possession of the ground, occupying a new house, or erecting a bridge. Agamemnon dedicated a tenth of Mycenae to the gods after he conquered the city.[54] First-fruits were sent regularly to Delphi and Delos by the Athenians,[55] it being one of the functions of Apollo to make the crops grow. Therefore, at the time of harvest tithe-offerings were showered upon him, and at his command the shrine of Demeter at Eleusis was regularly supplied with first-fruits.[56] Late in September or in October when the grapes were trodden in the wine-presses and the apples, plums and pears were ripe, a har-vest-home or Thalysia was held at the altar of Demeter on threshing-floors by farmers in the presence of a sheaf probably representing bounteous Mother-earth and the Corn-mother with corn-stalks and poppies in her hands.[57] This very ancient rustic domestic observance, which has changed little through the ages, has been celebrated when the threshing was ended and the first loaf, the *Thalysion arton*, was baked from the new corn, without regard for any particular date.[58] These loaves (*thargelos*) were associated with Demeter, who was known as 'the goddess with the great loaves', and were in the nature of first-fruit offerings; the same applied to the mixture of all the new fruits (*panspermia*) cooked in a pot and carried round as an offering to the gods to promote fertility during the forth-coming year.

In Attica these loaves gave their name to a festival, the Thar-gelia, celebrated in May, the last month but one of the year and called Thargelion. As it belonged to Apollo rather than to Demeter, it had, however, a different character. The central figure, called Pharmakos, was usually a criminal who was led through the streets, fed, flogged with green branches, and finally either expelled or killed, though the extreme penalty was never required in Athens. The purpose of the rite was to ward off all injurious influences from the crops that were about to ripen, and to drive away the evil that had accumulated during the year, including no doubt the supernatural dangers incurred in slaying the Corn-spirit at the harvest by way of anticipation. The Pharmakos, therefore, was both a sin-carrier and a sacrificial victim in an early agrarian vegetation rite. In its later form the cleansing of the town was followed by the *thargelia* being cooked and presented to Apollo as a thank-offering and for a good harvest.[59] In the background lies a primitive expulsion and fertility ritual to remove the tabus and sinister influences surrounding the new crops and to produce an abundant ingathering.

In the month of Pyanepsion (October) when ploughing began, beans were cooked in a pot at the Pyanepsia, or festival of fruit-gathering, and the *eiresione*, or Maypole, was carried in procession, decorated with figs, wine, oil and honey.[60] As the symbol of the first-fruits, it was set up before the temple of Apollo or a private house. There it remained for the rest of the year, except when it was carried in the spring festival of the Thargelia to foster the growth of the crops, until its life-giving power was exhausted in the autumn, when it was replaced by a new one. Once the crops had come to fruition and were ready to be reaped they had to be made accessible to man as common food, but their vitality also had to be transferred to the new harvest destined to spring from the garnered cereals and fruits. This was coupled with a general cleansing of houses, barns, receptacles and utensils, followed by rejoicing. Hence the dual significance of the sacrifice of the first-fruits and their attendant rites and symbols.

Rome

In ancient Rome purification rites in the form of lustrations and fumigations were combined with the offering of the first-fruits of the crops to the numina who were concerned with their welfare in order to render the year productive. This survived in the State cult, as, for example, in the practice of the Vestal Virgins gathering the first ripe ears of corn in May which were ground into flour by pounding. From the grist thus prepared at the Vestalia on June 9 they made a sacrificial cake or meal (*mola salsa*) which they mixed with salt prepared from brine with very great care for use at the Lupercalia, an ancient spring festival on February 15, in which purification and fecundity were combined.[61]

That a vegetation cultus lay behind that of the Vestal Virgins is indicated by their duties and functions, all of which belong to the oldest agricultural ritual. Moreover, their own temple on the north side of the Palatine Hill between the Via Sacra and the Via Nova was the most ancient temple in Rome, said to have been erected by the legendary King Numa in 716 B.C.,[62] on the model of a primitive round hut.[63] It was, however, most apparent in the preparation of the *mola salsa* culminating in the very primitive purificatory Argei cere- mony[64] on the Ides of May to drive away evil influences so prominent in first-fruit and harvest rites, and in the sweeping of the *penus*, or storehouse, in the temple where the *mola* was kept before it was closed at the end of the Vestalia. This was done to remove every vestige of the old corn in readiness for the first-fruits of the new harvest. They again appeared at the Consualia and the Obiconsivia, the late harvest festivals on August 21 and 24, when the grain was stored in the silos as a kind of harvest-home in honour of the gods who protected the stores.

The cult of Hercules in August at the *ara maxima* in the cattle market (Forum Boarium) in Rome near the church of Sta Maria in Cosmedin, suggests that the first-fruits developed into a system of tithes as in Israel and Greece. According to Dio- dorus Siculus 'Hercules, in gratitude for the kindness he had received from the inhabitants of the Palatine, foretold them that after his own departure to the gods all who should vow to dedicate a tithe of their substance would live a life of greater affluence thereafter, which has continued to prove true down even to our own time. For many of the Romans, not merely those of moderate means, but even some of the very wealthy, have vowed to dedicate to Hercules a tithe of their fortune, when that fortune amounted to thousands of talents.'[65] It is said that the god himself sacrificed a tithe of cattle on the altar, but as first- fruits are not known to have been offered to Hercules in parti- cular, it is likely that the altar was already connected with the practice before the urbanization of the city, and afterwards transferred to the god very much as the *mola salsa* sacrificial cakes were attributed to King Numa, who ordained that the spelt offered to the gods should be toasted.[66]

Ceres, as the goddess controlling the growth of the corn, was the recipient of the first ears reaped at the harvest. Until this offering had been made the new crops might not be eaten. Her cultus, however, centred in a numen representing the generative process, was established before Ceres was identified with Demeter in the temple on the Aventine Hill. This was introduced into Rome in 493 B.C. under Greek influence, and associated with Liber and Libera, representing the Eleusinian triad, Demeter, Kore and Iacchus (Dionysus), who in fact were old Italian deities connected with the growth of the crops.[67] So although her festival, the Cerealia (April 19), had lost its rustic character when it was established after the second Punic War, it is hardly surprising that a primitive feature derived from the earlier cult survived in the practice of tying burning torches to the tails of foxes and letting them loose in the Circus Maximus.[68] It may have had a cathartic significance in the protection of the crops, but the explanation of the obscure custom can only be very conjectural.

At the annual festival of Ceres in August, women clad in white robes and adorned with garlands of the first-fruits of the wheat crop, after having observed a strict rule of continence for nine nights, celebrated the return of Proserpine (Kore) from the underworld.[69] This may have been of Greek origin. It was probably then, when the ears had been reaped just before the heat of summer,[70] that the first-fruits of the corn harvest were offered to the goddess. This would be the most likely occasion for the rite to have been held, particularly if it included a dramatic enactment of the union of Pluto and Proserpine brought into relation with the ingathering of harvest.[71] Ceres had bestowed her gifts upon mankind and in return had every right to receive the first-fruits of their harvest before her bounty was enjoyed, just as the Greeks offered barley and wheat to Demeter and Persephone at Eleusis.

LIBATIONS AND LUSTRATIONS
Babylonia

Closely associated with these regenerative vegetation rites are the lustrations and libations employed either to give a fresh outpouring of life or to remove harmful and dangerous influences as a ritual purification. It is not surprising that water should have been regarded as at once a revivifying and cleansing agent, since vegetation has always depended on rain, rivers, fountains and springs, and water has always been used as a cleansing medium. As Langdon has pointed out, 'since in Babylonia as in Egypt the fertility of the soil depended upon irrigation, it is but natural to expect that the youthful god who represents the birth and death of nature would represent the beneficent waters which flooded the valleys of the Tigris and Euphrates in the later winter, and which ebbed away and nearly disappeared in the canals and rivers in the period of summer drought.'[72]

Thus Dumuzi, the Sumerian Tammuz, was 'the faithful son of the waters that came forth from the earth' who became the god of the fertilizing *bel girsu* which flooded the land in winter and died away in the summer. In this capacity he was the source and controller of vegetation *par excellence*,[73] while Ea, or Enki, the third of the great triad of gods, was 'the Lord of the watery deep' whose abode was in the Apsu (the abyss or subterranean ocean) which surrounded the earth, and whose cult-centre was Eridu at the head of the Persian Gulf. There his temple with its sacred tree stood where the 'sweet waters' of the rivers, believed to be under the earth, mingled with the 'bitter waters' of the sea, personified in Tiamat, as in the blending the Apsu with Tiamat in the primeval watery chaos. There the human race was fashioned from clay by Anu, the Sumerian Creator, and Ea, to whom the Persian Gulf was sacred as the source of all water, endowed all creatures with life.

Water, therefore, became the symbol of life and the supreme fertilizing agency, and as Ea was also the god of wisdom and the source of magical knowledge, it was efficacious in incantation, and in the delivery of human beings from demons and disease. It was also a means of purification, removing pollution and the miasma of substantive evil by its cleansing properties when sprinkled on the body, or on any object or place, and drawn from the Tigris and Euphrates or from a bubbling spring. Thus, when Inanna-Ishtar went to the underworld in search of Dumuzi-Tammuz and was reduced to a naked corpse by Ereshkigal, the queen of the nether regions, Ea fashioned two sexless creatures and sent them to her with the water of life to sprinkle on her body. She thereupon was revived and restored to earth.[74]

Egypt

In Egypt much the same situation obtained. All existence had emerged from the waters of Nun, the primordial abyss, and from them issued the annual inundation of the Nile, on which vegetation depended, which was equated with Osiris and with Isis as its creatrix. From Nun two mighty rivers flowed, one the Nile on earth and the other its heavenly counterpart flowing across the sky and through the underworld (Duat), along which the Sun-god Re pursued his daily and nightly courses, born afresh every morning as at the beginning of creation. Therefore, from Nun the divine and cosmic orders were established by a series of births in the realms of the gods, appearing from the original source of all life personified and materialized as the state of Chaos, Nun, which surrounded the world, until eventually in the New Kingdom it was confined to the subterranean Duat. It was also applied to the Nile, upon the waters of which Egypt depended for its vegetation. The ocean was also identified with Nun as was the sky in its watery aspect, 'the celestial ocean', the father of the gods, traversed by Re in his solar barque. It is not surprising, there-fore, that water was regarded as the source of life and, in the form of libations and lustrations, became an integral element in the institution of sacrifice.

Since man and vegetation everywhere depended upon the water supply for their sustenance and survival, it became equally efficacious in relation to the gods and the dead, or as a potent accessory to other offerings, extended to similar life/giving agents such as milk, oil and wine. The ritual of mum/mification was developed in order to render the corpse im/mortal. First the corpse was washed in Nile water; then the brain and the internal organs were extracted, and then it was taken out of the salt/bath to free it from all impurity. In the subsequent Opening of the Mouth ceremony the desic/cated body, or the portrait statue, was sprinkled with holy water from different vessels, as well as being censed, anointed with cedar and olive oil, and had natron, honey, wax and such like life/giving substances applied to it.[75]

This combination of purification and regeneration recurred in the royal Toilet ceremonies at Heliopolis when the Pharaoh as the high/priest of the Sun/god Re entered the temple of his heavenly Father to perform his ritual of renewal every morning. At birth the infant prince was washed in water from a sacred pool identified with that of the primeval ocean by priests im/personating the deities Thoth (or Seth) and Horus, in order to initiate him into his royal divine status. On the day of his accession he was publicly acknowledged by the Sun/god as his son and again purified with 'the water of life which is in the sky'. It was this ablution that was repeated every morning when at dawn he underwent his daily ceremonial lustration to unite him with Re/Atum before he ascended to the solar temple which symbolized the celestial realms. There he kindled a fire and, having placed incense on the burning charcoal in a brazier, he proceeded to the sanctuary to be asperged, censed, anointed, robed and crowned before ascend/ing the stair to the great window to behold his celestial Father. The earthly incarnation of the Sun/god underwent the same ritual processes as the god himself; and, similarly, the priests, as the deputies of the king, repeated these ceremonies in the daily temple liturgy in connexion with the cult/image in the shrine. In most of the temple reliefs the Pharaoh is represented as the celebrant of the rites, but in fact he only performed them in person on rare occasions. Nevertheless, what was done in the heavens and in the House of the Morning and in the temples on earth were all one and the same sacred action, and were for the purpose of rejuvenating the god, the king and the 'Two Lands' of Upper and Lower Egypt.[76]

The same rites were performed to ensure the dead king's daily rebirth. The corpse was washed and laid in the grave, and libations were poured out in the cult-chamber of the tomb-chapel by mortuary priests impersonating the gods who assisted at the lustration of the Sun-god. The deceased Pharaoh was then able to cross over the flooded Field of Aalu to the horizon where the ageing gods were reborn, and like them he himself was reborn, drinking the cool water of the primeval land of revivification. Thus, Osiris as the dead king was resuscitated by being washed at dawn in the water of life from such a pool, and then suckled by Isis and Nephthys; or imme-diately after the lustration he was restored with an indestruc-tible heavenly body and all his earthly defilements were washed away.[77] The priest, on pouring out the libation at the third hour of the night during the ceremony of the embalming of Osiris, said, addressing the god, 'Take to them thy cool water which is in this land, which begets all living things; yea, all things issue from it. Thou partakest thereof, thou livest thereon, thou art healthy thereby, thou breathest the air that is in it. It hath begotten thee, and thou camest forth living on all things thou desirest.' In the same manner the king was rebegotten and reborn as the son of the god, the living Horus,[78] having emerged from the womb of the sacred waters like his divine prototypes. It was in this context that the royal lustrations were performed.

Palestine

In Palestine, although in no part of the year is there drought comparable to that in Mesopotamia, serious conditions of famine periodically occur, especially in Judaea and the south on the edge of the desert. The north was described in the Old Testament as essentially 'the good land, a land of brooks of water, of fountains and depths, that spring out of the valleys and hills, a land of oil, olive and honey',[79] but drought was a recurrent phenomenon.[80] Therefore, when the rains failed, resort was made to ritual of the Tammuz type at the approach of the cool season. In the Canaanite Ras Shamra texts the seasons are represented as being under the joint control of Baal, the god of rain and fertility, 'the Rider of the Clouds', who ruled the earth from September to May, and his adversaries Mot, the god of aridity and death, and Prince Sea, who held dominion in the rainless summer. The struggle between them being perennial, neither could be finally and completely des-troyed. At the end of summer and the opening of the rainy season the calendrical cult drama was probably celebrated, as elsewhere in Western Asia, to establish the dominion of the beneficent Weather-god (Baal) and to ensure the return of the rain. The priest went to the sea and poured ladlefuls of water into basins, and carried them to his temple, after a ritual com-bat had been enacted depicting the victory of Baal over Mot. Then Baal opened the lattice in his mountain palace on Sapan to allow the rain to fall on the parched soil to rejuvenate its vegetation.[81]

Before he was introduced into Syria Baal was probably identified with the Hurrian Weather-god Hadad and the Akkadian Adad, the ancient Semitic Storm-god.[82] Once established in Palestine he controlled its weather, ordering a rift to be opened in the clouds and a lattice within his palace in the heavens to enable the rain to descend. The installation of windows in his house represents the mythological background of a rain-making ceremony at the autumnal festival when the windows in the temple at Ras Shamra were opened to simulate the opening of the lattices in heaven and the clefts in the clouds. Schaeffer, in fact, has suggested that the rain was intended to descend through the skylight in the roof on the face of the god depicted on a stele which stood in the sanctuary, representing Baal armed with lightning.[83]

In the absence of irrigation as in Egypt and Mesopotamia, the Canaanite peasants felt themselves to be absolutely depen-dent upon the divine powers who sent down the 'former rains' in autumn and the 'latter rains' in winter and spring. Hence the resort to libations and rain-making ceremonies, and the seasonal drama, to secure an adequate water supply, and also the struggle between two rival cults on Mount Carmel in the reign of Ahab and his Tyrian wife Jezebel. There, at an ancient sanctuary of Aleyan Baal at a time of prolonged drought, a ritual contest between the Canaanite Storm- and Weather-god and the Hebrew desert deity Yahweh was enacted in a sacrificial context in which, according to the nar- rative, after the pouring out of libations three times on the altar erected by Elijah in honour of the god of Israel, fire was sent down from heaven to consume the sacrifice, and immediately the drought ceased,[84] thereby establishing Yahweh as the con- troller of the weather in Israel.

Although the conflict between the two cults continued the Carmel legend shows that Yahweh, in spite of his desert tradition, was concerned with rain and vegetation, and, there- fore, libations and lustrations had their place and function in the Hebrew sacrificial system. The sources of rain were believed to be above the firmament, from there descending upon the earth when the lattices in the sky were opened,[85] as in the Ugaritic texts. Since it was a divine gift, full of regenerative power, able to make the desert blossom as the rose, it naturally was employed in conjunction with the prescribed ritual. There- fore, as in the Canaanite sanctuaries, a reservoir of water stood beside the sacred trees and asherah, so in the court of Solomon's temple there was a large basin called 'the sea' supported by twelve oxen and ten bronze carts decorated with lions, oxen and cherubim, and bearing lavers.[86] By pouring out water before Yahweh a sacrificial oblation was made, as in the case of Samuel at Mizpeh[87] and of David at Bethlehem, when three of his warriors risked their lives to obtain possession of the water from the sacred well there.[88] When this was done in the holy place the offering acquired even greater sanctity.[89] After the Exile on the last day of the Feast of Tabernacles (i.e. on Tishri 21) a pitcher of water was taken by priests from the pool of Siloam to the temple, and together with a wine oblation was solemnly poured out as a libation beside the altar in the presence of the congregation. Boisterous rejoicings followed.[90] Originally this was doubtless a rain-making cere-mony, since in the Talmud it is affirmed that the waters were offered to Yahweh that 'the rains of the year may be blessed to you.'[91]

After the destruction of the temple in A.D. 70 the obser-vance ceased, but a prayer modelled upon it was added to the liturgy for the Day of the Water-libation on the seventh day of the Feast, with a penitential note suggestive of an act of atone-ment rather than of rejoicing. But both before and after the cessation of the temple worship, the water libations associated with the festival were an expression of the belief that Yahweh as the Lord of creation was responsible for sending the rain to fertilize the earth, as in the sacred marriage ritual, a relic of which may be detected in the Samaritan liturgies.[92]

Greece

Although the Olympian gods in Greece, unlike Yahweh in Israel, never transcended the cosmos and the processes of nature, Zeus was an Indo-European Sky- and Weather-god who as 'the cloud-gatherer' poured the refreshing fertilizing rain on the earth from his exalted abode on Mount Olympus. Indeed, every hill-top and every town had its localized Zeus who gathered the clouds and produced the rain and the tempest. But water always has been scarce in Greece, and in addition to the great Sky-god as the rain-producer, the numer-ous rivers and springs also were sacred, and treated with such reverence that before an army ventured to cross a stream an offering had to be made to the indwelling divinity,[93] and horses and bulls were thrown into the sea to Poseidon.[94] In fact, no one should cross a river without making some oblation, however small, and washing his hands in its water. It was par-ticularly to the Earth-gods and goddesses that libations were poured out, as in the Minoan-Mycenaean Goddess cult where those attendant upon the Mountain-Mother are frequently depicted on seals, gems, rings and plaques pouring libations on a sacred pillar or cairn, or on the boughs of a tree, often between the horns of consecration on altars. This was done to make the rain of heaven fall on the thirsty vegetation.[95] On a bead-seal from Crete, for example, genii stand at either side of a tree holding jugs in their uplifted hands with what seems to be the orb of the sun on top of the tree.[96]

The practice of pouring libations over sacred cairns and pillars as an offering to the indwelling god developed in Late Minoan III in Crete into that of pouring the libations into a bowl resting on a column. On either side the bowl had two further supports which became the legs of a tripod, often having an anthropomorphic form, with a central stem. This was the prototype of the baetylic libation-table which survived until Roman times.[97] In Greece it appeared in Corinth with three lion-goddesses for its supports, and at Delphi with three serpents for its base,[98] the antecedent perhaps of that on which the Pythia exercised her oracular functions after drinking of the water from the subterranean spring and undergoing purifica-tion. Libations were offered to Zeus and the Olympians at banquets from the first of three mixing-bowls, to the heroes from the second, and to Zeus from the third,[99] probably as the final offering for the soul of the deceased like the cup of wine drunk at the end of the meal in the name of Agathos Daimon, or the 'Good Spirit', originally probably the ancestor of the family as the giver of fertility and wealth like Plouton.

The bottoms of amphorae were frequently perforated like the great Dipylon vases which stood over graves and contained funerary offerings, to enable the libations to be poured over the grave and so conveyed to the dead. The snakes entwined round the rims and base of the neck and the handle are suggestive of a funerary ritual, though the cylinders at Knossos and Gournia with snakes drinking from little cups attached to the sides appear to have been intended to receive libations for the Genius of the household.[100] At Gournia, in the centre of the sanc-tuary containing a primitive figure of the Snake-goddess Eileithyia with a Minoan bull-shaped skirt, stood a low earthen table with three legs and the base of a vase supporting a bowl for libations. Around it were three tubular vessels with a vertical row of three or four handles on either side. Above a large handle was a pair of horns of consecration, and one of the vessels was entwined with two snakes.[101]

Tubular vases recur at the household sanctuaries at Kumasa and Prinia. Gournia, however, was neither a house nor a palace shrine, and at Knossos the Snake Room, where the tubular vessels and libation-table were found, was in a private house. The Snake-goddess at Gournia was not the centre of a domestic cult, in spite of her equipment with a table of offering and tubular vessels. Here, it would seem, she was rather the chthonic Earth-mother, both the Goddess of fertility and Mis-tress of the nether regions. The vases without cups were hollow tubes through which, doubtless, offerings were poured on to the earth as libations to the chthonic Goddess, very much as at Asine a large jug decorated with parallel stripes stood on a ledge upside down, its bottom having been deliber-ately broken off to enable it to be used for libations.[102] At Phlius in the Peloponnese, Aras, the primal man, was invited to partake of the libations offered to him before the celebration of the mysteries of Demeter.[103] In Attica it was the custom for girls to bring libations to the tomb of Iphinoe before their marriage,[104] and wine was offered to gods, heroes and their wives at Olympia by libation-bearers every month.[105] But it was forbidden to make libations of wine to Zeus in the Erech-theum at Athens,[106] or to nymphs or mistresses, or on the common altar of all the gods.[107]

Rome

In ancient Rome the characteristic form of the *sacrificium* was the *lustratio*, or purification procession, to get rid of evil or hostile influences, and to maintain the sanctity of a sacred enclosure by encompassing it so as to draw a 'magic circle' round it. This happened at certain fixed times, usually in May, when the crops were ripening and were in the greatest need of supernatural protection. At the Ambarvalia three circuits were made round the boundaries of the fields with the pig, sheep and ox to be sacrificed, and prayer for the protection of the

fields from evil; a rustic ceremony that subsequently was transformed into the Amburbium which took the form first of the
purification of the army before setting out on a campaign, and
then of the purification of the trumpets of war and a census.[108]
The course of the *Luperci* round the Palatine Hill at the Lupercalia on February 15 had a similar significance, since its
purpose was to drive away evil influences and deliver from
barrenness women who were struck with the strips of goat's
hide which the *Luperci* carried on their circumambulations.

Again, when in March the *Salii* leapt about the Palatine and
Quirinal Hills to make the crops grow, and visited the Forum
and the Capitol arrayed in their bronze armour and red and
purple cloaks, this was in the nature of a *lustratio* of the sacred
shields (*ancilia*) they carried in their left hands. Although these
shields were not actually taken into battle, the general in
command at the outbreak of hostilities went to the *sacrarium*
where they were kept and called upon Mars to come to his
aid.[109] Other cities besides Rome had their *Salii* in the service
of Hercules instead of that of Mars, to promote the well-being
of vegetation and to drive away blight and infertility in the
spring, as well as to secure victory on the field of battle. This
may be a reason for their often having been associated with
dancing maidens, *Saliae virgines*. But since the *lustratio* was
essentially an agricultural institution, when it survived in the
State cult of an urbanized community it lost much of its
original purpose and significance concerning the crops and
fruits of the earth, the flocks and the herds. Nevertheless, as the
word indicates, the derivation being from *luere*, 'to free' or
'loose', the fundamental conception was that of removing
harmful taints, conditions or influences by means of a purifying
or desacralizing agent, be it in relation to a person, property or
condition.[110]

Thus, the shepherds' festival known as the Parilia on April
21, began with an elaborate lustration of the sheep and cattle
comparable to that among herdsmen at Beltane in Scotland on
May 1.[111] According to Ovid's account of the proceedings,
the sheep and the people were sprinkled with water, and

towards evening the ground was cleansed and carefully swept with brooms made of twigs of laurel. The folds were adorned with leaves and boughs, and the door with a wreath. Sulphur was then ignited and burnt with olive wood, laurel and rose-mary to purify the flock in its smoke. Offerings of a basket of millet and cakes of millet, a pail of milk and meat (*dapes*) were accompanied in the later rite with a prayer to Pales, the guardian of flocks and herds, said four times by the shepherd, who then washed his hands in 'living water' or the morning dew before drinking a bowl of milk and wine. The flocks, having been fumigated, were driven through the bonfires to cleanse them, followed by the shepherds who jumped over them three times facing east to complete the *lustratio*; the festival con-cluding with a feast in the open air.[112]

The Pavilia, although one of the chief festivals in the Roman calendar, always retained its pastoral and rural character and purpose designed for the care and protection of the flock and shepherds, that the sheep might be kept free from disease, not fall a prey to wolves, and the dogs be watchful; that grass and herbs be plentiful, the udders of the cows full of milk, the rams lustful and the ewes prolific, the wool thick and soft, and the water supply adequate. As a *lustratio* the emphasis was on cleansing from sacred taints, broken tabus, and pollutions of various kinds, together with harmful supernatural forces. Pro-ductivity of the sheep and cattle when they were turned out to pasture in the spring was stressed in the prayer to Pales, as well as protection against the onslaughts of wolves. Therefore, in its Roman form the *lustratio* combined purification and protection against external evil influences, with the well-being of the flocks and herds and the prosperity of the household.

Christendom

The Christian Church retained many of the water obser-vances that were established in Judaism and the Graeco-Roman world, and placed its own interpretation on them, giving them a new significance without materially altering their character. Thus, water was still used for expiatory and purificatory purposes, as it had been throughout its long cultic history. The initial sacrament of Baptism was regarded as a 'washing of regeneration',[113] a new spiritual birth of 'water and the Spirit', foreshadowed by the Noachian Flood and the passage of Israel through the Red Sea. When in the second century the water was consecrated[114] and the Holy Spirit invoked to sanctify it, the way was opened for holy water to be employed for the blessing and dedication of altars, churches, houses and sacred objects, for exorcisms, asperging at the beginning of Mass, and in mortuary rites, while unblessed water was also used ceremonially for the washing of the fingers of the celebrant at the offertory and of the vessels after the Communion in and after the tenth century, and for rinsing the mouth at the reception of the Blessed Sacrament, as in some Eastern usages, and in the Communion of the Sick.[115]

After baptism, the ceremonial washing of the feet of the catechumens (*Mandatum*) was performed by clerics in minor orders, or by lay persons,[116] and this practice was long maintained in Gaul, Milan and Ireland. In the fourth century, as is clear from the Council of Hippo in 393, it was performed at the commemoration of the institution of the Eucharist in Holy Week on Maundy Thursday when the *Mandatum* became liturgical practice in cathedrals and religious houses; now in the revised Order of Holy Week extended to parish churches after the Gospel in the Evening Mass of the Lord's Supper. These ablutions, however, are distinct from sprinkling and lustration with holy water consecrated for the purpose of conveying spiritual influences and sanctifying grace, defending the person or object from all demonic forces.

CHAPTER VII

Mortuary Sacrificial Ritual

THE CULT OF THE DEAD

THE extension of the life-giving process to the dead brought the mortuary cultus into relation with the institution of sacrifice at a very early period, the quest of newness of life in this world and in the hereafter being inseparable. Indeed, belief in the re-birth of man is apparently almost as old as the human race. In the archaeological record there are indications of mortuary practices suggesting the existence of a cult of the dead going back to the beginning of the Palaeolithic. Moreover, from the available evidence it seems that not only was the body often laid to rest in a carefully prepared grave and provided with the food and implements that would be required in the after-life, but the brain was extracted from the cranium as the seat of special potency and eaten sacramentally to imbibe the qualities of the deceased.[1]

The Palaeolithic Grave Equipment

Mortuary ritual was mainly concerned to feed the dead and to reanimate the corpse. Behind it lay a combination of emotions of fear, respect, veneration, and sometimes doubtless of affec-tion and a genuine desire for the well-being of the departed whose death was lamented. At first it was enough to inter the body with some care and protection from molestation, as at La Ferrassie in the Dordogne where the corpses had been sur-rounded with slabs of stone and covered with flakes of bone or another stone, the skeletons being orientated east to west, and equipped with implements. In front of the grave a ditch con-tained bones and ashes, perhaps the remains of a funerary feast.[2] Similarly, at Le Moustier on the right bank of the Vézère a Neanderthal youth was placed in a recumbent posi-tion with his head resting on a pillow of flint flakes and a fine hand-axe near the left arm. In the grave were wild ox bones, charred and split.[3]

At this stage human survival was considered to require only food and tools but in the Upper Palaeolithic the more advanced Crô-Magnons and the allied types of *Homo sapiens* were often interred in a deposit of ochreous earths or sprinkled with red ochre, as at Paviland in South Wales or in the caves at Grimaldi between Menton and Ventimiglia, where they were also surrounded with quantities of shells, including cowries.[4] Similar ceremonial interments have been found in the Dordogne and in Central Europe; attempts were made to make the body serviceable for its owner's use by supplying it with vitalizing agents such as ochreous powder, the surrogate of blood, and shells connected with the female principle, employed as life-giving charms.

This mortuary equipment and offerings indicate a regard for the dead that went beyond fear. The Neanderthals had begun to look forward to survival after death requiring food and tools, and made provision as they were able for these needs. The Crô-Magnons went a stage further in the development of the cult of the dead by offerings of magico-religious life-bestowing substances or objects to effect the reanimation of the mortal remains. Burial in the flexed position, the binding of the body having been done in some cases before rigor mortis had set in, may have been a precaution against the ghost 'walking' and exercising vengeance on the living for any neglect of adequate offerings, or to pay off old scores. Conversely, the preservation of the skull seems to have been inspired by a desire to retain a potent trophy of the departed, while brain-extraction probably was a means of communion with them, or of imbibing their qualities and strength.

Egyptian Funerary Offerings

With the rise of civilization in the Fertile Crescent, mortuary ritual assumed more elaborate proportions. This became most apparent in ancient Egypt. The corpse was preserved by a highly technical process of mummification, and skilfully designed plastered heads, death masks and portrait statues made as permanent simulacra of the deceased. In the Fourth Dynasty life-sized figures were made by modelling the heads in limestone or mud and placing them in the burial chambers with the mummy to ensure the continuation of the existence of the occu, pant should the body disintegrate or become unrecognizable.[5] In view of the importance attached to the head as the seat of the soul-substance particular significance was given to a permanent simulacrum of it in stucco resin, or some similar durable material, as a part of the mortuary offerings inserted in the *serdab*, or statue-house, at the top of the shaft of the mastaba tomb. As immortality was extended from the Pharaoh and the nobility to commoners, lavish offerings of food and drink were made, together with ushabti figures of servants to take the place of the deceased when he might be called upon to do servile work in the after-life, later represented in the form of a mummy impersonating the dead.

At first the offerings were placed in the tomb, and in the mastabas a chapel and storeroom on the east side were pro, vided to contain the provisions for those buried in them, while in the great royal pyramids a 'temple of offerings' consisting of several rooms stood in the front on the east side. As early as the First Dynasty mortuary chapels were attached to royal tombs and those of nobles, and by the time of the Empire anyone who could afford them caused them to be erected and endowed by a son for offerings of food and drink, cult objects, weapons, ornaments, ushabtis, and articles of clothing, to be made to his father after his death for use in the next world. The entrails also were preserved in canopic jars protected in the tomb by four funerary genii, children of Horus. The *ba* (soul) of the deceased was thought to have access to the grave goods through a 'false door' in the tomb, and to procure for himself the articles de, picted on the walls of the necropolis, made accessible by the recitation of the liturgy.[6] This followed the pattern of the daily toilet ceremonial in the House of the Morning[7] based on 'The Opening of the Mouth' ritual, originally performed for the Pharaoh and the nobles, and hardly likely to have formed part of the obsequies of commoners except on comparatively rare occasions. When it was used it included anointing, censing and feeding, a procession with lamentations to the tomb after the embalming had been completed in the 'House of Gold' or 'mortuary workshop', and sacrifices and a meal to give nourishment to the *ba*.[8]

The Feeding of the Ka

The gods, first the Pharaohs and then the dead in general, were thought to be in heaven, on the earth and under the earth, equipped with an imperishable body and/or a portrait statue, and an immortal *ba* or ghost, in addition to a protective guardian genius, the *ka*, guiding their fortunes here and here-after. Offerings were centred in the tomb as the place on earth which was continually visited by the *ba* to receive the gifts. Resurrection of the body is not mentioned, though it was thought to be preserved by the sacrifices.[9] However, the *ka* born with a man lived on in the tomb and subsisted on the offerings; thus the regular provision of food for this purpose became a duty of supreme importance. Rich men employed a *ka*-priest to perform these functions daily with unfailing regularity to discourage the *ka* from leaving the tomb and going into the cemetery or the town in search of sustenance.

The deceased and his *ka*, then, were not supposed to be in the celestial realms subsisting on divine food, since they were so dependent upon the mortuary sacrifices on earth. Nevertheless, the *ba* left the body at death, and is usually represented in the form of a human-headed bird, or some other external manifesta-tion, though it retained the likeness of the person from whom it emerged.[10] Its normal abode appears to have been in heaven, but it could move about at will and return to its physical mummified body in the tomb to partake of the offerings, assuming for the time being material form. So it had a quasi-independent existence after the dissolution of the body at death, effected by the funerary ceremonies enacting the reconstitution of the dismembered body of Osiris and the reanimation of his mummy with the aid of the Eye of Horus, the most potent life-giving object.[11]

The Preservation of the Body

The Pharaoh was regarded as a human and divine being, the implications of which duality were later transmitted to the immortality of mankind in general causing endless confusion concerning the relationship between mind and body. For the purpose of the mortuary ritual the corruptible physical body, or its simulacrum, was rendered as imperishable as possible, and adequate provision was made for the incorruptible immortal element in its constitution, designated the *ka*. It was this belief that found expression in the supply of offerings for the deceased at the tombs from Predynastic times to the Ptolemaic period.

MESOPOTAMIA

Mesopotamian Obsequies

In Mesopotamia the cult of the dead never attained the prominence and importance it had in the valley of the Nile. This was partly due to climatic and geographical factors. With the exception of the royal tombs at Ur[12] no indications have survived of a developed mortuary ritual with elaborate offerings and monumental graves at all comparable with those in Anau and Egypt. The Sumerians were content to lay the body to rest, often in the flexed position, clad in its ordinary clothes and wrapped in a mat with a bowl of water and a few personal belongings in a simple earth grave or small brick vault. When these interments were made under the floor in the house of the deceased, the obsequies performed and the flooring relaid, no further cultus appears to have been practised. Family vaults were bricked up after each burial and the food vessels placed outside before the earth was filled in.[13] Few cemeteries have been discovered in Mesopotamia, and at Hassuna near Mosul in Assyria west of the Tigris; while interments have been discovered at all levels in the late prehistoric mound, there are no traces of funerary furniture or any uniformity of burial. In level III two skeletons had been flung into a grain bin and in level

IV a skull was in a rubbish pit.[14] Similarly, at Samarra on the Tigris north of Baghdad badly preserved graves with no goods or orientation were found underneath the pavements of Mos/ lem houses.

The mound of Gawra near Nineveh north/east of Mosul was used as a burial ground throughout the greater part of its inhabited history, and in addition to the very large number of simpler graves there were eighty more elaborately constructed tombs of sun/dried mud/bricks or stone with a domed roof, and sometimes a rectangular chamber attached to them for ritual purposes. Most of them were orientated on a north/west– south/east axis, but the bodies in them were placed in different directions in respective strata. In eight of them green or blue pigments had been laid on the body, and in three there were traces of grain, two of barley and one of wheat, probably the remains of food offerings. Among the mortuary gifts vessels, mace/heads, and symbols made of stone, obsidian and other materials were abundant. There were also bone and ivory combs, gold and ivory hairpins, gold, obsidian and lapis lazuli pendants, seals and beads. The simple graves were poorly fur/ nished, the equipment consisting mainly of beads, stone bowls, and other vessels, and a few gold ornaments, while in stratum XI a grave containing the body of a child revealed the remains of a sacrifice. Surrounding some of the temples and under the floors were large numbers of burials. Others were the nuclei of cemeteries, possibly because in them human sacrifices had been offered to chthonic deities.[15] This, however, was not a wide/ spread practice in Mesopotamia, in spite of the spectacular holocaust in the royal tombs at Ur.

The cemetery at Ur, which goes back to the Jemdet Nasr and Uruk periods in the fourth millennium B.C., contained stone vessels, lead cups, painted pots with sharp angular out/ lines, lug handles and spouts, and an inverted lead tumbler over the mouth of one of the pots. Later the stone vessels became more numerous and varied in form and decoration, until in the uppermost level they were replaced by cups, bowls and vases in limestone, diorite, steatite and alabaster.[16] With the body were

personal belongings, beads, ear-rings, pins and knives, together with food and drink offerings and toilet articles, to
satisfy the material needs in the after-life. Social standing was
indicated by the quantity and quality of the grave goods and
the offerings. In the subsequent graves the pottery, metal vases,
ornaments, tools and weapons were richer than in those of the
Sargonic period, though without vessels for food and drink
offerings, these being confined to the principal burials, probably those of the Sumerian rulers, like the mausolea of the Third
Dynasty of Ur. These kings appear to have been accompanied
by their retinue with a complex mortuary ritual, lasting several
days after the vaults had been sealed or bricked up, which was
held in a temporary superstructure designed for the purpose.
The kings having been deified, their cultus was perpetuated
in a permanent annexe equipped with offering-tables in the
chambers.

Mortuary Sacrifice at Ur

In the Isin and Larsa periods (*c.* 1960–1830 B.C.) when the
Elamites conquered Ibin-Sin, the last of the Ur Dynasty, the
dead were buried in a long narrow paved yard at the back of
private houses, the penthouse roof covering one end of it being
used as a mortuary chapel. In the tomb in front of the chapel
food and drink offerings were made in clay pots, but each time
the vault was reopened for a new interment the body of its pre-
decessor was thrown into the corner. At the back against the
wall stood a table for offerings with cups and small plates still
found *in situ*, and above it a fireplace on which incense was
burnt. In one corner was a mud-brick altar screened apparently
with curtains, and everywhere there were terracotta figures and
reliefs of gods and of votaries.[17] At the death of a man his
eldest son became the priest of the household, and it was his
duty to pour out oil to his father, and to make offerings to the
ancestral divine patron of the family who acted as their inter-
cessor with the great gods. The cultus, in fact, was similar to
that at the wayside shrines at street corners, with their votive
offerings of models of chariots, beds, clay rattles, mace-heads

and whetstones, necklaces, beads, incense-burners, pedestals with a hollow at the top for libations, a brick altar and clay cups. Goddess figures served by a visiting priest were main, tained by voluntary subscriptions supplementing the endow, ment of the founder. But the purpose of the mortuary ritual and its offerings was essentially for the benefit of a deceased mem, ber of a family and dedicated to its patron, whereas the wayside shrines were consecrated to lesser departmental gods invoked on specific occasions for particular needs.

The Babylonian Land of No-return

In Babylonia and Assyria the grave was regarded as a *cul-de, sac*. It was constructed beneath the earth with huge walls and strongly guarded gates secured by bolts, or a hollow mountain difficult to approach. There all the dwellers, whatever their social status, were huddled together in the dust in a semi, conscious condition. It was thought that nothing could be done by those who were alive and remained on earth, and this mood of despair found expression in the lamentation texts and Tammuz liturgies; in the mourning for Marduk at the Akitu festival[18] in Babylon; and in the Gilgamesh Epic where the failure of the founder of the city of Erech to attain the boon of immortality is recorded. Enkidu was led to the House of Dark, ness, the abode of Irkalla; they fed on dust and clay, and were clothed like birds with wings for garments but unable to escape.[19] The contents of the old Babylonian version of the Gilgamesh Epic of the first half of the second millennium B.C. go back substantially to Sumerian sources,[20] where, in the poem 'Gilgamesh, Enkidu and the Nether World' the appear, ance of the shade of Enkidu to Gilgamesh is described.[21]

The Rite de Passage *through the Waters of Death*

The Babylonian and Assyrian conception of the after-life probably represents a devolution from an earlier, more hope, ful, outlook when a conscious life of activity was sought rather than a mere existence under most uninspiring and undesirable conditions. The Akkadian legend in its final form on twelve tablets was the product of a long literary process which seems to incorporate elements from Sumerian and Semitic sources, unified around the hero of Erech. The adventures of Gil-gamesh and Utnapishtim (Enkidu) were combined with the Tammuz theme and the Deluge myth in a quest of immortal-ity in what seems to be a *rite de passage* through the waters of death to emphasize the importance of the obsequies and the prescribed mortuary ritual. The conviction that by divine decree mankind had lost immortality for ever was so firmly established that even the relentless endeavours of Gilgamesh ended in failure and frustration, as did the strivings of another semi-divine hero Adapa, the son of Ea, who inadvertently refused the food of life when it was offered to him, and so had to return to earth as a mortal doomed ultimately to virtual extinction.[22]

If such privileged and exalted figures failed, lesser mortals could not hope to succeed. Nothing short of a special divine intervention secured the release of Inanna-Ishtar, the queen of heaven, from her pitiable state in the nether regions, and throughout Babylonian and Assyrian mortuary myth and ritual the fundamental theme is that of frustration ending in despair. Because the fate of the unburied dead was too dread-ful to contemplate, the funerary rites and their offerings had to be duly performed to make escape possible from the pangs of hunger beyond the grave. Moreover, unless this was done and they were adequately supplied with food and drink, and their virtues extolled, they would take revenge on the living. This explains the presence in almost every tomb of the water jar with the bowl of clay or bronze beside it, and the care taken to guard the vaults against dust and air. In the Persian and Greek periods these offerings tended to diminish as ornaments in-creased, but proper burial remained essential. The worst thing that could be done to an enemy was to leave his body exposed on the field of battle, or to desecrate his grave and to mutilate his corpse.

The funerary ritual consisted in a priest in the guise of Ea asperging and censing the body to protect it and the grave from demonic attacks. Originally, as elsewhere, they were primarily life-giving rather than cathartic rites; but the sombre and sinister aspects of the after-life became more prominent, and so lamentation was stressed and extended from three to seven days. Dirges were sung by professional singers, reference being made to the journey of Ishtar to the nether world, and to Gilgamesh weeping for his friend Enkidu. Ashurbanipal visited the graves of his ancestors with his clothes rent and poured out libations to them; a practice that was frequently adopted at the festival of Tammuz when lamentations for the dying god were made, and a dirge in memory of the dead was sung. Thus, in Babylonia the obsequies, although in the nature of a *rite de passage*, were essentially gloomy and funereal. All that could be done for the dead was to protect them against the attacks of demons and to keep them from hunger and thirst.

PALESTINE

Funerary Rites and Beliefs among the Ancient Hebrews

Immediately before the Exile, when the prophetic movement was dominant, the cult of the dead among the Hebrews was very like that of the Babylonians. The ancient Hebrews, how-ever, believed in a conscious survival of the individual after death, and attached supreme importance to burial and the prescribed funerary rites. They too maintained that not to be buried, or for the body to be mutilated, was the greatest evil that could befall a man, but it is not clear exactly how and when the Babylonian conception of a shadowy existence in Sheol, the Hebrew Land of No-return, became the prevalent belief. Prior to the monarchy, as among the Canaanites, cave burial was widely adopted, often in the contracted position, and the body was placed on shelves or benches along the wall or in a hollow on the floor.[23] Access was by a vertical shaft or a gallery, and when chambered tombs were constructed they were modelled on the general plan of dwelling-houses and similarly equipped with food and personal belongings. Food and drink offerings, in fact, survived sporadically as late as the second century B.C., as is indicated in the Tobit legend.[24] The grave goods at

Gezer, Jericho, Ain Shemesh, Beth Shemesh and elsewhere in Palestine show that the practice was very deeply laid in the mortuary ritual.[25] Kings had elaborately chambered tombs; commoners appear to have been interred in public burial places with meagre equipment and little protection, as is demonstrated at Gezer. Relatives usually provided the dead with food and other requirements and the food was regularly renewed. The existence of pits containing the bones of animals suggests either a funeral feast or possibly a sacrificial offering on behalf of the deceased.[26]

Generally family graves were located as near the home as possible. As in Mesopotamia, Samuel was buried in his house at Rama, Joab in his house in the desert, and Asahel and Ahithophel were interred in their fathers' sepulchres,[27] but David had his own grave in Jerusalem rather than in Bethle hem, his native town. Afterwards except in the case of Heze kiah and his descendants, the kings of Judah were buried with their fathers in the capital.[28] Libations and other offerings sug gestive of a cultus were made at the traditional ancestral graves of the Patriarchs and their wives—those of Abraham and Sarah, Isaac and Rebekah, Jacob and Leah in the sanctuary at Mamre while the tomb of Rachel at Ephrath (Bethlehem) was marked by a sacred pillar said to have been erected by Jacob. On the grave of the nurse of Rebekah at Bethel there was a sacred oak at which divination was practised, and at the tomb of Joseph at Shechem rites of a similar nature were performed.[29]

Sheol and the Illustrious Dead

To mutilate, burn or leave unburied a corpse prevented the soul from attaining rest and peace either in the tomb or in the land of Shades (Sheol). Probably the original purpose of funerary offerings was to provide the deceased with food and the things he had required when alive before any attempt was made to show particular respect and veneration to illustrious ancestors. Among the Hebrews ancestor worship never seems to have been definitely established in spite of the erection of *mazzebóth*, planting trees and making libations on famous graves.[30] Incense was offered to a departed king until the end of the monarchy,[31] doubtless originally as a life-giving agent, and the repetition of public mourning rites on the anniversary of the death of a ruler may have arisen from private laments for a father in a patrilineal family. If ancestor worship existed it was not a permanent heritage in Israel, and the cult of the dead was independent of it both in origin and content.

The underlying belief was that the dead were not only active and conscious but also endowed with supernatural power and knowledge, and under particular circumstances they could and did return to their bodies and manifest themselves to the living.[32] This was the reason for the mortuary offerings, feasts, libations and mourning customs, some propitiatory, others apo-tropaic, based on respect for and fear of the supernatural powers ascribed to them capable of bringing famine and barrenness;[33] also for their being consulted about the course of present and future events. This might be done through the instrumentality of a 'familiar spirit', or *'ob*. For example, on the night before the fatal battle on Mount Gilboa, Saul sought out a medium at Endor to acquire occult knowledge of his fate from the shade of Samuel, in spite of his having 'put away those that had familiar spirits, and the wizards, out of the land' because of the incompatibility of necromantic practices and divination with the monotheistic worship of Yahweh.[34] Necromancy, however, continued to flourish in Israel, as elsewhere among the contemporary Semites,[35] until after the Exile, when it was effectively discredited and eliminated in Judaism.

It was to prevent this traffic with the dead that the Hebrew prophets and the Deuteronomic legislation denounced the ancient mortuary ritual, and in the pre-exilic literature Sheol was often represented as a state of forgetfulness, silence and ignorance in which 'the dead know not anything'.[36] From being *elohim* endowed with supernatural power and know-ledge the dead became *rephaim*, or shadowy, feeble shades devoid of memory.[37] Formerly the name *rephaim* had a con-notation of strength,[38] equivalent to that displayed by the

nephilim, or 'sons of the gods', and was applicable to the illustrious dead before it was applied to the 'weak ones' in Sheol,
after the earlier conception of the departed as *elohim* had been
abandoned.[39] Even after the prophetic denunciation shades
were regarded as having some knowledge and foresight about
events on earth, as in the case of Samuel at Endor who is
represented as leaving Saul in no doubt about his fate.

The cult of the dead and its mortuary ritual continued to
exercise its influence until the universal sovereignty of Yahweh
was extended to include the nether regions,[40] which eventually were divided into different compartments with appropriate
rewards and punishments for the righteous and the wicked.[41]
The late Jewish conception of death, however, was never
clearly defined, although belief in some kind of after-life usually
has been held, and importance attached to the disposal of the
body and to mourning ceremonies. The corpse had to be 'laid
out', washed and anointed in the prescribed manner,[42] the
eyes closed,[43] and the body clad in a shroud or grave-clothes.[44]
Herod was covered with purple and buried with his crown and
sceptre.[45] Aristobulus was adorned with ornaments[46] though
grave goods of this nature were subsequently forbidden by
Rabbi Gamaliel II. Cremation has never been adopted; only
the worst of criminals were burned after death.[47]

The carrying of the body to the grave on a bier was the pious
duty of the relatives and friends accompanied by trumpets,
professional wailing women, and the delivery of a funeral
oration in the court of the synagogue.[48] A fast has sometimes
been observed during the obsequies, ending with a feast of
'funeral baked meats' for the mourners.[49] Mourning, however,
has generally been a prolonged procedure beginning with
abstention from work for a week involving fasting, condo-
lences, and the reading of the book of Job, while a son repeats
publicly a *Kaddish* in honour of his deceased father for eleven
months. But while the performance of these customs and rites,
most of which have survived through the ages, has been
thought to have an atoning value for the sins of the departed,
they have never been incorporated in the sacrificial cultus.

GREECE

The Minoan-Mycenaean Tendance of the Dead

In Greece the conception of immortality developed along much the same lines as in Israel, the Homeric shades being the coun/ terpart of the Hebrew *rephaim*, in their respective nether regions. As among the early Hebrews, a more defined cult of the dead and mortuary ritual was practised in Mycenaean times. A wealth of funerary equipment has been recovered from the royal Helladic shaft/graves and the Mycenaean tholoi testify/ fying to the veneration bestowed upon the princes and heroes with whom they were associated. This may have been stimu/ lated by Egyptian influences, apparent in the Hagia Triada sarcophagus in Crete,[50] but in any case in the second half of the second millennium B.C. the kings at Mycenae were buried with an equipment similar to that of the gods.

Recent excavations in the Grave Circle west of the tomb of Clytemnestra near the Lion Gate have brought to light Middle Helladic shaft/graves (*c.* 1650–1500 B.C.) with the skeletons of adults and children and rich furnishings *in situ* (vases, gold ornaments, an ivory plaque, a silver jug, bronze swords and daggers), and in some of them a succession of interments at regular intervals.[51] The obsequies seem to have concluded with a funeral feast, and the goblet containing the libation was broken at the doorway of the chamber. At Drachmani and Dendrea near Medea sacrificial pits filled with the charred remains and ashes of burnt/offerings show that an elaborate cultus was practised, including sacrificial gifts made at the tombs on certain days subsequent to the obsequies at the time of death. Mycenaean shaft/graves were provided with means of conveying libations and other offerings to the deceased after burial. Moreover, as Farnell has pointed out, when as at Menidi in Attica this tendance was continued for many genera/ tions and had ceased to be a family responsibility, it developed into actual worship in a hero or ancestral cult.[52] Recesses in the wall of the dromos near the doorway of Mycenaean cham/ ber tombs sometimes contained fragments of animal bones, sherds, vases and other objects indicative of a continued cult, as are the sacrificial pits filled with the ashes of charcoal mixed with earth and vases,[53] though some of them were used as receptacles for human remains removed from the chambers.[54]

There is no real evidence to suggest, despite the abundant traces of fire in most of the tombs, that the bodies had been cremated, either on the mainland or in Crete.[55] The offerings had been burnt in or before the graves but the corpses had been inhumed without incineration. It was not until after the Mycenaean era that the widespread custom of cremation in the Bronze Age was established in Greece. The closest parallels of the Mycenaean chamber tombs are the Egyptian rock-cut graves of the Middle Kingdom[56] and the funeral offerings and customs also were predominantly Egyptian[57] in the Early Bronze Age (1500–1400 B.C.). The great tholoi, on the other hand, may have been constructed for the Mycenaean rulers more or less independently on the mainland on the plan of the Grave Circles covered with a corbel vault and a mound. Burial in rock chambers and the accompanying offerings and grave goods were adopted by the populace and a hero cult was becoming established at Mycenae. Egyptian prototypes lay behind the round chambers hewn in the rock shaped in the form of the Grave Circles; moreover, the mortuary ritual had Egyptian affinities very different from the simple Helladic belief in human survival requiring relatively meagre equipment in the slab cists or shallow pits cut in the rock.

Cremation and the Homeric Shades

The Mycenaean methods of disposal and tendance of the dead contrast with those recorded in the Homeric literature when inhumation had given place to cremation. At first the funerary furniture and offerings were burned with the corpse on the pyre while the shaft-graves, chamber tombs and tholoi were reduced to a mound surmounted with a menhir covering the urn in which the ashes of the deceased had been deposited.[58] Already in the pre-Homeric period when the floor of the chamber was filled with bodies and offerings, fresh interments were heaped up against the walls or pushed into side chambers, niches or the dromos to make room for the later burials, objects of value not infrequently being appropriated by the relatives. This suggests that when the flesh had decayed the psyche was thought to leave the grave, and was no longer in need of offer-ings, having made its abode in the nether world where they had no significance.

It is clear that Mycenaean burial rites survived in the time of Homer. The account of the funeral of Patroclos in the *Iliad*[59] recounts that after the body had been washed and anointed, the eyes and mouth closed, the corpse clothed and laid in state on a bier, and a feast held, Patroclos was burnt on the pyre to-gether with four horses, nine dogs and twelve Trojan captives slaughtered for the purpose by Achilles, in addition to sheep and oxen. This immolation may have been just a piece of ostentatious barbarism on the part of Achilles, condemned by Homer as an 'evil deed', but, as Nilsson maintains, it is much more likely to have been a carry-over from the sacrificial rites performed at the tomb of the prince of Midea near Dendra,[60] which, as we have seen, included human and animal victims consumed by fire. The description certainly suggests Mycenaean obsequies; Achilles, as the chief mourner, fasted and re-mained unwashed throughout the ceremony,[61] and wailing women accompanied the procession to the pyre of the bier which was carried by warriors with shorn hair.[62] The burning of the body of the hero may have been suggested by the earlier custom of burning the offerings in the tomb.

The psyche of Patroclos was represented as standing all night over Achilles 'marvellously like himself' rather than as an insubstantial phantom in Homeric fashion. This shows that a conscious after-life was presupposed requiring mortuary offer-ings on an extensive scale. After the establishment of crema-tion, although some of the Mycenaean funerary customs lingererd on, the predominant conception of death became that of passing to the nether regions in which, as in the Babylonian Land of No-return and the Hebrew Sheol, the feeble witless shades flocked together like bats incapable of joy or sorrow. The mother of Odysseus gazed vacantly at her son, and only

when the phantoms drank blood as a vitalizing agent did consciousness return to them.[63] An exception was made in the
case of Teiresias, the blind seer of Thebes to whom Persephone
gave reason (*nous*) as a special gift, and a few favoured heroes
like Kadmos, Harmonia, Herakles and Menelaus, who were
promised Elysium in the delectable Isles of the Blest.[64] But
these heroic figures retained their bodies and sometimes escaped
death altogether as well as a disembodied existence in Hades.
For the rest, destined to become shades, mortuary offerings were
of little avail.

This, like the corresponding interlude in Israel, was a temporary phase, generally thought to have been introduced by
the Dorian Indo-European invasion when it became partly
established.[65, 66] In sub-Mycenaean times it was only a spora-
dic practice existing alongside with inhumation.[67] But whether
or not the custom was inherited from semi-nomadic immigrants
from the northern or Eurasian grasslands, or from the Troad,
where it prevailed in and after the fourteenth century B.C., it
did not originate in a desire to liberate the soul from the body.
In practice it tended to foster the belief in the spirit as an independent entity temporarily housed in the body and wafted to
the celestial realms, as in the Tyrian version of the legend of
Herakles.[68]

It was, nevertheless, an ancient and widespread method of
disposal. It was in vogue side by side with the notion of a life
of continued activity. Tendance in the grave was capable of
freeing the vital essence alike in man and in sacrificial offerings.
The final destination of the soul has not always been in a sky-
world where cremation has been adopted, though it is true
that when the practice became the established procedure belief
in the sustenance and resurrection of the physical body dimin-
ished together with mortuary ritual centred in the conception
of personal immortality. A few ashes in an urn and possibly
some charred bones, in striking contrast to the skilfully preserved mummies in the Nile valley, and carefully embalmed or
naturally desiccated corpses elsewhere, made it difficult to inde-
finitely maintain gifts and sacrificial offerings to the deceased.

Ritual often persists after its significance has disappeared. In Greece cremation and inhumation flourished together, and in the classical obsequies of Patroclos, as we have seen, an elabo⁄rate tendance combined with the conception of the psyche as a phantom shade independent of the physical body, found ex⁄pression in the Homeric custom of cremation. Blood and wine were poured on the ashes as a libation in honour of the departed hero, and sacrifices were offered to give life and nourishment to his psyche, just as Circe made Odysseus promise to the gib⁄bering shades that he would offer a barren heifer on their behalf on his return from Ithaca.⁶⁹ The revivification of the dead by blood as a vital essence is implied, though it cannot be reconciled with the Homeric picture of the shadow⁄life of the disembodied souls. Unlike the Hebrew prophets and psalmists, the Greek writers and their bards had no desire to suppress the cult of the dead for theological and necromantic reasons, or to exclude the gods from Hades, which was under the control of Pluto and Persephone. In the Homeric Age interest was centred in this life, and poems were the songs of the brave days of old when gods and heroes freely intermingled, telling especially of the adventures of the Trojan hero and his relations with his former companions; they were not a descrip⁄tion of the land of the dead and the precise nature and destiny of the soul. Therefore, while for the purposes of entertainment and the use of noble language they were superb, they failed to provide for the deeper spiritual needs of mankind, or to inspire a mortuary cultus to give expression to these hopes and require⁄ments, however much the earlier funerary customs may have survived in the classic period.

The Mystery Cultus

Graeco⁄oriental mystery cults offered an explicit means of obtaining a happier lot beyond the grave through a process of ritual initiation. For this reason they played very much the same role as the apocalyptic movement in post⁄exilic Judaism. As Plutarch said, 'death and initiation clearly closely correspond, word for word and thing for thing. At first there are wander⁄

ings and laborious circuits, and journeyings through the dark, full of misgivings, where there is no consummation; then before the very end, come terrors of every kind, shivers and trembling, and sweat and amazement. After this, a wonderful light meets the wanderer; he is admitted into pure meadow lands, where are voices and dances, and the majesty of holy sounds and sacred visions. Here the newly initiated, all rites completed, is at large.'[70]

Eleusinian Initiation

At Eleusis this was attained by a myth and ritual going back to a Mycenaean origin with a Minoan background; in it an idealized continuation of terrestrial life was maintained, as against the shadowy existence in the Homeric subterranean realms from which the daughter of Demeter had been delivered with as beneficial effects for her initiates as for vegetation in the spring. Although the ritual of the Mysteries originally was concerned with the death and rebirth of the corn, it acquired a mortuary significance. In its post-Athenian form initiation conferred a regeneration that endured beyond the grave. The orator Isocrates in the fourth century B.C. reminded the Athenians of what they owed to Demeter,[71] just as Pindar and Sophocles bore witness to the blessed state of those in the hereafter who had beheld the saving rites which brought peace at the last.[72] Again, the Homeric Hymn declared: 'happy is he among men upon earth who has seen these mysteries; but he who is uninitiated and who has no part in them, never has like good things once he is dead, down in darkness and gloom.'[73]

As the seed buried in the earth fertilized by Demeter sprang up to new life, so for her initiates the grave was but the beginning of a happier and fuller existence in the delectable meadows of Persephone. Little is definitely known about what was done and said when the *mystae* were assembled in the Telesterion at Eleusis for the closing act of the drama of initiation. There, seated on sheepskins covering the steps along the four sides of the great hall, they underwent a profound mystic experience.

They emerged with a new hope and assurance of having attained a quality of life, destined to issue in a blissful immortality. It would seem that the hierophant, with his long hair wreathed with myrtle and tied at the forehead with a broad fillet, and clad in vestments resembling those worn by the deacon in the Eastern Orthodox Church, from time to time emerged from the Anacteron in the centre of the hall to address them and reveal to them secret sacred objects. During the course of the ritual the abduction of Kore by Pluto may have been reenacted by the hierophant and the hierophantess, while it is possible, if the Christian writer Hippolytus is to be trusted as an exponent of the symbolism drawn from Gnostic sources,[74] that an ear of corn was reaped in silence. In any case, as Cicero (who was himself an initiate) affirms, 'among the many excellent and divine gifts of Athens to the life of men, nothing is better than those Mysteries by which we are drawn from savagery to civilization. They are rightly called initiation (beginning) because we have not only received the method of living with joy, but also of dying with better hope.'[75]

The initiation rites were in the nature of a prefiguration of initiation into the next life as a *rite de passage* like the quest and adventures of Gilgamesh through the waters of death in the Akkadian legend.[76] Thus, the *mystae* were required to undergo a period of segregation like the mourners in the mortuary ritual. This involved fasting, instruction and purification with water drawn from the sacred well Kallichoron, concluding with a torchlight procession to the seashore in imitation of the sorrowful search of Demeter for her abducted daughter, in order to be brought into union with the passion of the Mothergoddess. Both initiation and the cult of the dead were virtually a sacrificial process with a sacramental significance securing rebirth to a higher status through a death and resurrection ritual. In this process the preliminary rites were mainly cathartic, but once purification had been accomplished the transition was effected by the revelation of the sacred sights in the Telesterion *ex opere operato*. By this *dromenon*, the salvation of the initiate was attained. Therefore, as the cynic Diogenes remarked, 'the robber Pataikon, because he was initiated, would fare better after death than Epaminondas', an uninitiated just man; or, in the words of Plato, 'he who arrives in Hades uninitiated and without having participated in the mysteries lies in filth'. This applied to the mortuary ritual in general as well as to the Mys-tery initiations, the two being part of the same process. The Mysteries flourished in the Graeco-Roman world because there was 'a brooding consciousness of failure, of the futility of human effort, of the load of human sin, the ineluctability of penalty, of gods estranged, and the need of reconciliation and purification';[77] the cult of the dead, particularly in its sacri-ficial aspects, gave emotional relief and satisfaction in the recur-rent crises aroused by the mystery of death. The grave was the dark and dangerous portal through which all must pass, and the mortuary cultus had as its purpose the liberation of the deceased from terrestrial existence, launching him safely and securely on his new career in the after-life.

ROME

Funeral Rites in Ancient Rome

To these ends the methods of disposal of the body and their associated rites might vary but the aim was the same. In Italy, as in Greece, cremation and inhumation were both practised. Sometimes this was as a result of racial and cultural inheri-tances, as in the case of the Terramara people in the Po valley and the Villanovans on the east side of the Apennines near Bologna, both of whom in the Late Bronze Age and the Early Iron Age normally cremated whereas the Etruscans and the Picenes inhumed.[78] But no hard and fast rule obtained, as frequently urn fields and inhumation cemeteries occurred in the same localities belonging to the same period and race, the opposed practices apparently having no marked influence on the conception of the soul and the location of the after-life. The rites of cremation and inhumation took much the same form, granted that cremation was practised chiefly by the educated and well-to-do section of the community while the poor and slaves were buried in earth graves or thrown into *puticuli* (communal ossuaries or holes) *en masse*,[79] with neither obsequies nor any clearly defined beliefs and hopes about a future life. Warde Fowler, in fact, has maintained that before the age of Augustus there were two attitudes to immortality, the one learned and philosophical, derived from Pythagoreanism, dis-seminated by the Neo-Stoicism of Posidonius (*c.* 135–50 B.C.), the other popular and poetic based on Greek ideas of a gloomy underworld with dreaded penalties for wrong-doing depicted on the Etruscan tombs.[80] The former is alleged to have rested on a dualism of a body incarcerating an immortal soul which was capable of making its escape at death to an existence of eternal bliss, sometimes of becoming deified. This was as-sisted by the cremation of the body. To free the ignorant masses from the alleged terrors of the popular hell Lucretius (94–55 B.C.) sought to demonstrate the destruction of the soul at death, it being a material entity as an integral part of the body.[81]

Manes *and the* Mundus

A distinction did, no doubt, exist between the educated and the uneducated sections of society respecting death and its aftermath. But it can hardly have been clear cut. From the available archaeological evidence it would seem that the ancient Romans regarded the tomb in which their body or ashes were deposited as the abode of the deceased whose funeral rites had been duly performed. There, in their *domus aeterna*, they continued to live as they had lived before death, and therefore required the things they had needed on earth. The grave goods buried with the corpse or burnt on the pyre, fol-lowed by the periodical offerings of food and drink at anni-versaries, included eggs, beans, honey, milk and wine. But as the spirits of the dead (*manes*) were regarded as ethereal beings like the Greek shades, bloodless *anima* or *spiritus* (i.e. breath), they required dark blood to be revived and strengthened, afforded by sacrifices at the tomb particularly of dark victims. With the aid of these mortuary rites they were able to join the undifferentiated mass of *manes*, or 'kindly ones', as opposed to the *lemures* and *larvae* who as wandering, restless ghosts were liable to haunt the living and their former abodes. But the *manes*, though generally beneficent, on special occasions could roam about, and on August 24, October 5 and November 8 when the circular pit on the Palatine Hill in Rome, known as the *mundus*, was opened to allow them to return to their homes, it was with much relief apparently that at the end of the pre/ carious visitation they were safely installed in their own realm, and the *mundus* was closed securely by 'the stone of death' (*lapis manalis*).[82]

On three days in May (9th, 11th, 13th) an ancient rite known as the Lemuria was celebrated in order to drive the *lemures* from the house. The head of the household cast black beans over his shoulder at midnight nine times after an ablu/ tion, saying 'with these beans I redeem myself and my family'. Then again washing his hands he clanged brass vessels to com/ plete the expulsion ritual with the words, 'ghosts of my fathers, depart'.[83] In a later festival, the Parentalia, on February 13–21, culminating on the 21st with the Feralia, or Feast of All Souls, offerings were made at the graves of the dead, and the funeral rites were performed at the tomb while the Vestal Virgins made a sacrifice at the tomb of Tarpeia, a chthonian goddess.[84] The next day a feast, the Caristia, was held as a renewal of the funeral feast, and a family gathering in which offerings were made collectively to the *Lares*, or spirits of the farm,[85] one of which, the *Lar familiaris*, became the guardian of the house.[86]

In Rome the funeral of prominent people among the upper classes was primarily a social event; its ceremonies were repro/ duced in the Parentalia. After the wailing (*conclamatio*) the corpse was dressed, arrayed in the toga, and carried in proces/ sion to the family tomb, or to the place of cremation outside the city, accompanied by the mourners and relatives. The pollu/ tion of death had to be swept out of the house with a special broom by the heir, and after a dirge had been sung a death mask might be taken of the face of the deceased and kept in a niche near the atrium of the house. Outside the entrance of the house a cypress, or pine,branch was hung as a sign of mourn, ing until the obsequies had been completed. Ornaments, weapons and other possessions and offerings were placed on an elaborate pyre, which was ignited by one of the relatives, or, in the case of an official, by an important civic dignitary. A funeral feast then was held in the family tomb,chapel, or at the home. On the anniversary of the death the tomb was visited by the members of the family and offerings were made of water, wine, oil, milk, honey and flowers, together with words of farewell.[87]

Cemeteries and Catacombs

Such elaborate public mortuary rites were confined to im, portant people in the late Republic and early Empire, and the State,festival, but in a very much simplified form. Ordinary funerals of the upper and middle classes followed much the same sequence, without the processions, death masks and dis, plays of wealth and ostentatious magnificence. At the other end of the social scale labourers and slaves were buried in pit,graves outside the Servian Wall on the Esquiline plain in a great necropolis in cheap coffins with little or no ritual.[88] In the Augustine age cremation became the normal mode of dis, posal of the dead, until, under Christian influences, it died out, and resort was made to burial in the extensive catacombs, as the subterranean cemeteries have been called, in the north,east and south of the capital, notably in the neighbourhood of the Appian Way under the basilica of St Sebastian ad catac, combas. In the fourth and fifth centuries A.D. these were used by Christians and Jews for interment, though some of them resemble Etruscan necropoli. They consist of labyrinthine gal, leries covering more than 300 miles, often arranged in tiers one above the other, the bodies being placed in niches (*loculi*) hewn in the rock, holding two or three bodies. Small chambers off the galleries (*cubiculi*) became family tombs for the more im, portant members of the community, and the walls were often decorated with Christian symbols and stucco paintings. Burial places were sacrosanct in Roman legislation, and the bodies of many of the martyrs were buried in the catacombs. In the fourth century the Eucharist was celebrated there on the anniversaries of their deaths.

CHRISTIANITY

Burial in the Early Christian Church

The importance attached to decent burial by the Early Church was in accord with the deeply engrained hope of resurrection after the body had rested in the grave and the soul had under/ gone a period of preparation and purification requisite for entry into the final state of heavenly bliss and the attainment of the Beatific Vision. The physical body was regarded as 'the temple of the Holy Ghost' capable of being made 'a living sacrifice, holy, acceptable to God', and destined to be raised in glory if among the redeemed at the Judgment.[89] It was treated with due care and respect. The eyes were closed, the corpse was washed, swathed and wrapped in a linen sheet with myrrh and aloes by the female mourners, and laid on a couch in an upper room of the house for not less then eight hours before inter/ ment.[90] It was then carried to the grave outside the town by young men accompanied by relatives and friends. In Jewish practice the body was buried with lamentation, wailing and other noisy displays of grief.[91] It was laid to rest in a rock/cut tomb, a cave or simple grave, death being looked upon as a sleep from which the dead in Christ would be awakened by the blast of the last trump at the Parousia.[92] Christians believed that death was the entrance to a higher and enduring life of eternal bliss in which spiritual bodies were no longer depen/ dent upon material sustenance, and so they anticipated it with joy. For them, funerals were occasions of happiness rather than of condolence, and it was not until about the eighth century that more doleful elements were introduced in the Office of the Dead and in the mourning customs.

Commemorations of the Martyrs and the Faithful Departed

When the Church spread into the Graeco/Roman world in the sub/apostolic period, the current mortuary practices of

Jews and pagans were generally adopted, though by the middle of the third century the Church had acquired its own ceme-teries and erected chapels at the tombs of the martyrs. The honour and veneration bestowed on martyrs are shown by the erection of *memoria*, or tombstones, with an inscription record-ing the manner of their deaths and sufferings and their witness to the Faith. *Diptychs*, or tablets containing the names and location of the martyrs; the *Commendatio*, or funeral oration; the *Passiones*, or necrology giving details of their cases, developed into *Martyrologies* in the form of official registers of the mar-tyrs, each local church having its own Calendar with the names of its martyrs and place of martyrdom under the date of the anniversary observed as a festival. The Commemorations were read by the deacon from the ambo at the Eucharist cele-brated in honour of each saint, who often was depicted on the tombstone with outstretched arms as an *orante* praying for those who sought his intercession.[93]

As the nobles in Ancient Egypt endeavoured to be buried near the Pharaoh, so the early Christians regarded it as a privilege to be laid to rest in the catacombs or cemeteries hal-lowed by the mortal remains of the martyrs. There they assembled not only to venerate these illustrious confessors but also to commend the souls of all the faithful departed to the mercy of God. If they died unbaptized their surviving friends or relatives might undergo the sacramental initiation on their behalf.[94]

Although prayers beseeching refreshment and peace for the souls of the faithful abound in the inscriptions of the cata-combs and in the early liturgies, intercession was never made for the martyrs because they were thought to have attained the Beatific Vision by virtue of their voluntary death in defence of the Faith. In due course their *panegyrics* were collected together as *Martyrologies*, or Acts of the Martyrs, and were soon ex-tended to contain the birthdays of all the saints preserved as permanent records of the whole Church. The calendars, or *monologion*, as they were called in Eastern Christendom, on the other hand, were texts of the feasts kept in particular districts

with their dates. The earliest of these chronological lists of fes/
tivals occurs in a compilation in A.D. 354 representing the re/
publication of an edition of 336 designed and illustrated by a
Roman calligrapher, Furius Dionysius Philocalus, which
brought the Roman pagan calendar and its observances into
relation with the list of the deaths of the bishops of Rome from
St Peter to Liberius in 366.[95] Thus, the mortuary ritual played
an important part in the development in Christendom of the
Calendar and the Liturgical Year.

Development of the Mortuary Ritual

This chronological document and similar local lists formed a
conspectus of the shrines, which from the second century A.D.
occurred in the catacombs to which the faithful resorted for the
celebration of the Eucharist at the funeral of the martyrs and on
the anniversaries of their deaths. At the end of the penal times
the relics were transferred to the churches erected in honour and
under the patronage of the saint commemorated. After the
final peace of the Church had been granted by Constantine in
313, the cemeteries both below and above ground were em/
bellished with basilicas preserving some of the features of the
catacombs and their cultus, including the epigraphs engraved
in honour of the martyrs in the Philocalian Calendar. As the
catacombs ceased to be places of burial at the beginning of the
fifth century they became sanctuaries of the martyrs to which
pilgrims flocked from all parts of the Roman world, until in
the ninth century the bodies of the martyrs were removed from
them, after the Lombard invasion of the Campagna, and
translated to the churches in the city.

Meanwhile the mortuary ritual had undergone considerable
development. At the death of Constantine in 337 elaborate
ceremonies were held at his interment at Constantinople when
'the body was placed in the principal chamber of the palace
and surrounded by candles, and encircled by a numerous
retinue of attendants who watched around it incessantly night
and day.' It was then taken in procession to the church dedi/
cated to the Twelve Apostles, and followed by vast multitudes,

the coffin being surrounded by spearmen and infantry. On arrival at the church the obsequies were performed by the hierarchy in the presence of the huge congregation of the faith-ful.[96] These rites included the customary *eulogium*, and since the second century in North Africa the Holy Sacrifice was offered for the benefit of the departed.[97] Similar ceremonies were held at the entombment of both the Latin and Greek Fathers of the Church (e.g. St Basil of Caesarea, St Gregory of Nazianzus, St Ambrose). Thus, the body of St Basil was carried high above the crowds on the occasion of his funeral because they were eager to seize the hem of his garment, or to touch his shadow or the bier which bore his holy remains to the tomb of his fathers, amid loud lamentation and psalmody. Yet behind these signs of mourning there was joy. It was hoped that in the eternal world he was 'offering sacrifices and praying for the people'.[98]

Funerary feasts, or *agapae*, were common in the third century, death being described as 'the putting away of all pains and the escape from all temptations'. 'We celebrate the day of death', says Origen, 'because those who seem to die do not really die. For that reason we both make memorials of the saints and also devoutly commemorate our parents and friends who die in faith, both rejoicing over their state of refreshment and also entreating for ourselves a pious consummation in faith.'[99] Similarly, St Cyprian (d. 258) affirmed that mourning was inappropriate for those who had been released from the world since 'while appearing to lose they have really gained ground, as travellers and navigators are wont to do'.[100] Therefore, Christian obsequies consisted of a triumphal procession with torches and incense and cries of 'Alleluia', and the waving of branches of palm, the singing of praises and antiphons, and with the refrain 'Requiem aeternam dona eis Domine, et lux perpetua luceat eis' instead of the 'Gloria Patri', with the songs of Hezekiah, Zechariah, and lessons from the book of Job and Nocturns ending with the responses, 'Libera me, Domine, de viis inferni, qui portas aereas confregisti et visi-taste infernum et dedisti eis lumen', etc.

The Office of the Dead and the Requiem Mass

Under the influence of St Augustine (354-430), there was a more sombre element in the mortuary rites, the emphasis being on judgment, and the remission of sins contracted in this mor- tal life. This became more pronounced after the eighth century, and by the Middle Ages it had become predominant, find- ing expression in the Office of the Dead beginning with *Placebo*, the traditional title of the Vespers of the Dead, derived from the antiphon (Ps. cxvi, 9), 'Placebo Domino in regione vivorum', with which it opened. This was followed on the morning of the funeral, or commemoration, by the *Dirge*, as the Matins and Lauds were called, and the Mass of Requiem and absolution of the dead. Black then replaced white as the litur- gical colour, and the procession was in the nature of a sombre cortège. The offering of the Holy Sacrifice for the dead was repeated on the third, seventh and thirtieth days after death, with 'a year's mind', reviving the ancient custom of commemo- rating the dead in accordance with the progress of the soul in the various stages of the after-life,[101] and the practice of second- ary burial. In spite of the opposition of the Fathers of the Church to these Jewish and pagan survivals, popular belief and practice ultimately prevailed, and a Christian interpretation was placed upon the custom, connecting the third day with the Resurrection of Christ and the fortieth day with his Ascension, while the seventh and thirtieth days have the sanc- tion of the Old Testament and so were substituted, except in the East, for the ninth and fortieth days in the earlier sequence.

The Feast of All Souls

At first Masses for the dead were indistinguishable from other Masses, but with the introduction of an appropriate Introit, Sequence, Offertory, Communion, and Post-Communion commemorations, they acquired their distinctive characteris- tics, taking their name from the opening antiphon—'Requiem, aeternam dona eis Domine.' The selection of the magnificent poem, the *Dies Irae* (the Day of Judgment), for the Sequence, the work of a Franciscan in the thirteenth century, placed the emphasis on purgation. Originally it was intended for private devotional use, and its first appearance in the Mass for the Dead is that of Venice in 1493, before it became a permanent feature in the Roman rite on the day of decease or burial, on the anniversary of the death, and on the Feast of All Souls on November 2. This annual commemoration of the faithful departed was first observed in Benedictine Religious Houses under the influence of Odilo, the Abbot of Cluny (*c.* 962–1048), who in 988 introduced it as a local solemnity. With the approval of Pope Sylvester II (999–1003) and his successors, it was soon accepted throughout the Western Church, and by the thirteenth century it was established everywhere. Eventu-ally two Masses were allowed to be said on this day, a privi-lege which since 1915 has been extended to the saying of three Masses by all priests of the Latin rite, religious and secular alike. It was also the rule for the Office of the Dead to be said daily in Religious Houses, largely under the influence of Cluny.

Many popular customs have survived concerning the Chris-tian commemoration of the dead. For example, on the Feast of All Saints (All Hallows) on November 1, lamps are lit on graves, torches and candles are burned in the houses, and the bells tolled until midnight. In Brittany a procession is made to the charnel-house after Vespers of the Dead on the Eve of All Souls, and a dirge is chanted in Breton. A large log is kept alight all night on the hearth, around which the family talk of their departed relatives, and 'singers of death' parade the streets urging the people in the houses to pray for the souls in pur-gatory. Food is provided for the holy souls in the kitchen, who are thought to return and warm themselves by the fire.[102] Like the processions with lighted candles, the offering of soul-cakes to the dead on the Eve of All Souls' Day has been widely prac-tised in Northern and Central Europe.[103] Behind all form of mortuary ritual lies the belief that the fate of the deceased is assured very largely by the sacrificial offerings—the *oratio pro defundis*—made by the living on behalf of the dead. As a *rite de passage* its purpose has been to secure a happy destiny for the soul, freed from the trammels of earthly existence yet to some extent influenced and determined by conduct and conditions in life and rites performed by the living. In Christianity eternal life is regarded as a divine gift bestowed by God on man as a new creation[104] brought into direct relation with the redemptive offering of Christ and its anamnesis in time and space.

CHAPTER VIII

The Eucharistic Sacrifice

THE emergence of more spiritual, ethical and refined conceptions of the institution of sacrifice in the higher monotheistic
religions inevitably produced a reaction against the cruder and
crueller forms of blood-offerings. This was most apparent in
Zoroastrianism; in the prophetic movement in Israel and its
rabbinical aftermath; and in Christianity where the bloody
self-offering of Calvary became the bloodless eucharistic sacrifice. In Islam animal sacrifice is confined to the end of the pilgrimage to Mecca, on the tenth day of Mina, and to occasional
offerings in times of epidemic, sickness, or at the naming of a
child at the Aqipa ceremony.

Zarathushtra and Animal Sacrifice

Thus, Zarathushtra (Zoroaster) denounced the cruelty involved in the sacrifice of the ox with 'fury, violence and shouts
of joy'[1] in a drunken orgy described as the work of 'the followers of the Lie,'[2] inherited from the ancient Indo-Iranian
cultus of pre-Avestan times. The Prophet was in deadly opposition to the old religion of the marauding nomads who preyed
on the flocks and herds of his settled pastoral herdsmen, as were
the pre-exilic Hebrew prophets two centuries earlier in their
diatribes against the sacrificial worship of the local sanctuaries
at Bethel and Gilgal.[3] He did not condemn the current mode
of slaughtering the bulls dedicated to the altar, since it continued to be practised in a more humane manner.[4] The victim, instead of being slain with a knife, was first struck with a
log to stun it that it might be spared the fear and pain of having
its throat cut.[5]

Zarathushtra declared furthermore that offerings of cattle
should not be made indiscriminately, impulsively and in-
ordinately, nor should the flesh of the immolated animal be

eaten by the laity, or combined with the consumption of the sacred Haoma plant, the drink of immortality, as had formerly been the custom by the hated worshippers of the *daevas*, the ancient Iranian gods.[6] Nevertheless, in the later Avesta after the death of Zarathushtra, it was forbidden to burn the victim. It had to be taken limb by limb and seethed, placed on a carpet of clover, either, according to Herodotus, by the sacrificer, or, as Strabo affirmed, by the Magi. A hymn of praise and thanks/giving was then sung to Ahura Mazda as a theogony, and the flesh was consumed by the offerer and the Magus, and assigned to different gods.[7]

The Achaemenian kings in Persia appear to have offered sacrifices on a grand scale, estimated by Greek writers at a thou/sand cattle, horses and asses daily, though this may perhaps have been an exaggeration.[8] The victims seem to have been dedicated to the Greek counterparts of the Iranian deities and their sacred flesh eaten in commemorative banquets on state occasions.[9] The descriptions of the rites and the altar suggest that in and after the fifth century B.C. Greek cult practices had been adopted, but nevertheless, relics of an earlier Persian method of sacrificing animals can be detected, going back to the Indo/Iranian period when the immolation was made on the top of mountains to a sky/god, who later may have been associated with Ahura Mazda under Mazdaean influence, and brought into conjunction with the fire cult ritual that predominated in Zoroastrianism.

Haoma

The principal offering, however, was the Haoma, or Yasna ceremony, which constituted the central act of Zoroastrian worship, and consisted in the pounding of the sacred plant regarded by the Indo/Iranians as the elixir of life, the beverage of immortality from whom death flees (*durosha*). The word Haoma (Sanskrit *Soma*) comes from the root *hu* (Sanskrit *Su*), 'to pound' or 'squeeze'. In the Avesta it is used to denote a prophet (*Duraosha*) and a plant (*Zaire*) discovered by him;[10] and also a heroic figure (Haoma Khvarenangha and Haoma

Frashmi),[11] the designations being more or less interchange-
able. As a god he was the son of Ahura Mazda[12] who became
the first priest of the cult and the first to proclaim 'the Good
religion' to the world.[13] It was he who found the plant on the
Elburg mountain in the Caucasus and pounded it in a mortar
and so extracted its life-giving juice, thereby making available
for mankind the boon of immortality by a sacrificial act of
sacramental self-giving. In the Yasna ceremony which he
instituted in honour of Ahura Mazda and all the lesser divine
beings (*asuras*), he immolated himself incarnate in the Haoma
plant, and from his perpetually broken body streamed forth
the very life of his divine essence, giving wisdom, courage,
health, greatness, inspiration and exhilaration, 'making both
soul and body immortal in righteousness'.[14]

The Yasna Ceremony

In its pre-Avestan form in India the Soma cult extolled in the
ninth book of the Rig-Veda was associated with the *daevas* and
especially with Indra who derived from it his strength and
exalted position in the Vedic pantheon, becoming violently
drunk in the process.[15] Therefore, in Indo-Iranian times it
would seem to have had an orgiastic character which underwent very considerable modification in Iran under Zoroastrian
influences without losing its original sacrificial and sacramental
qualities as the source of divine power alike for gods and men.
Indeed, acquiring a personality of its own it was deified, and
the sacrificial immolation of the Haoma was made the core of
the liturgical ceremony. This was followed by its sacramental
consumption, first by the priests and then by the congregation
as a solemn act of communion rather than as formerly in a
drunken orgy. In the established liturgical rite the twigs of the
sacred plant have to be consecrated and the juice prepared after
it has been extracted and strained in order to be offered sacrificially. This is accompanied by an oblation of bread (*Draona*)
dedicated to the god Sraosha. Three sections of chapter xxiv
of the *Yasht*, the liturgical text, are recited, and a hymn of
praise of the sacred juice is sung, which is then consumed by

the priests. There follows a profession of faith in Ahura Mazda as the Wise Lord who created the ox and man and abjured the *daevas*. This having been done during the morning or at mid-night, the second preparation and straining of the Haoma juice begins with the recitation of three ancient and most sacred prayers ascribed to Zarathushtra and a repetition of the pre-vious consecration and solemn consumption while chapters xxv to xxvii of the *Yasna* are recited by the laity as well as by the priests.[16]

In the Vedic Soma rite all the priests, sixteen in number, must partake of the sacred drink; the two principal Brah-mins imbibe very large quantities. In the Iranian Yasna ceremony and the modern sacrament, only a very little of it is drunk by one of the two Parsee priests. Again, none of it is thrown into the fire before drinking it as offerings to the Vedic gods, as in India. It is sufficient to show it to the fire before drinking it. As no Zoroastrian sacrificial rites could be per-formed in the evening, the third Brahmanic libation was omitted, but until the Yasna ceremony came to an end in the late afternoon a strict fast was made from dawn until sunset by the officiating priests,[17] during which sleep was forbidden and the utterance of profane words.

This remarkable anticipation of the Mass in Christianity constituted the principal act of sacrificial worship and sacra-mental communion in the Avestan liturgy from post-Gathic times to the present day. In it, the sacred Haoma was regarded as a god incarnate in a life-giving earthly embodiment taking the form of a plant, in which he was slain, as the victim, to confer immortality on his votaries by bestowing upon them his own divine life. He was also the eternal priest in that he per-petually gave himself in a sacrificial oblation as the son of Ahura Mazda, the Wise Lord, in a cult that was instituted by the Sun-god Vivahvant in the golden age at the beginning of time.[18] The cult is the antecedent of the offering of the bull Hadhayans by the Saviour Saoshyant. At the final consum-mation a white Haoma would be produced from its fat by which all just men would be made perfect and immortal.[19]

The Mithraic Sacramental Meal

Haoma as the intermediary *par excellence* between god and man, found a place and sacerdotal function in the worship of Mithras in the capacity of 'the healing, fair, lordly, immaculate priest of Ahura Mazda', with 'golden eyes, prompt to sacrifice with a mighty voice, loud in song, reaching to the heavenly lights, encompassing the whole earth, and penetrating all the seven climes'.[20] From the Yasna ceremony in which Mithras participated, the Mithraic sacramental meal was derived, wine taking the place of the Haoma, and Mithras himself raised to a divine status co-equal with Ahura Mazda as a participant in the Haoma sacrificial cult. Offerings of 'small cattle and large, and of flying birds' were made to him, accompanying the Haoma libations and liturgical prayers, and preceded by puri-ficatory ablutions and flagellations. Not until the degree known as 'Lion' was attained could communion be given to the ini-tiates of Mithras in the oblation of bread, wine and water.

In a bas-relief published by Cumont[21] two people are repre-sented stretched upon a couch covered with pillows before whom a tripod is placed bearing four tiny loaves, each marked with a cross. Around them are grouped initiates of the differ-ent orders, and one of them, the Persian, presents to the two a drinking-horn; while a second vessel is held in the hands of one of the communicants. These love-feasts, or *agape*, evidently were the ritual commemoration of the banquet which Mithras celebrated with the Sun before he ascended to heaven with the rest of the immortals. In this mystical banquet the sacred wine gave not only vigour of body and material prosperity, but also wisdom of mind, the power to combat the malignant spirits, and immortality to the neophytes.

This close resemblance between the Mithraic banquet, the Zoroastrian Haoma ceremony, and the Christian Eucharist might suggest plagiarism, as in fact it did to the early Fathers of the Church. Mithraism was to some extent influenced by Christian beliefs and practices, and this is particularly apparent in the analogies in the ritual meals in the two hostile move-ments. But their origins were very different. The antecedents of Mithraism were Vedic and Iranian, and as a Mystery cult providing a link between a sacramental religion and morality, it emerged from a combination of Mazdaean dualism, Magian and oriental astrology and Zurvanism. Passing into the Roman world at the turn of the era (*c.* 67 B.C.) from Asia Minor, where it had been diffused through Persia in the Hellenistic period, it spread westward along the trade-routes, especially in the Danubian provinces and in the military stations *en route*. By the time it reached Europe, however, Mithras had acquired the nature and status of a Mystery divinity with ethical attributes and a sacramental cultus with Babylonian astrological accretions.

As the god of light in perpetual conflict with the powers of darkness he became *sol invictus*, the invincible sun, bestowing the *hvareno*, or nimbus, dispensing its heavenly light on kings and emperors and his worshippers, and the mediator between the celestial powers and the human race.[22] The chief act of worship was his capture and the slaying of the bull, the first creature created by Ormuzd (Ahura Mazda). This sacrifice was the central event in the cult-legend represented in the *tauroctonus*, the bas-relief at Heddenheim and elsewhere depict-ing the virile youthful hero with conical Persian cap and flying garment, in the act of killing the bull, but displaying an expression of pathos as though reluctant to perform the offer-ing. A dog is shown springing towards the wound in its side, while a scorpion attacks the genitals of the victim and a serpent drinks its blood. A raven sits nearby, and from the tail of the bull germinating ears of corn emerge, and the blood gives life to the vine. The scene is interpreted by Cumont as the seed of the bull producing the different species of animals. The soul of the bull, under the protection of the dog, the faithful com-panion of Mithras, ascended into the celestial spheres. By his sacrificial act Mithras liberated the blood of the bull from which all life sprang, notably the fruit of the vine for the sacra-mental banquet, and he became the guide and protector of the souls of men in quest of immortality. He secured for his initiates ascent through seven spheres to the supreme heaven, the plenitude of the mystic beatific vision. There the celestial banquet with the Sun and his heavenly allies was celebrated of which the sacred meal of bread, water and wine in the initia' tion rites, consecrated by priests called 'fathers', no doubt was the earthly counterpart. In one scene, in fact, Mithras stands beside the slain bull holding a drinking-horn in his left hand, receiving a bunch of grapes from Ahura Mazda.

Little is known about the Mithraic liturgies from the monu' ments and texts. In the Hermetic literature a few extracts occur related to the beginning and end of the world, with Mithras as the inaugurator of the new order destined to last for ever. The cult-legend culminating in the slaying of the bull is all that remains enshrined in the iconography. It depicts the birth of Mithras from a rock witnessed by shepherds, his investiture by the Sun-god whom he had vanquished, the capture of the primeval bull leading on to the *tauroctonus*, the mystic banquet, and the figures of the god and goddesses associated with the cult.[23]

It is possible that the Mithraic sacrament owed something to Christian influences but the cult was more ancient than the Zoroastrian liturgy in which it was the central feature. There' fore, it had an independent history, and did not escape some measure of censure by Zarathushtra in respect of the bull sacri' fice, before it was reincorporated in the Mazdaean cultus and so passed into Mithraism. There it acquired an ethical charac' ter. Mithras inspired the devotion of a military fraternity who found in him and his worship strength to fight successfully on the field of battle and to prevail against their own passions and temptations. By virtue of their initiation they secured immor' tality in union with him at the final consummation when evil would be destroyed and good become eternally triumphant.

THE EUCHARIST

Christianity

It is true that Christianity and Mithraism had much in com' mon, but Mithraism was rooted in oriental polytheistic mytho' logy, Mithras himself being devoid of reality as a historical character. Christianity, on the other hand, arose as a sect within Judaism, the theology of which was based on the ethical monotheism of the Hebrew prophets, coupled with the Messianic hopes and eschatology of Hellenistic Judaism. This was related to a highly spiritualized reinterpretation of the sacred drama of death and resurrection of the Near Eastern religions and those of the Graeco-Roman world, reassembled around the historic personality of Christ. At the centre lay its doctrine of the Incarnation, issuing in the all-sufficient atoning sacrifice of its Founder at a particular moment in time and space, commemorated in a bloodless sacrifice instituted and commanded by him to be continued in perpetuity on earth and in the eternal world.

The Eucharist in the New Testament

From the first, the Eucharist was a weekly celebration of the Last Supper. The course of events is recorded in minute detail in the four independent though closely related accounts in the Gospel narratives, and while they contain puzzling discrepancies there is no doubt that they are dealing with actual historical events of relatively recent occurrence. The earliest record of the ordinance is that mentioned by St Paul in his first letter to the Corinthians, probably written in A.D. 55, and therefore within about twenty years of the crucifixion.[24] By that time certain abuses had arisen due mainly, it seems, to the combination of the Eucharist with a common meal which, as in the Iranian Haoma ceremony, became an occasion of drunkenness and gluttony. There were also heresies and divisions among the Corinthian Christians. All these irregularities led the Apostle to declare that by such conduct they were eating and drinking damnation to themselves, 'not discerning the Lord's body'.[25]

To rectify this unedifying state of affairs he recalled the original institution of the eucharistic 'Lord's Supper' on the night of the betrayal when Jesus 'took bread, and having given thanks, broke it and said: This is My body which is for you; this do in remembrance of Me. In like manner also the cup after supper, saying: This cup is the new covenant in My blood; this do, as oft as ye drink it, in remembrance of Me. For as often as ye eat this bread and drink this cup, ye do show forth (καταγγέλλετε) the Lord's death till He come.' Then followed the admonition: 'Wherefore whosoever eats the bread and drinks the cup of the Lord unworthily shall be guilty of the body and blood of the Lord.'[26]

From this it would seem that the Corinthians had departed from the purpose and significance of the assembling together in one another's houses on the first day of the week for 'the break﹨ing of the bread' as a solemn sacramental fellowship, repeating the actions Christ performed and the words he uttered in the Upper Room on Maundy Thursday evening.[27] St Paul sought to restore it by separating it from the social meal and recalling its most sacred nature and intention.

The Gospel narratives of the original meal present difficul﹨ties both as regards their respective presentation of the events and in relation to the Pauline tradition. In St Mark xiv, 22–5, compiled between A.D. 65 and 70, Jesus is said to have taken bread, blessed and broken it, and given it to the apostles gathered together with him to partake of the Paschal meal. He declared the bread to be his body, and taking the cup and having given thanks, he gave it to them, commanding them to drink it as his blood of the new testament (i.e. covenant), 'which is shed for many'. Henceforth he would not drink of the fruit of the vine until the day he would drink it anew in the kingdom of God.

The Lucan and Matthaean narratives are an expanded ver﹨sion of this Marcan logion, derived in the first instance perhaps from a very primitive Christian liturgy of Palestinian origin. But the account in St Luke xxii, 15–20, written probably about ten years later, seems to be independent of the Marcan text as it mentions a preliminary cup of blessing before the con﹨secration of the bread, and in such important manuscripts as the Graeco﹨Latin Codex Bezae (D), the Old Latin Manu﹨scripts, the Curetonian Syriac version, and certain cursive manuscripts,[28] the words 'do this in remembrance of Me' are omitted. It may be that at a very early date the Pauline tradition

(1 Cor. xi, 34 ff.) was incorporated in the shorter Lucan text which breaks off in the middle of verse 19 after the delivery of the bread. The Matthaean version, on the other hand, is merely an elaboration of the earlier Marcan narrative.

Thus, the Synoptic tradition is in substantial agreement about the actions performed by Christ at the Supper though the precise order of the blessing of the bread and the cup, and more particularly the date and character of the meal, raise difficulties. According to the Marcan, Matthaean and Pauline accounts, the eucharistic action consisted of Jesus taking bread, giving thanks over it, breaking it, and distributing it to the disciples, saying certain words. This was followed by his taking a cup of wine and water, giving thanks over it, handing it to his apostles, and saying the words recorded. In the Lucan variant two cups are mentioned. This makes the rite a 'ten- action' scheme, or a different 'seven-action' with a single cup before the bread.[29] But the same words are said to have been spoken in the delivery of the bread, 'This is My Body', and with a slight variation in that of the cup, but explaining that his Blood of the covenant is shed for them, thereby showing that his approaching death was to be the sacrifice by which the kingdom of God was to be inaugurated. To this the Matthaean narrative adds, 'unto remission of sins', and all three record the eschatological saying about his not drinking of the fruit of the vine until the kingdom is established.

The Two Chronologies

The Synoptists are also in agreement that the gathering was held on 'the first day of unleavened bread when they sacrificed the Passover',[30] i.e. on the 15th of Nisan. The Fourth Gospel, on the other hand, without making any attempt to describe the proceedings, maintains that the gathering occurred 'before the feast of the Passover',[31] and alleges that to prevent their re- maining at the scene of execution over the feast, 'for the day of the Sabbath was a high day', the bodies were to be taken down from the crosses before sunset on the Preparation (i.e. on Nisan 14),[32] about the time that the lambs would be killed.

If this is correct then the Lord's Supper could not have been the actual meal, but rather a preliminary *Chaburah*, or quasi-religious gathering of friends, in preparation for the coming festival.

The two chronologies are mutually exclusive and expert opinion is still divided, in spite of attempts to reconcile them. Chwolson has suggested that since the 15th of Nisan fell on a Sabbath that year Christ and his disciples, unlike the Sadducees, followed the custom of the Pharisees in celebrating the Passover on the 14th.[33] But in fact all that was done on such an occasion was to put forward the killing of the lambs from four to six hours rather than to alter the date of the observance. It is true, as Jeremias contends, that the meal as recorded to some extent had a Paschal character,[34] but it is extremely difficult to reconcile the subsequent course of events—the arrest, trials and crucifixion—with the Paschal requirements. Even though a dangerous and rebellious teacher could be executed on a festival,[35] the priests and people would be too much occupied at that moment with their Passover duties and observances to conduct a public trial involving popular demonstrations on a large scale and the bearing of arms on a holy day. Furthermore, although the Synoptic tradition places the Supper on the night of the 14th of Nisan, it contains the warning of the Sanhedrin against taking action on the feast day lest there should be a riot,[36] while in St Luke xxii, 15 f., reference is made to Jesus' unfulfilled desire to share in the Passover with his disciples.[37] It is also worth remarking that no mention whatsoever is made of a lamb in either the Marcan or the Matthaean accounts of the meal.

The Chaburah *Meal*

The Johannine date (Nisan 15) remains the most probable; this means that the Last Supper occurred on the eve of the festival. In that case the gathering would appear to have been in the nature of a *Chaburah*, and it has been widely held that it took the form of a *Kiddush* ceremony as a preparation for the Passover, consisting of two blessings: (i) the benediction over

the wine, or *Kiddush*-cup, drunk at sunset,[38] and (ii) the sanctification of the day. After the cup had been passed round by
the head of the household, or president of the group, two loaves
reminiscent of the double portion of manna in the wilderness
were taken, one of which was cut in pieces and distributed to
the company, and the other reserved to the next day. The blessings were a 'grace' or 'thanksgiving for the creation of the fruit
of the wine, and the bringing forth of bread from the earth'.[39]
But the *Kiddush* immediately precedes the actual celebration of
a festival or sabbath, and to put it forward a whole day would
be a very unusual procedure. In this case it could be argued that
Christ, knowing that the blow might fall at any moment, and
having an intense desire to eat this Passover with his disciples
before he was arrested,[40] gathered them together on the Thursday evening for a special *Chaburah* which took the form of a
Kiddush and included a dish of bitter herbs and fruit juices, the
distribution of unleavened bread and the prescribed cups of
wine with the solemn washing of hands, and, it would
seem, the *mandatum*, or feet ablution, the ceremony concluding
with the singing of the last part of the Hallel (Psalms cxiii–
cxviii).

It would seem that he was in the habit of assembling them
frequently as a *Chaburah* for a common meal to discuss the
Messianic mission in its various aspects, and to give charity
from the common purse. On the Johannine interpretation the
Lord's Supper was one of these gatherings brought into very
close relation with the impending Paschal celebration. The
stories of the miraculous feeding of a great multitude appear to
have been connected with ritual meals of this kind, and it is
significant that in the Fourth Gospel the eucharistic discourse
in chapter vi occurs in this context, while earlier St Paul connected the Eucharist with the 'spiritual food' or manna, which
sustained Israel in the desert, where the feeding miracles are
said to have occurred. Moreover, according to the fourth
evangelist the feeding of the five thousand took place about the
time of the Passover.[41] If the events were regarded as anticipatory of the coming Messianic banquet,[42] a sacramental

interpretation is possible, and the whole setting of the miracles indicates a mystical significance. Thus, in this Gospel this is the only occasion before the resurrection when Jesus is called ὁ κυρίος (Lord), and the loaves are described as ἄρτον ('one loaf') in the singular,[43] as in 1 Cor. x, 16 f., and xi, 27, symbolizing the unity of the Christian community. Because the disciples 'understood not concerning the loaves' they were rebuked for the hardness of their hearts,[44] while judgment was passed on the crowd for following Jesus not because they saw σημεῖν but because they 'ate of the loaves and were filled'.[45] Contrasting the barley loaves with 'the true bread' (i.e. Jesus) they were exhorted to 'labour not for the meat that perisheth', for 'the flesh profiteth nothing; the ῥήματα of the Logos, made flesh, are spirit and life.'

It would seem, then, that the origin of the Eucharist must be sought not in the Last Supper, be it *Kiddush* or Passover, but in what lies behind the *Chaburoth*, or group gatherings of Jesus and his disciples, and ultimately reached its climax in the cenaculum on the night of the betrayal when the new covenant sacrifice was inaugurated and the heavenly banquet in the kingdom was anticipated on the eve of the Passion. St Paul and the Synoptists agree that it was then that the rite was institated, but it represented the final *Chaburah* when the ceremony reached its consummation in the eucharistic 'breaking of the bread' as the central act of Christian worship at which the risen and ascended Lord vouchsafed his presence and the Church offered the *anamnesis* of his death and resurrection until his return at the *Parousia*. But whatever may have been the precise nature of the Maundy Thursday gathering, certain departures from the normal order of the Jewish observance, Paschal or *Kiddush*, occurred. Either the meal did not begin with bread and wine, and Jesus blessed these elements when they came; or, if the meal began with the blessing of the bread and wine, the duplication of the blessings suggests an innovation implying that the previous blessings, *Kiddush* or otherwise, were invalid, and they were repeated because afterwards they were to have a new significance.

The New Covenant and its Sacrifice

If it were a *Kiddush* ceremony, the Eucharist was made a new *Kiddush* by identifying the cup with the blood of the covenant. This introduced a new division of time because Jewish chronology was divided into two parts: (i) from the Creation to the Exodus, and (ii) from the Exodus onwards. As Lietzmann says, in offering himself like the Paschal lamb at the last of the solemn banquets with his disciples Christ in effect said, 'I am the victim, whose blood is shed for you, i.e. for the faithful, that a new covenant may be sealed with God; and whose body is slain for you.'[46] Thus, he interpreted his own death as the event which would establish the New Covenant, as his words over the bread and the cup made explicit. Thereby the Passover was abrogated and in its place the Eucharist was instituted as the continuation of the former *Chaburah* meals with Jesus as the true Paschal Lamb. Whether or not the Lord's Supper was in fact the Paschal meal, it soon became interpreted in these terms as the Synoptic narratives and the Pauline teaching show. Christ, having been sacrificed as the true Passover brought about by the shedding of his blood a redemption greater than the deliverance from Egypt. Meanwhile the Eucharist was the perpetual memorial (*anamnesis*) of the sacrifice, replacing the Passover in the New Israel till the kingdom would be established in all its fullness at the end of time, and God would become allinall.[47] Then the heavenly offering would have accomplished its purpose and the eternal priesthood of Christ would be complete.[48]

Along these lines a eucharistic theology was gradually formulated in the Apostolic Church centred in the 'breaking of the bread' at the weekly *Chaburah*. The original disciples who foregathered week by week recalled with increasing vividness the unique occasion when they assembled with their Master for the last time on the eve of the passion and the impending Paschal celebration. This gave their weekly *Chaburah*, or 'breaking of the bread', a sacrificial and sacramental significance in Pauline terms irrespective of anything that had been said on the original occasion about the repetition of the rite. It must have seemed to them that as they assembled on the first day of the week they were fulfilling the prophecy of Malachi offering a pure sacrifice in every place.[49] The gathering was inseparable from the *Chaburoth* they had so often had with Jesus in their midst as their host, which according to their own tradition had been continued and renewed after the Easter miracle (e.g. at the Emmaus evening meal).[50]

The Anamnesis *and the* Agape

When the movement spread in the Graeco-Roman world, the *Chaburah* fellowship meal underwent changes calculated to bring the sacrificial and sacramental elements into greater prominence. Since only the eleven apostles had been present in the Upper Room on Maundy Thursday evening, exactly what took place there and its specific occasion were in the nature of oral tradition rather than personal remembrance or recorded history. For Gentile converts were more concerned with the death and resurrection of Christ conceived in Mystery concepts than with the Jewish background of the events. From the Judaeo-Christian conception of the rite it was but a step to the identification of the broken bread and the poured-out cup with the flesh and blood of the victim offered on Calvary. In this *anamnesis*, as the former Covenant had been sealed with blood, so the eucharistic wine could be none other than the blood of Christ in which he sealed the New Covenant.[51] It was at this point that the respective approaches of Jewish and Gentile Christians met.

The Last Supper was undoubtedly a ceremonial meal, and if the intention of Jesus at the time of the institution, like the date and nature of the gathering, is not clear, it was certainly continued by the disciples and the Apostolic Church. At first it was primarily a ritual meal of a quasi-religious character, but as this combination of Eucharist and *Agape*, or 'love-feast', gave rise to abuses and heresies, after the Pauline reform at Corinth the *Agape* became a separate social gathering, or 'charity supper', as it was called by St Augustine, while the

Eucharist developed as a sacrificial-sacramental rite. Both had their origin in the common fellowship meals of the feeding-story type, in which perhaps the breaking of the bread came first in the Pauline ordinance, then the meal proper, and finally the blessing of the cup; the Eucharist being 'after supper'. At Troas, as at Corinth, the common meal (δεῖπνον) was in the evening, and it was followed by a very lengthy discourse by St Paul, who subsequently celebrated the Eucharist.[52]

In the sub-Apostolic *Didache*, or 'Teaching of the Twelve Apostles' (*c.* A.D. 100–140), the two were still associated, but the Eucharist (here first called by this name, ευχαριστίας), is the centre of worship and 'thanksgiving' is offered to God over the cup 'for the holy vine of David, Thy servant', and over the bread (in the form of a loaf symbolizing unity) 'for the life and knowledge made known through Jesus Thy servant'. Then comes a prayer for the gathering of the Church from the ends of the earth into the kingdom of God, and 'after ye are filled' at the end of the common meal, a third prayer sums up the earlier thanksgivings. Finally, that 'the sacrifice may be pure' confession of sins must be made.[53]

Although in this very obscure document the practice of some isolated Christian community, probably in Syria, appears to have been described before the Eucharist and *Agape* had been separated, the 'thanksgiving' is given the title of a 'sacrifice' (θυσία). It is restricted to the baptized members of the community, and celebrated on the 'Lord's Day'. Much the same situation is suggested in the Ignatian Letters (*c.* A.D. 108) where emphasis is given to the bishop, or one appointed by him, as the celebrant.[54] But by the middle of the second century the separation was complete, and the fellowship meal had by then tended to drop out altogether. Justin Martyr and Irenaeus derive the eucharistic oblation from the Last Supper, and equate the bread and wine with the body and blood of Christ. For Justin Martyr the oblation was a commemoration of the passion of Christ; for Irenaeus an offering of the first-fruits as an act of thanksgiving for creation and redemption.[55] The words 'do this in memory of Me' now acquired a sacrificial interpretation—ποιεῖν (do) and ἀνάμνησις (memorial)—and were related to the morning and evening sacrifice in Juda/ism.[56] This connexion probably was further suggested by the weekly Jewish *Kiddush* commemoration of the Sabbath with its memorial of the Creation and the Exodus in its Paschal set/ting. The blessing of the wine is reminiscent of the vegetation ritual and the sacrifice of the first/fruits with their life/giving and renewing sacramental attributes consumed to assimilate the life/principle. It only remained to identify Christ with the Paschal Lamb of the New Covenant for the eating of the flesh and the presentation of the blood of the divine Victim to become integral in the sacrificial eucharistic action.

The Church, as the Body of Christ sharing in the eternal royal priesthood of its Founder, recognized that its first duty as the worshipping community was to offer up spiritual sacri/fices acceptable to God by Jesus Christ.[57] As E. K. Cham/bers has said, 'From the fourth century, the central and most solemn rite of that worship was the Mass, an essential dramatic commemoration of one of the most critical moments in the life of the Founder. It is His very acts and words that day by day throughout the year the officiating priest resumes in the face of the people. And when the conception of the Mass developed until, instead of a mere symbolical commemoration, it was looked upon as an actual repetition of the initial sacrifice, the dramatic character was only intensified.'[58]

THE DEVELOPMENT OF THE LITURGY

In North Africa Cyprian (c. A.D. 258) referred to the Euchar/ist as 'the sacrifice of the Lord's body and blood', the priest offering to God the Father in the Church a true and full sacri/fice 'repeating what Christ the High Priest after the order of Melchizedec did on the Cross'.[59] A century later this was con/firmed in the *Euchologion* of Sarapion where the liturgical obla/tion of the bread was described as 'making the likeness of the death' in order to effect a sacrificial reconciliation between God and those who offered the bread and the cup in 'the likeness of the Blood for the remission of sins'. Similarly, St Cyril of

Jerusalem (A.D. 350) called 'the bloodless service' the 'holy and awful sacrifice of propitiation' in which, by the invocation of the Holy Spirit (*Epiklesis*), the bread and wine became the body and blood of Christ as the water was changed into wine at Cana of Galilee.[60] Although it was said to be sacrificed for sins and 'the loving God propitiated' thereby, the self-offering on the Cross is not repeated, as St Chrysostom (407) was care-ful to maintain, the eucharistic memorial being one and the same sacrifice pleaded in the heavenly and spiritual realms of the eternal world.[61]

Oriental Liturgies

In the East the liturgical action took the form of an elaborate sacred drama reproducing the salient features of the Christian sacrifice as a *dromenon* in response to the command 'do this in remembrance of Me'. The emphasis was laid increasingly on the transformation (μεταστοιχειοῦν) of the elements by the consecration, through the operation of the Holy Spirit. This was stressed by Gregory of Nyssa, in the parallel he drew between the Eucharist and the Incarnation; it found liturgical expression in the Invocation as the focal point of the rite. In his account of the *missa fidelium* in the fourth century at Jerusalem St Cyril refers to the washing of the hands of the bishop and priests surrounding the altar as a preliminary oblation, followed by the kiss of peace and the Preface opening with the *Sursum corda*. After the *Sanctus* no mention is made in the eucharistic prayer of the Creation, Incarnation and the Passion, or of the institution and *anamnesis*. 'Then having sanctified ourselves with these spiritual hymns [i.e. the *Sanctus*] we beseech the loving God to send forth the Holy Spirit upon the gifts lying before us, that He may make (ποιεῖν) the bread the body of Christ, and the wine the blood of Christ. For whatsoever the Holy Spirit touches is sanctified and changed.'[62]

This strange omission is explained by Brightman and other liturgists on the assumption that Cyril was only expounding the salient points of the rite, concentrating on the form of In-vocation as the essential feature.[63] Gregory Dix, on the other hand, thinks that at Jerusalem these elements were absent, the Invocation following immediately upon the *Sanctus*.[64] But as he had already dealt with the words of institution in his earlier 'catecheses' to the catechumens,[65] Cyril may not have thought it necessary to include them in his description of the Palestinian liturgy, and it is clear that he regarded the consecration as effecting a real change in the elements, through the operation of the Holy Spirit. After the consummation of the unbloody spiritual sacrifice at the Invocation, intercessions followed for the peace of the world, the sick and afflicted, the priests, magistrates, the army and the emperor, for the saints, apostles, and martyrs, the catechumens and penitents, the seasons and the fruits of the earth, concluding with a doxology. The *Pater Noster* having been recited, together with a Diaconal liturgy, the Benedictus, and probably the Fraction, Communion was given by the bishop assisted by the deacon, to the priests, deacons, lectors, virgins, widows, children, and then to the whole congregation, introduced with the formula 'holy things for holy persons', and accompanied by the singing of Psalm xxxiii. Much the same order appears to have been adopted in Syria, judging from the references to the Eucharist in the *Didascalion Apostolorum*, while St Chrysostom shows that at Antioch at the end of the fourth century the liturgy began with Biblical lections and a sermon, prefaced by a salutation, after which the *missa fidelium* commenced with a long litany said by the deacon. The Anaphora included the Preface, the *Sursum corda*, the *Sanctus*, the words of institution, and the Invocation of the Holy Spirit, completing the consecration; the 'common sacrifice' concluding with the commemoration of the martyrs, priests, confessors, and the faithful departed, the *Pater Noster*, and the Fraction before the Communion.[66]

Another source of information for the Syrian liturgy occurs in the eighth book of the *Apostolic Constitutions*, compiled probably in the latter part of the fourth century, and conforming closely to that of St Chrysostom, being, in fact, an elaborate version of the Antiochene liturgy (viii, 3–27), but with Arian traits. The compiler was not inclined to follow formulae, and treated the Creed and the *Gloria in Excelsis* freely. In the prayers his own hand is discernible, the literary style resembling that of the spurious Ignatian Epistles, with perhaps some Jewish liturgical affinities.[67]

Taking the evidence collectively, the oriental liturgies sug' gest a pattern of sacrificial eucharistic worship in which the bishop occupied the central position with the presbyters on either side of him, and the deacons in attendance. The lector read the lessons from the Old Testament and the Acts of the Apostles or Epistles, and the Gospels from a 'high place', and the priests the homilies and finally the sermon by the bishop. After the dismissal of all but the faithful the liturgy proceeded, beginning with petitions by the deacon for the Church, the several estates of men, the sick and sinners; and followed by the kiss of peace, and ablutions and admonitions. The Ana' phora opened with the salutation and the *Sursum corda* preced' ing the eucharistic prayer and its commemorations, and leading on to the *Sanctus*. The Bishop then continued the 'thanks' giving' for redemption wrought by the Incarnation and Passion concluding with the words of institution. The *anamnesis* of the death, resurrection and ascension, looking forward to the *Parousia*, carried the liturgical action on to the Invocation and Epiklesis, ending with the Doxology, the Intercessions, the Benedictus and Communion and the final dismissal.

The Conversion Theory
In the West the work of the Holy Spirit in the consecration of the sacred elements, so prominent in the East, was obscured by the emphasis given to the words of institution, 'This is My Body' and 'This is My Blood', effecting the conversion. St Ambrose, bishop of Milan in the last half of the fourth cen' tury (374–397), maintained that the elements were 'trans' figured' by the recital of the actual words of Christ uttered originally by him at the Last Supper,[68] and repeated by the priest at each consecration. His illustrious convert St Augustine, bishop of Hippo from 395 to 430, regarded the Eucharist as the sacrifice of the body and blood of Christ, but he made a

distinction between the supernatural gift and the means by which it is bestowed;[69] between the sign and the thing signified. In the Western Church, however, the 'conversion theory' became predominant, and with it a propitiatory emphasis on the inter, pretation of the eucharistic sacrifice, the Mass being regarded as a renewal of the self-offering of Christ on the Cross. But the symbolical view was never wholly excluded, and in some form or other it reappeared, as, for example, in Paschasius Radbert's book *On the Body and Blood of the Lord*, first published in 931. There, in conjunction with the conversion theory, it was affirmed that the change in the elements at the consecration into the flesh born of Mary was not apparent to the senses, the sacerdotal gift being of a spiritual character.

The Doctrine of Transubstantiation

In the early Middle Ages the controversy was pursued, notably by Ratramnus, also a monk of Corbie, who attacked the cor, poreal doctrine of Paschasius, denying any miraculous material transformation of the bread and wine and affirming an invisible 'real presence' along the lines of Tertullian, Jerome, Ambrose and Augustine in the West. Popular thought in the eleventh century had moved in the direction of the conversion doctrine, and Ratramnus and his ally Berengar of Tours were condemned and made to recant. Nevertheless, the Berengarian controversy raised crucial issues which eventu, ally led to the framing of the definition of Transubstantiation at the Fourth Lateran Council in 1215 as *de fide*. This opened the way for a scholastic examination of the philosophical basis of the doctrine, and, indeed, of the sacramental principle in general, in Aristotelian terms. It remained for St Thomas Aquinas (1227-74), maintaining the scholastic distinction between *substantia* and *accidentia*, to affirm that the whole Christ, body and blood, was present in each of the species of the consecrated Elements by concomitance, but he denied that the presence was localized, being only *per modium substantiae* (i.e. 'after the manner of a substance'). Therefore, 'He is not moved in the sacrament *per se* but only *per accidens*, in relation to the move, ment of the outward and visible signs in which He vouchsafes His presence.' Similarly, at the Fraction his heavenly body is not broken.[70]

This metaphysical interpretation sufficed so long as the Aris/totelian principles on which it was based were maintained unchallenged, and it left more or less unimpaired the popular eucharistic devotion that was so firmly established and prac/tised in the thirteenth century. Moreover, the emphasis on the eucharistic sacrifice in the Roman liturgy kept the way open for theological and philosophical speculations about the sacra/mental presence in the elements without conflicting with the daily offering of the Mass at the altar. All that mattered was that the Body and Blood of Christ should be offered to God the Father in the prescribed manner, irrespective of precisely how and when the transformation of the species occurred.

The Medieval Mass

In this new trend of medieval eucharistic thought Albertus Magnus (1200–80) led the way. Concentrating upon the text of the *Ordo* he deprecated the excessive allegorical exposi/tion of the ceremonial, and stressed the co/offering of the con/gregation with Christ in the sacrifice of the Mass.[71] The oblation of the Cross once offered and being perfect and in/finite needed no renewal, but the faithful must offer themselves to the Father in union with the divine Victim as a 'holy priesthood offering spiritual sacrifices acceptable to God through Jesus Christ'.[72] Allegory and the expiatory theory held the field, and the doctrine of transubstantiation increas/ingly became the subject of metaphysical speculation, with a rising tide of miraculous Hosts in popular devotional credu/lity. However, Albertus had directed attention to the threefold structure of the liturgy—the *introitus* up to the collects, the *instructio* to the end of the Creed, leading to the *oblatio* in which the consecration was the culminating point, with the Preface as the conclusion of the Offertory.

The stress on the atoning death of Christ gave the entire eucharistic action a redemptive significance. It represented the enactment of the Passion, interpreted allegorically, from the Preparation to the Fraction and its sequel, carried sometimes to arbitrary lengths of mystical imagination obscuring the real *anamnesis* and the self-oblation of the worshippers, who were content to be spectators of the sacred drama enacted in the seclusion of the sanctuary. Hence the significance attached to the Elevation of the Elements at the consecration at the end of the twelfth century, given literary expression in the Grail legend in medieval romance. With the introduction of processions of the Blessed Sacrament the Host was exposed for veneration in a monstrance, and after the institution of the Feast of Corpus Christi in 1264 on the Thursday after Trinity Sunday, Ex-position became an observance independent of the Mass as well as sometimes in conjunction with it.

The ancient practice of commemorating the martyrs and the faithful departed in the liturgy, particularly on the anniversaries of their deaths,[73] was eventually extended to the day of burial in the Gelasian and Roman Sacramentaries,[74] and acquired a propitiatory character. With the institution of All Souls' Day on November 2 and its acceptance everywhere in the thirteenth century as a general commemoration of the faithful departed, coupled with the development of the doctrine of purgatory in its popular medieval form, Requiem Masses tended to be endowed and said in increasing numbers. The establishment of chantries in the fourteenth and fifteenth centuries served by priests whose function it was to multiply solitary Masses for the souls of the founders and their friends and relatives made the 'sacrifices of the Masses' for the dead virtually an actuarial system in popular practice, although not endorsed by the best theologians. Many of the chantries were centres of education, but they were liable to abuses alike in faith and practice, and unquestionably they were one of the chief contributory causes of the Reformation reaction against the Mass as a sacrificial liturgical institution.

A good deal of confusion arose concerning the efficacy of the sacrifice of the Cross for the forgiveness of original sin and that of the eucharistic offering availing for actual sins. While it may have some expiatory character, it has been generally agreed by theologians that it cannot be regarded as accomplish, ing the forgiveness of mortal sins unless it is accompanied by contrition and repentance.[75] Each Mass is not a sacrifice inde, pendent of or additional to the sacrifice of the Cross; the self, oblation of Christ is alone all-sufficient. Nevertheless, in Catholic Christendom throughout the world, in West and East alike, it has always been steadfastly maintained that the Eucharist is a true and proper sacrifice. The formularies of the Church of England are in fact capable of this interpretation, if less explicit than those of the Council of Trent. The con, tinental Reformers either repudiated the doctrine altogether as relentlessly as that of transubstantiation, or explained it in an unreal sense as a subjective sacramental memorial feast. The representation and pleading of the sacrifice of the Cross before God the Father was maintained, and reaffirmed by the Anglican episcopate in 1896, while the medieval 'sacrifices of the Masses' were condemned in untempered language in Articles 28 and 31.

The Anglican Liturgies

In England the reforming party was at first mainly Lutheran in tendency, but Cranmer soon veered towards the Zwinglian eucharistic position under the influence of Ridley. After the death of Henry VIII and the accession of Edward VI in 1547, and with the influx of Continental reformers, this became rapidly apparent. Following ancient custom the chalice was restored to the laity, and an 'Order of Communion' in the ver, nacular drawn up by Bucer, a Lutheran from Strasbourg with Zwinglian sympathies, was instituted by royal proclamation in May 1548. This consisted of a general confession and absolu, tion, some sentences from the New Testament known as 'The Comfortable Words', a 'prayer of humble access', the formula of administration of Communion in both kinds and the blessing, interpolated in the Latin (Sarum) Mass. The way was thus prepared for the introduction of the First Prayer Book of Edward VI in 1549, in which 'The Lord's Supper, commonly called the Mass' replaced the Sarum rite without materially altering the structure of the medieval liturgy.

The Introits, Collects, Epistles and Gospels were for the most part taken from the Sarum Missal, and the ninefold *Kyrie eleison* was retained with the *Gloria in Excelsis* in its original place before the collects. Then came the Nicene Creed and the Sermon or Homily, concluding with an Exhortation before the Offertory, which consisted of sentences from Holy Scripture concerned with almsgiving rather than with the oblation of the bread and wine to be consecrated. From this point, which originally was the beginning of the Mass of the Faithful after the dismissal of the catechumens, the rite pro-ceeded along the customary lines with the *Sursum corda*, the *Sanctus*, and five proper Prefaces for the principal festivals, leading up to the Canon, which was unchanged except for the introduction of a long intercession for 'the whole state of Christ's Church', and including the words of institution and the *Te igitur* and *Momento* in the vernacular, followed by the Lord's Prayer in the usual manner. The wording, however, was slightly altered to place a Zwinglian emphasis on the remembrance of the Passion and the innumerable benefits obtained from the merits and death of Christ, together with the remission of sins through faith in his blood. Moreover, the offering was said to be of 'ourselves, our souls and bodies' as 'a reasonable, holy and lively sacrifice' so that 'whosoever shall be partakers of this Holy Communion may worthily receive the most precious Body and Blood of Thy Son Jesus Christ; and be fulfilled with Thy grace and heavenly benediction', not-withstanding our unworthiness 'through our manifold sins to offer unto Thee any sacrifice.' After the 'Our Father', the Order of Communion drawn up in the previous year was inserted, while the *Agnus Dei* was sung by the choir. Then came the administration, followed by some post-communion sentences from Holy Writ, a prayer of thanksgiving and the blessing.

This skilful attempt to place a vernacular version in the traditional setting of the Latin Mass, with the priest still wear-ing the eucharistic vestments and performing the rite in the customary manner with a few important verbal modifications in the Canon in a Zwinglian direction, was in fact only a tem-porary expedient. Nowhere was it well received. The country clergy, the peasants and the laity at large resented the new Prayer Book, dismissing it as 'naught but a Christmas game', and rising in rebellion in the West Country and elsewhere against the innovations; e.g. the giving of Communion in two species at every Mass, the abolition of the Holy Week cere-monies, the Stations of the Cross, the Candlemas Procession and the Blessing and Distribution of Ashes on Ash Wednes-day, together with the transformation of the Divine Office into a greatly shortened form of Morning and Evening Prayer.

The Reforming Party was no less dissatisfied, complaining that 'the ceremonies and form of administering the Holy Eucharist scarcely differed from those observed in the celebra-tion of the Catholic Mass'. The 1549 rite had been devised, it was declared, 'that the people might not think anything of the latter had been removed or cut away, but should believe that what had formerly been read in Latin was now being read in English.' The opposition of the Protestant Reformers may have been to some extent justified, as the Henrican bishops and theologians recognize that the rite was capable of a Catholic interpretation, though they voted against the 1549 Book. Calvin denounced it as 'puerile and frivolous', and Bucer inveighed against the retention of the vestments, prayers for the dead, and the invocation of the Holy Spirit in the Prayer of Consecration.

Encouraged by the support of the government and the worth-less Warwick, who had succeeded the more moderate Protector Somerset, an iconoclastic movement was initiated largely under Calvinistic guidance, in which the medieval service books were destroyed, churches were stripped of their ornaments, statues and stained-glass windows were broken and treasuries ran-sacked. A new 'Order for the administration of the Lord's Supper or Holy Communion' was drawn up in which the altar was transformed into a table standing in the body of the church in Protestant fashion. The 1549 Prayer Book was revised with the result that the Canon of the Mass was dislocated by the Communion following immediately after the Prayer of Consecration, thereby removing the sacrificial memorial of the eucharistic offering. The *Agnus Dei* and the co-mixture of the Host in the chalice were eliminated, and the Fraction accompanied the words of institution at the Consecra-tion instead of being a separate action in the traditional manner and place before the co-mixture. The *Gloria in Excelsis* was moved to the conclusion of the service before the blessing, while the Ten Commandments were substituted for the ninefold *Kyrie*. New words of administration were inserted and subse-quently an unauthorized rubric was added printed in heavy black type (commonly called the 'Black Rubric') denying the doctrine of the Real Presence, probably largely at the instiga-tion of John Knox. To complete the reaction the vestments were abolished. But before this Second Prayer Book received the sanction of Convocation, Edward VI died (1552), and with the accession of Mary Tudor the Latin Mass was restored before any of the drastic changes had been enforced.

When it was revived by Elizabeth I in 1559, after the death of Mary, it was subjected to some modifications. It is probable that the Queen's intention was to restore the First Prayer Book of 1549, or to make it the basis of the new revision. In the hope of placating the returned Protestant exiles, however, the Second Book was taken as the model with the omission of the Black Rubric, and the words of administration from the 1549 rite were prefixed to those of 1552. The most significant concession to Catholic practice, however, was the inclusion in the new Act of Uniformity of a rubric declaring that 'such ornaments of the Church and of the ministers thereof, shall be retained, and be in use, as was in this Church of England by the authority of parliament in the second year of the reign of King Edward the sixth' (i.e. 1549). This 'Ornaments Rubric' was inserted in the 1559 reissue at the beginning of the Order of Morning and Evening Prayer, and if the injunction had been carried out, as it has been in the majority of Anglican churches and cathe-drals during the last century, in outward appearance and modes of worship the services in England would have been comparatively little changed by the Reformation upheaval in the sixteenth century, particularly if the 1549 liturgy had been re-introduced.

The 'Elizabethan Settlement', however, was a compromise that satisfied nobody, and was never really put into operation. At that time it had never dawned upon anyone that there could be more than one religion in a country, and an attempt was made to combine in one comprehensive liturgical experiment, ancient and medieval, Catholic, Lutheran and Zwinglian elements, expressed in the magnificent language of the period and adorned with the traditional ceremonial. Formularies were made as vague as possible in the hope of embracing all opposed groups and factions. But after what had happened since 1553 it was courting disaster to levy a fine of a shilling for non-attendance on Sundays at a composite liturgical rite which had been compiled and authorized without even consultation with Convocation, and after nine lay and nine spiritual peers voted against the innovations, the bill being carried in the Lords by only three votes.

To the Marian episcopate and its influential clerical and lay adherents the compromise appeared to abolish 'the doctrine and form of religion in which our fathers were born, brought up and lived', and to put in their place 'something lately brought in, allowed nowhere, nor put in practice, but in this realm only; but a small time and against the minds of all catholic men.' To the more advanced and thorough-going Reformers even the 1552 Prayer Book was no less abhorrent, having been devised according to John Knox, the leader of the Genevan Calvinist school in Scotland, 'rather for the up-holding of massing priests than for any good instruction which the simple people can receive thereof.' For this section of the community nothing short of the elimination of the entire Catholic structure of the Mass and its underlying theology sufficed. Thus, Peter Martyr (1500–62), the Edwardian Regius Professor at Oxford, in his polemic repudiated the Mass as 'a feigned and damnable imitation of the Lord's Sup-per', not to be tolerated in any shape or form. With such diametrically opposed groups, and a very uncertain middle section of opinion, the Elizabethan Settlement was in a pre, carious position.

The one thing that the Queen and her ecclesiastical advisers appear to have been agreed upon, and were quite resolute about, was the maintenance and continuity of the Apostolic ministry and all that this involved in the perpetuation of the eucharistic faith and practice. In the Preface to the First Edwardian Ordinal, which was based on the pre-Reformation Pontificals and retained in the subsequent revisions, it was affirmed that 'it is evident unto all men diligently reading Holy Scripture and ancient authors that from the Apostles' time there have been these three orders of ministers in Christ's Church: Bishops, Priests and Deacons. Therefore, to the intent that these Orders may be continued, and reverently used and esteemed in the Church of England, it is requisite that no man (not being this present Bishop, Priest or Deacon) shall execute any of them, except he be called, tried, examined and admitted, according to the form hereafter following, or hath had formerly Episcopal Consecration or Ordination.' Extreme care was taken to secure the valid election of Matthew Parker and the proper quorum of bishops who had held sees in the reign of Edward VI secured to raise him to the episcopate at Lambeth Palace on December 17, 1559. These included two (Barlow of Bath and Wells and Hodgkin of Bedford) who had been consecrated themselves by the pre-Reformation Ordinal.[76]

It was this insistence on the continuity of the Apostolic suc, cession and Episcopal ordination that constituted the main cause of Puritan opposition to the Elizabethan Settlement. As against the Calvinist, Lutheran and Zwinglian doctrine of the ministry and the Eucharist, which had been adopted by the English Puritans, the crucial term 'priest' was retained in the Ordinal and throughout the Prayer Book. The celebration of the Eucharist was confined exclusively to the priesthood, as was the giving of absolution to the penitent, while Ordination and Confirmation continued to be specifically episcopal ministries. The insertion of the Ornaments Rubric, if not strictly enforced, at least made provision for the retention of the sacerdotal vest/ ments and the traditional Catholic arrangement and adorn/ ment of the sanctuary and chancel. This was done in the face of violent opposition from the reforming Puritan party, thereby making possible a return to the *status quo* of the Ornaments Rubric which has now become more or less the Anglican norm in the appointment of its churches and in the vestures of its sacred ministry.

After the Cromwellian interlude, during which the Book of Common Prayer was replaced by the Puritan 'Directory for Public Worship' (in 1645) for sixteen years, only a few minor changes were made in 1662 when the Elizabethan rite was restored. The rubrics were made more precise and explicit, and as a concession to the Puritans the Black Rubric was re/ inserted, but with the important distinction between a cor/ poreal and a real presence of Christ in the Blessed Sacrament. All holders of ecclesiastical offices were required to be episco/ pally ordained within two years, and a greater emphasis was placed on the distinction between the orders of bishop and priest. No attempt, however, was made to restore the *anamnesis* and the traditional arrangement of the Canon with the Frac/ tion and co/mixture after the Prayer of Consecration, as in the 1549 liturgy, or to transfer the *Gloria in Excelsis* to its original position after the *Kyries*.

In spite of a good many anomalies, however, the seventeenth century was the heyday of Anglicanism, and it was in the reign of Elizabeth I that its distinctive faith and practice were formulated, and in the Jacobean and Caroline period estab/ lished. Before and after the Commonwealth the Anglican, or Caroline, Divines evolved a theology and liturgical movement designed to express the peculiar position of the English Church as a *via media* between the opposing disciplines of Rome and Geneva, centred in the Book of Common Prayer and Episco/ pacy. They accepted the Elizabethan Settlement and its liturgy without apology or reservations, not only as a political and ecclesiastical necessity but also as expressing the Anglican interpretation of Catholic truth in accordance with its own

tradition, history and milieu. However mutilated, disintegrated
and ambiguous the 1662 Liturgy might be in its final form
after the Restoration, it represented the genius of Anglicanism
with its own order and structure, and capable of a dignified
ceremonial presentation of the Eucharistic Sacrifice as it was
conceived at this period in England.

Although the seventeenth-century liturgists differed concerning the particular point at which the consecration was effected
and the oblation was offered, it was affirmed that the Eucharist
was a propitiatory sacrifice for the whole Church, living and
departed.[77] Jeremy Taylor (1613–67), who in 1638 had
adorned the altar of his church at Uppingham with a fair linen
cloth, a silk damask frontal, and costly plate,[78] maintained that
'as Christ is a priest in Heaven for ever and yet does not sacrifice Himself afresh nor yet without a sacrifice could He be a
Priest, but by a daily ministration and intercession represents
His sacrifice to God and offers Himself as sacrificed, so He does
upon earth by the ministry of His servants. By prayers and the
sacrament He is represented or offered up to God as sacrificed,
which in effect is a celebration of His death, and the applying
it to the present and future necessities of the Church as we are
capable by a ministry like to His in Heaven. It follows, then,
that the celebration of this sacrifice be in its proportion an
instrument of applying the proper sacrifice to all the purposes
which it first designed. It is ministerially and by application an
instrument propitiatory; it is eucharistically; it is an homage
and an act of adoration; it is impetratory and obtains for us and
for the whole Church, all the benefits of the sacrifice which is
now celebrated and applied.'[79]

Unlike most of the Anglican divines in the seventeenth century, Jeremy Taylor brought the Eucharistic Sacrifice into relation with the Resurrection instead of the Consecration. It was
this latter Caroline interpretation of the rite which found adequate expression in the 1662 liturgical sequence, as the eucharistic action was completed with a repetition of the Last Supper.
Therefore, an *anamnesis* after the Prayer of Consecration was
superfluous. The Communion, following immediately, was

the proper sequel to the offering that had been made, with the Prayer of Oblation as the post-communion and the *Gloria in Excelsis* as the fitting act of thanksgiving for the benefits of Christ's death bestowed in 'the Christian Sacrifice', as the Eucharist was frequently designated by them. Similarly, an *Epiklesis* after the words of consecration, as in the oriental and Scottish liturgies, was not required since the work of the Holy Spirit was regarded as operative throughout the entire rite.

While this emphasis on the unbloody sacrificial commemoration of the Passion was in line with the 1559 and 1662 liturgical pattern, and could claim medieval and Patristic precedents, as was stressed by Jewel[80] and Hooker,[81] and their Caroline successors, it was exposed to the danger of making the Eucharist merely the memorial of the Last Supper; a Communion Service of the 1552 type in which the sacrificial significance was deliberately obliterated. This was recognized by Thorndike (1598–1672), who, like Cosin (1594–1677) and Overall (1560–1619), favoured the Canon in the First Prayer Book of 1549, and laid the foundations of the Scottish liturgy of 1637 and that of the Non-jurors.

It was generally agreed by the Anglican liturgists in the seventeenth century that the Eucharist was a renewal and representation rather than a commemoration of Calvary, in which the whole Church on earth presents before God the sacrificial oblation of the death and passion of the Redeemer, and in union with him the individual members offer themselves as part of his Mystical Body. Their conception of the *anamnesis* in the structure of the liturgy may have been defective and contrary to liturgical tradition, but at least, in the words of Thorndike, they made the Eucharist 'the crown of public service', and succeeded in making their contemporaries liturgically minded. Their doctrinal approach for the most part was, however, Calvinistic concerning the Real Presence, though a succession of divines in the seventeenth and eighteenth centuries made various attempts to return to the 1549 position, the first being as early as 1637 in the experimental Scottish Liturgy. This was followed by that of the Non-jurors in 1718 after their

secession from the National Church on the arrival of the Calvinistic William Prince of Orange at the abdication of James
II. They went back to the eastern *Apostolic Constitutions* and the
Liturgy of St James, and carried on abortive negotiations for
reunion with the Eastern Orthodox Church. Their liturgical
efforts, however, influenced the revision of the Scottish Liturgy
in 1764 and its subsequent versions in 1912 and 1929. As a
result the Prayer for the Church has been transferred in it to the
end of the Prayer of Consecration in the form of an oblation,
with the *Epiklesis* in the Eastern position.

The American revision of 1929 corresponds to the Scottish
pattern in its structure except that the Prayer for the Church is
retained in its former (1552) place and the invocation of the
Holy Spirit has been shortened. In the latest (1935) version,
the Lord's Prayer and Prayer of Humble Access have been
placed before the Communion immediately after the Consecration Prayer and its *anamnesis*. The South African rite (1920 and
1929) has kept rather nearer to the 1662 order, with an *Epiklesis* after the oblation following upon the words of institution
and the Fraction, and emphasis placed on the sacramental gifts
about to be received.

The ill-fated English alternative rite approved by Convocation and the House of Lords but rejected in the Commons in
1927 largely as a result of strenuous Protestant opposition,
approximated to the South African Liturgy, particularly in
the introduction of the *Epiklesis* in the oblation after the consecration. This reversal of Western practice was a contributory
factor in its rejection as it ranged an influential section of
Anglo-Catholic opinion on the side of the Protestant oppo-
nents of the compromise. Nevertheless, in the structure of the
Canon it maintained the traditional pattern with the *anamnesis* and the Lord's Prayer before the Communion of the
priest and people, as in the 1549 rite and its medieval and early
prototypes. Though it was not accepted by Parliament it
received the consent of the Upper and Lower Houses of Convocation and is authorized by most bishops as an alternative to
the 1662 rite.

Apart from these various liturgical expressions of the sacri﹣ ficial interpretation of the Eucharist, it was affirmed in the official reply of the Archbishops to Leo XIII, formally accepted by the Lambeth Conference in 1930,[82] that 'we truly teach the doctrine of the Eucharistic Sacrifice and do not believe it to be a "rude commemoration of the Sacrifice of the Cross", an opinion which seems to be attributed to us by the quotation made from the Council [Trent]. But we think it sufficient in the Liturgy which we use in celebrating the Holy Eucharist—while lifting up our hearts to the Lord, and when now consecrating the gifts already offered that they may become to us the Body and Blood of our Lord Jesus Christ— to signify the sacrifice which is offered at that point of the ser﹣ vice in such terms as these. We continue a perpetual memory of the precious death of Christ Who is our Advocate with the Father and the propitiation for our sins, according to His pre﹣ cept, until His coming again. For first we offer the sacrifice of praise and thanksgiving; then next we plead and represent before the Father the Sacrifice of the Cross, and by it we con﹣ fidently entreat remission of sins and all other benefits of the Lord's Passion for all the whole Church; and lastly we offer the sacrifice of ourselves to the Creator of all things which we have already signified by the oblations of His creatures. This whole action in which the people has necessarily to take its part with the Priest, we are accustomed to call the Eucharistic Sacrifice.'[83]

The Tridentine Reform
The ecclesiastical upheaval in the sixteenth century in Western Europe was not confined to those who repudiated the papal jurisdiction, and the Counter﹣Reformation within Roman Catholicism gave rise to a liturgical reform to meet the wide﹣ spread dissatisfaction with the Mass books, and to reconsider the doctrine of Eucharistic Sacrifice. With the invention of printing the Missal ceased to be copied by hand, and with the wide distribution of copies the variations and errors in the pro﹣ vincial texts became apparent. To examine the urgent need of

administrative, moral, doctrinal and liturgical reforms an Oecumenical Council was convened by Paul III at Trent, which, after some delay, assembled on December 13, 1545, and remained in session for more than eighteen years.

During the course of the protracted proceedings the question of the Missal came under review in 1546-7, the sacraments in general were defined at Session VII, and Session XIII in 1551 was devoted to the Eucharist. Transubstantiation was affirmed and the Lutheran, Zwinglian and Calvinist doctrines were unequivocally rejected, while in 1562 at Session XXII the sacrificial offering of the Mass was declared to be propitiatory and impetratory, anathematizing 'any who said it was only a memorial meal or sacrifice of praise and thanksgiving', and 'ought not to be offered for the living and the dead, for sins and punishments, satisfactions, and other necessities'.[84] On the contrary it is a sacrifice having the power of atonement and petition, offered by Christ himself at the Last Supper, and committed to the Apostles and their successors for all time, so that through their ministry he makes his heavenly offering available within his mystical body the Church. It is also the means whereby honour is done to the saints and their inter-cession with God obtained. The expiatory efficacy is *ex opere operato* wiping out mortal sin of those who are truly contrite and have been absolved, and taking away temporal punish-ments incurred from those in a state of grace.

Arising out of these discussions about the Sacrifice of the Mass a commission was appointed to investigate the abuses in connexion with the liturgical books. The Council had clearly defined the objective character and efficacy of the offering in its several aspects, and it now remained for the celebration of the liturgy and the multitudinous diocesan and provincial Missals to be put in order without disturbing the Canon and traditional structure of the Roman rite along the lines indicated during the Tridentine sessions and by numerous synods. These included the elimination of legendary material in the propers, formularies of questionable origin and content, in Votive Masses, and all the varieties and vagaries that made for the confusion of the celebrant and the bewilderment of the congregation. A long list of items and practices requiring attention was drawn up, but as the Council had been so interminable, approaching twenty years in duration, it was impossible at this very late stage in the proceedings to deal with all the minutiae that had been collected for consideration, much of which was highly contro⁄ versial. Therefore, all that could be attempted was to present at Session XXII a greatly reduced *Decritum de observandis et evitandis in celebratione missae* on September 17, 1562, as a supplement to the Canons on the Sacrifice of the Mass, avoid⁄ ing any attempt at a reform of the Missal. Two years later a papal decree was issued appointing a further commission to carry on the revision and eventually in 1570 the Roman Missal was promulgated as the uniform Liturgy by a Bull of Pope Pius V.

In it some ceremonial and ritual accretions were eradicated, but although it was said to have been reformed 'according to the custom and rite of the holy Fathers', it remained essentially a simplification of the Roman rite with little done to remedy its historical defects. The *Ordo Missae* in fact retained the tradi⁄ tional liturgical practice of Italy very much as did such per⁄ mitted medieval variants established for over two hundred years as those of the churches of Braga in Portugal, Lyons in France, Cologne and Trier in Germany, and Liège in Bel⁄ gium. Founded on the early Roman Sacramentaries, the changes and additions in the *Ordo Missae* did not substantially alter its original character, and while several revised editions of the Missal have been issued, the text and ceremonies have sur⁄ vived with only minor corrections, as in the case of the Ambrosian rite in Milan and even the Iberian Mozarabic remnant of Gallican type used annually in one of the chapels of the cathedral at Toledo, which are fundamentally Roman.

The reform did have the effect of providing the entire Latin Church with a unified Liturgy, notwithstanding these local and monastic variations, representing a combination of medie⁄ val eucharistic worship and that of the Early Church, while admitting influxes from non⁄Roman Latin Catholicism.

From the end of the sixteenth century the Ordinary of the Mass has been fixed, and by the institution of the Sacred Congrega-tion of Rites in 1588 by Sixtus V many doubts and difficulties concerning the performance of liturgical functions inherent in such a gigantic unification have been resolved. It issues dis-pensations and privileges when and where these are deemed necessary or desirable, but its principal function is to interpret the rubrics and formularies and regulate the ordinances of the Missal, the proper hours for celebrating Mass, and the ordering of particular events such as the Holy Week ceremonies.

The Liturgical Movement

Arising out of the Tridentine reform, the greater prominence given to the localized presence of Christ in the Blessed Sacra-ment, which found expression in popular piety in an extra-liturgical cultus, has tended to obscure and lessen the active participation of the laity in the sacrificial and sacramental wor-ship of the altar. To make the liturgy better known and better lived among the faithful a Liturgical Movement has been initiated during the present century with the object of bringing the Mass into closer relation with the congregation, and secur-ing for it its proper place in the daily life of the worshipping community.[85] Arising in Belgium at the end of the last cen-tury, it spread rapidly to Germany, Holland, Italy, Spain, England and America, and its influence has been felt in the Anglican Communion and among Lutherans in Germany and Sweden.

The prohibition to translate the Ordinary of the Mass into the vernacular ceased to be enforced in 1897. Prayers in the liturgy became increasingly used by the laity in conjunction with those recited in Latin by the celebrant at the altar. This led to the responses being made audibly, and ultimately to the development of the *Missa Recitata* (or *Dialogata*) as a community Mass in which the congregation, instead of saying the rosary and private devotions which have no particular eucharistic reference, followed the rite and themselves repeated in their own language the words sung by the choir at a *Missa Cantata* or at a

High Mass. As early as 1833 when the French ultramontane Benedictine P. L. P. Guéranger became Abbot of Solesmes and made a determined and successful stand for the replace, ment of local diocesan uses by the one Roman rite, attention was being increasingly focused on the rendering of the liturgy; and on the election of Giuseppa Melchior Sarto to the papacy as Pius X in 1903, he issued an encyclical in which he declared that 'in order to restore the true Christian spirit the faithful must be brought back to the first and indispensable source of that spirit, the active participation of the faithful in the holy mysteries and in the public and solemn prayer of the Church'. If 'frequent and even daily Communion' was to be encouraged, as Pius decreed in 1905, its rightful place must be in the eucharistic context, and not as a separate and indepen, dent act from the tabernacle out of Mass. The restoration of plain,chant was urged, in place of the secular music frequently introduced into the rendering of the liturgy, and a revision of the chant books was undertaken by the monks of Solesmes.[86]

In Belgium these reforms were ardently promoted at the Benedictine Abbey of Mont César, Louvain, and at the Abbey of Maria Leach in the Rhineland. A systematic study of the liturgy was combined with liturgical worship along the approved lines, and a literary campaign was initiated to edu, cate the clergy and laity on the place and function of the Mass in the corporate life of the Church, and in the underlying principles of the movement, uniting the eucharistic movement with the redemptive work of Christ in the soul and in the world. While this acquired episcopal approval and regulation, it opened the way for a new type of variation in liturgical practice, but care was taken not to tamper with the text or rubrics in the *Missale Romanum*. This was sacrosanct, and the priest at the altar had to perform his sacerdotal functions strictly in accord with the prescribed rite interpreted as a collec, tive act of worship.

Once the principles underlying the movement were widely accepted, they began to find expression not only in the Com, munity Mass (*Dialogata*) and in Communion being given in the traditional place at the end of the Canon, but also in such transformations as the moving of the altar away from the east wall of the sanctuary to enable the celebrant to adopt a westward position behind it facing the congregation. The intention of this return to the practice of the Early Church was to emphasize the essential function of the laity in eucharistic worship, and with this end in view drastic simplification of High Mass was discussed at a liturgical conference at Lugano in 1953 to give the congregation a more active part in the rite. In 1951 far-reaching alterations and simplifications were begun in the Holy Week liturgy which resulted in the Restored Holy Week Ordo issued in 1955. Two years later evening Masses were introduced involving a new ordering of the rules governing the fast before Communion amounting to a reversal of the hitherto firmly established rule that the Blessed Sacrament must be the first food of the day. It is true that in the Primitive Church and in the early Middle Ages on Maundy Thursday, Easter, Pentecost, and on the Ember Sundays, Mass was said late in the evening. This created a precedent for what was introduced as a pastoral necessity under present-day conditions, after very careful instruction in the meaning and purpose of this startling modification of a rigidly observed discipline.

The increasing demand for the vernacular in the Mass has created another problem in spite of the fact that Latin has never been the only liturgical language in the Western Church. Old Slavonic, for example, has been adopted among the Slavic Uniates since the time of SS. Cyril and Methodius in the ninth century, and in Germany the long-standing custom of singing in German gave rise eventually to the *Singmesse*. Nevertheless, the fact remains that Latin was the universal literary language in Western Christendom, and was regarded as the proper tongue for the liturgy and divine worship in general, peculiarly appropriate for the Roman rite of which the Latin Canon was and is the core. It is hardly surprising that so ancient and firmly entrenched a feature should be regarded as an integral element, not to be lightly surrendered to the changing circumstances and conditions of a non-classical age. Moreover, since

Leo XIII in 1897 sanctioned the provision of vernacular translations of the Missal it has not been difficult for the words of the priest at the altar to be followed by the congregation provided they are spoken audibly. Inaudibility is now a greater hindrance to liturgical participation in the rite on the part of the laity than ignorance of the language employed by the celebrant, especially when the *Gloria in Excelsis*, the *Credo* and the *Sanctus* are sung or said in the vernacular in the *Missa Recitata*. Then Latin is confined mainly to the Canon thereby retaining the ancient liturgical language for the most numinous nucleus of the *Mysterium Fidei*.

CHAPTER IX

The Sacramental Principle

Sacraments and Sacramentals

ETYMOLOGICALLY, 'sacrament' is an ambiguous term, which requires clarification before we consider its relation to the institution of sacrifice. In Roman law, as we have seen, the word *sacramentum* was used to describe a legal religious sanction in which a man placed his life or property in the hands of the supernatural powers who upheld justice and honoured solemn engagements and contracts. It then became an oath of allegiance taken by soldiers to their *imperator*, sworn under a formula having a religious connotation. In the Early Church it was given a numinous and esoteric interpretation when the Latin *sacer* was brought into conjunction with the Greek *mysterion*. Thus, it became a convenient term for efficacious sacred signs or symbols which convey something 'hidden'—a mys' terious potency transmitted through material instruments as appointed channels of divine grace in a ritual observance. In this sense it acquired 'all the richness of the significance of *mysterion*'[1] and in the third century A.D. it was adopted by the Church for its appointed ordinances instituted by Christ as 'effective signs' to impart certain specific spiritual benefits to those who participated in them.

In the twelfth century the sacraments were narrowed down by Peter Lombard in 1159 to seven rites—Baptism, Con' firmation, the Eucharist, Penance, Holy Orders, Matrimony, and Extreme Unction. This became the recognized enumera' tion in the West, accepted by St Thomas Aquinas and officially adopted at the Council of Florence in 1439. It was confirmed by the Council of Trent in the sixteenth century and by the Vatican Council in 1870. Any ceremony, action or object endowing a person or thing with a sacred character was given the title 'sacramental', but was differentiated from the seven sacraments by not being of Dominical institution and not conveying divine grace *ex opere operato*, or conferring an indelible 'character' on the soul, as did Baptism, Confirma‑ tion and Holy Orders. They are spiritually efficacious only for the particular purposes for which they are used, and include the uses of holy water, incense, vestments, lights, exorcisms, anointing, confessing, making the sign of the cross, saying the rosary, the stations of the cross, the giving of alms, fasting and abstinence.

Thus, the sacramental principle has a wider range than the sevenfold system of medieval Western Christendom, which was reduced by the Continental Reformers in the sixteenth century to Baptism and the Eucharist as alone of undisputed Dominical institution. The underlying principle, however, is by no means confined to any Christian interpretation, whether Catholic or Protestant, Western or Eastern. All the deepest emotions, experiences and evaluations of human beings in every state of culture and in all religions find expression in actions, objects and external rites believed to be the vehicles conveying spiritual benefits to the recipients, so that 'inward' and 'outward' experience meet in a higher unity.

Sacraments and Symbols

Mental and spiritual activity is only known as embodied, the embodiment being not a symbol but an 'effectual sign' of that which it confers, effecting what it signifies. Thought cannot exist without a localized centre, or thinking object, which mediates and conditions the initial responses and presents objects, sounds, smells and other components of its experience and consciousness to the senses or to the imagination. The human mind functions symbolically, but, as Dr Edwyn Bevan has pointed out, there are two different kinds of symbols. There are visible objects or sounds which stand for something of which we already have direct knowledge, such as, for instance, the Union Jack or the Cenotaph. These are more than just a multicoloured piece of cloth or a block of stone. They are the emblems of the nation and events they symbolize but they do not give the patriotic Briton any information about his country, or the part it has played in the world. They remind him, nevertheless, of qualities of which he is already aware and which are appreciated by him as national values. Other kinds of symbol give specific information about the things they symbolize, conveying knowledge not hitherto known to those who see them, or of what is beyond the range of human experience.[2]

The sacramental principle belongs to the latter category. Since 'no man has seen God at any time', the spiritual world can normally only be visualized and made actual under tem, poral conditions by means of symbols or signs. Certain 'rare souls' with unusual mystical gifts or occult powers appear to be able to reach a perception of the timeless, spaceless presence of the transcendental without these material aids. Even the Hindu mystics often resort to such devices as yoga in the con, templation of the Infinite, while in Western Christendom those who have attained the heights of mystical experience (e.g. St Thomas Aquinas, St Teresa of Avila, St John of the Cross, St Bernard) have had regular recourse to the prescribed sacra, mental institutions of the Church. Since human beings are accustomed to think symbolically and make pictures out of the materials presented to the senses normally, Ultimate Reality and the mysterious presence of the *numen* are perceived phenomenally by means of effectual signs through the instru, mentality of matter.

The 'Communio' in Primitive Society

In primitive society everyday events have been given a sacra, mental significance by investing them with a supernatural meaning in relation to the ultimate source of all beneficence. Temporal needs depend on a proper relation being maintained with the unseen powers. The well,being of society demands the recognition of a hierarchy of values of which the lower is always dependent on the higher and the highest is self, sufficient. This transcendent source of values outside and above human life, essential to the stability of the whole scheme, becomes operative in a sacramental system in which the material is instrumental to the actualization of the spiritual and guarantees the validity of the outward experience, so that the purposive order holds its own against the merely casual. To partake of the flesh of a sacrificial victim or to consume a cereal image of a vegetation deity as in Mexico,[3] makes the eater a recipient of divine life and its qualities, granting his initial premises, just as, in the mortuary ritual, portions of the dead may be eaten to imbibe their attributes, or sometimes to ensure their reincarnation. Conversely, mourners allow their blood to fall on the corpse in order to give new life to the deceased and to renew the blood covenant with a departed kinsman.[4]

In this cycle of sacramental ideas and practices, as in their counterparts in the institution of sacrifice, the giving, conserving and promotion of life are fundamental. Thus, the eating of sacred food, like the ritual shedding of blood, is the means whereby life is bestowed through the vitality inherent in it, and at the same time a bond of union is established with the sacred order. In hunting communities, as, for example, under Palaeolithic conditions, these observances have been concentrated mainly on the control of the chase, the propagation of the species, and the maintenance of right relations with the transcendental source of the means of subsistence through visible and tangible sacramental objects and channels, be they visual representations or mimetic dances and other ritual actions. In such rites the chief actors assume the role of the supernatural beings on whom the group depends for the maintenance of its life. By a ritual imitation of what is urgently required (e.g. the killing of the prey, the propagation of the species, the acquisition of strength and power) desired results are accomplished by the wish discharging itself on efficacious symbols. The performers impersonate the thing represented, and to complete the identification they may wear objects charged with the appropriate potency, and partake sacramentally of sacred food having the same qualities. In this way a vital union with the source of strength is established. When it is done in a communal ceremony the life of the entire community is renewed by communion with the beneficent powers.

Blood, as we have seen, has been regarded almost everywhere as the vehicle of life and consciousness, and so it has been the means of effecting a bond of soul-substance between a human group and its supernatural ally. It is poured out sacrificially and consumed sacramentally to promote and preserve life, causing the sacred species to increase and multiply by ritual revivification, and so control is exercised over the food supply. Similarly, when the life and security of an individual is bound up with his guardian divinity, or *nagual*, the tutelary spirit is the link connecting him with the transcendental world in a more personal capacity.

While the totem is not a sacrificial victim,[5] it is a potent agent in effecting communion with the sacred order by virtue of its central position in the tribal fellowship at once human and divine. To consume its holy flesh, or certain parts of it especially impregnated with its soul-substance, is to assimilate the inherent qualities—life, strength, courage, wisdom, etc.—and this mystic power establishes *communio*. Life is essentially a whole, and primitive man thinks and acts collectively, making no distinction between spiritual and secular communion. 'Soul-substance' implies 'soul-power' and efficaciousness,[6] and so is a sacramental agent supplying powers wherein man is deficient. To kill and eat the totem is normally forbidden except under very carefully prescribed conditions and for the purpose of strengthening the bond of union by drawing upon this inexhaustible reservoir of ancestral power. This may require an apology, as at the well-known Ainu and Gilyah bear festival in which the cub, regarded as the guardian spirit of the community, was slain ceremonially and its flesh solemnly eaten after it had been treated with the utmost kindness and respect, suckled by a woman, and despatched with the greatest deference as the ambassador of the people to the sacred species to obtain a good hunting season for the group with which it had been so intimately associated.[7]

When this involves the sacrificial slaying of a member of the sacred species, as in the case of the Ainu bear cub or that of the turtle regarded by the Zuñi of Arizona as a lost child or parent, sister or brother, great-grandfather or great-grandmother,[8] lamentation and apologetic amends are required for the loss sustained by all concerned for the common good. But, as we have seen,[9] the ritual shedding of blood is the giving rather than the taking of life, and the outpouring of the vital essence and the reception of the sacred flesh are the means whereby life is given to promote and conserve life and consolidate the sacra-mental covenant. From this primary conception and intention an elaboration of ritual and belief has emerged having for its purpose the bestowal of spiritual grace through efficacious signs, often in very intimate association with the institution of sacrifice.

Totemism is only one mode of expression of the sacramental principle in primitive society. In it the communion sought is with the sacred ally rather than with the food itself, and through the totem with the members of the clan. Man is reach-ing out towards the inward and spiritual through the outward and visible in an attempt to establish a sacramental covenant, a religious bond or *sacramentum*, with the transcendent species by means of a ritual in which the totem and the totemites lose their separate identities in a common ancestry. The mainten-ance and increase of the food supply is the primary purpose of the rites but these temporal needs can be supplied only if proper relations exist between man and the supernatural powers. The action moves on a sacramental plane, where man is dependent upon a higher order of reality for his physical as well as his spiritual sustenance. The stability of the social organism, the health of society and the means of subsistence demand the recognition of a hierarchy of values of which the lower is dependent upon the higher and the highest is self-sufficient. This finds expression in a sacramental system in which the material is the instrument and channel of the spiritual.

SACRAMENTAL REGENERATION

As husbandry and herding replaced hunting and food-gathering as the basic economy in agricultural and pastoral civilization, the fertility of the soil and the succession of the seasons and their several pursuits—tilling, sowing and reaping —became the centres of interest and of the ritual organization. Nature was no less precarious for the farmer than for the hunter; consequently, seed-time and harvest were approached with the emotional anxiety formerly displayed at the breeding and pluvial seasons. A ritual technique, which assumed a sacrificial and sacramental form, was devised to prevent sterility and promote fertility, and to secure a safely gathered and abundant harvest, followed by a renewal of the generative process in nature. Around this cultus a death and resurrection drama in due course developed, notably in the Fertile Crescent in and after the fourth millennium B.C., in which sacramental regeneration was the dominant theme.

The Annual Festival in Mesopotamia and Egypt

In nature and man alike the same process of decay and regeneration is manifest; a perpetual dying to be reborn. The notion of a kind of never-dying spirit in all things has arisen; vegetation and the human community becoming a continuous cycle of existence comparable to the succession of the seasons. In this sequence birth, maturity, death and rebirth constitute a transition marked by a series of *rites de passage* in which the creative process is repeated through sacramental acts of renewal. Thus, in the background of the New Year rites in Mesopotamia, for example, long before the creation story had taken its later shape around the very ancient seasonal ritual going back to Neolithic times,[10] the death and resurrection of the god who was the embodiment of fecundity were enacted. Marduk, it is true, was never conceived as a single cosmic power like Atum-Re in Egypt, any more than the king was the dynamic centre of the social structure in Babylonia—as was the Pharaoh in the Nile valley. Neither the rulers in the city-states, nor the government, nor the gods had the assured and secure position in an immutable order with the same deity as the unchanging transcendental unifying principle as in the Egyptian solar theology or the Osirian-Horus relationship and function of the divine king. But in both civilizations the transition at the critical stages of each new season were effected by *rites de passage* in which the king in his sacral capacity was the principal actor in the sacred drama.

Because the reigning Pharaoh in Egypt personified the fruc-tifying waters of the inundation which contained all the potentialities of life, he was 'the herdsman of everyone without evil in his heart' whom the Sun-god 'appointed to be the shepherd of the land to keep alive the people and the folk'.[11] The first responsibility of the herdsman was to maintain the food supply. Therefore, he produced the life-giving waters, and at the Harvest Festival presented to the gods the sheaf of grain which symbolized the fruits of the earth and the fertility of the land.[12] In Mesopotamia, on the other hand, 'mother earth' rather than the sun being the inexhaustible source of new life, the goddess personified the reproductive forces in nature and mankind. It was she in the capacity of Inanna-Ishtar who renewed vegetation, promoted the growth of the crops and the propagation of man and beast symbolized in the union with the shepherd-god Dumuzi-Tammuz, the incarnation of the creative powers of spring at the turn of the year, delivering the earth from the blight of sterility.[13]

In Sumer, the sacred marriage of the king in the capacity of Dumuzi and the priestess of Inanna was a sacramental renewal of 'the life of all lands'.[14] This was only accomplished after a struggle between the opposed forces in nature, those of fecundity and barrenness, enacted by human beings with whom the conflicting powers were identified. This involved the imprisonment of Marduk (in the role of Dumuzi-Tam-muz) in the mountain of death, and the abdication and humiliation of his earthly counterpart, the king, and the descent of Inanna-Ishtar to the underworld, with reciprocal effects in a contemporary state of chaos and strife in the city during this period of the New Year Festival in Babylon. Before the release of the god, the reinstallation of the king and his sacred marriage with the queen or the priestess were enacted in the Akitu drama at the conclusion of the spring renewal rites.

The Annual Festival in the Ancient Near East represented the centre and climax of all the religious activities of the year when the king engaged in a sacred combat with his spiritual foes, like the gods in the creation story enacted as part of the drama. Having won the victory he was re-established on the throne, led forth in triumph, and to ensure the fruitfulness of the earth and the multiplication of man and beast a ritual marriage was celebrated with the queen or a priestess. The Fes-tival was held in the spring or the autumn and so coincided with the annual sowing or reaping, often associated with the first-fruit and harvest rites, including sometimes a drastic puri-fication of the entire community by way of preparation for the desacralization of the new crops for common use, and the removal of the harmful contagions of the old year by a *rite de séparation*, preceding a sacramental meal.[15] A similar ritual occurred at the season of sowing of which the Saturnalia probably was a survival.

In Egypt the regeneration of the Pharaoh was performed daily in the 'Toilet ceremonies' when the accession rites were re-peated with the sacramental ablutions with water from the primeval ocean (Nun) that 'begat all living things', and the censing of the cultus-image and the food and drink offerings,[16] in order that the king as the reigning Horus might be re-begotten and reborn as the son of the Sun-god. The water used for the lustrations was, in fact, regarded as the womb of the Sky-goddess from which the prince was born, begotten by the seed of Atum-Re.[17] The Nile inundation, being the vital fluid that issued from Osiris and regenerated the fertile soil, was identified with Isis, the wife of Osiris and creatrix of the Nile flood, who caused it to bring forth abundance every year. Therefore, a festival of the goddess was held when the waters of the river began to rise at the summer solstice, her tears shed when she mourned for Osiris making it swell and overflow,[18] equated with the appearance in the sky of the dog star Sirius (Sothis) on June 15 at the beginning of the new year.

In Egypt and in Mesopotamia the annual rise and fall of the respective rivers spreading fertilizing mud over the fields from which luxuriant growth sprang, were connected with the dying and reviving gods, Osiris and Tammuz, enacted in the sacramental drama. In such countries where the existence of vegetation and the human species was centred in the water supply, unless the autumnal rains continued uninterruptedly for several months the rivers could not fill the network of irri-gation canals which carried the water to the fields, and star-vation would follow. It is not surprising that the rivers and their waters acquired a sacramental significance in the regenera-tion of the parched and arid soil. From this the extension of the process to the sacral king as the dynamic centre of the com-munity and of the natural order was almost inevitable, since he was regarded as the early embodiment of the dying and reviving saviour-god who was the author and giver of life in all its aspects.

The Graeco-oriental Mystery Cults

(a) *The Eleusinia.* In the Graeco-oriental Mystery cults, lustrations never assumed the same importance as in the Egyptian and Babylonian sacramental ritual. During the preparation of the Eleusinian *mystae* at Athens on the 14th of Boedromion, neophytes underwent preliminary purification by bathing in the sea, each being accompanied by a young pig which he offered as a sacrifice to Demeter and Kore. On the 19th they went in procession along the *via sacra* to Eleusis; baths were taken by one section of them at Cephissus, by another at a bath near the statue of Anemocritus by the tomb of Scirus. On reaching Eleusis they were asperged with water from the well of Kallichoron where Demeter in the guise of an old woman was said to have met the daughters of the Archon Keleos. In due course the *mystae* were taken to the sea again, fasting and carrying lighted torches in commemoration of Demeter's search for Kore. This may have been intended to bring them into union with the passion of the Mother-goddess as a preparation for the supreme revelation in the Telesterion.

The things spoken and done there remain an enigma.[19] In the museum at Eleusis there is a statue of Demeter sprinkling water from a shell on a man who presumably was a neophyte, but like the drinking of the *kykeon*—a gruel of meal and water —it appears to have been a preparation for rather than the climax of the initiation. They emerged ultimately from the mystic experience with a new assurance of having attained salva‑ tion and the hope of a blissful immortality, but in what it con‑ sisted can only be conjectured from the few hints in the later literature, much of which is post‑Christian. But there is nothing to suggest that the ritual rebirth was effected by a sacramental lustration, or that the *mystae* partook of the divine substance of the Goddess in a sacred meal. There are vague hints that a sacred marriage was celebrated between the hierophant im‑ personating Zeus and a priestess assuming the role of Demeter to bring the neophytes into a mystic communion with the divinities portrayed and resulting in the birth of a holy child Iacchos or Brimo.[20] But neither contemporary writers nor vase‑painters betrayed the most secret and intimate disclosures, and since the accounts of Hippolytus and the early Christian Fathers were derived largely from Gnostic sources Farnell probably has good reason for rejecting their evidence as untrust‑ worthy.[21] However, the suggestion of Jevons that Demeter was a corn‑totem and that the *kykeon* made from the grain was regarded as her divine substance partaken of sacramentally by the *mystae* is without any foundation.[22]

From the general character of the ritual it is clear that the Mystery was connected with the seasonal drama in which a sacred marriage was a prominent feature.[23] It would not be surprising, therefore, if the annual autumnal celebration cul‑ minated in a symbolic sacramental union of the hierophant and a priestess with the mysterious child Iacchos, or Brimo, represented as the issue, though the origin of the Zeus‑born Iacchos is very obscure in spite of his prominence in later times as 'the daemon of Demeter'.[24] The name has been supposed to have been derived from the ritual cry of the *mystae* and to mean 'the god of the loud cry' (ἰαχεῖν), invoked with cries of triumph during the procession from Athens to Eleusis. But although he was said to be the son (or consort) of Demeter, of

Persephone, and of Dionysus, he was in fact a new god in the Mysteries when they were incorporated in the official religion of Athens as a Pan-Hellenic cult. Moreover, because his name, Iacchos, was similar to Bacchos, the title of Dionysus, he was identified with the tumultuous Thracian or Phrygian son of Zeus and Semele, the god of wealth, joy and prosperity, as well as of wine and vegetation.[25] It was only later that Iacchos became an independent object of worship as the son of Zeus and Persephone,[26] like others of the numerous Dionysoi.

(b) *The Dionysiac.* What happened to the image of the god when it reached Eleusis we are not told. It is clear that he had no abiding home there, or, indeed, originally any place in the Mysteries. He was essentially an Athenian and Dionysian figure, and it was only when the Eleusian rites acquired a syn-cretistic character after the union of Athens with Eleusis in 600 B.C. that he was incorporated into them. His Thraco-Phrygian background then constituted a link with the ecstatic and mystical forms of oriental worship, foreign to the Hellenic temperament. The Dionysiac religion was essentially orgias-tic; the regeneration of the *Maenads* or *Bacchae* being effected by becoming possessed by the spirit of Dionysus in the self-abandonment of the ecstatic rites. Clad in fawn-skins and taking in their hands the *thyrsos*, or rod, adorned with a bunch of ivy, the emblem of the god, the female votaries went to the moun-tains to engage in tumultuous dancing in their long flowing garments with horns fixed to their heads and snakes wreathed round them, and were roused to mania by the beating of the tympanum and the strains of the flute. In this state of wild exaltation, stimulated by the free flowing of wine, in the dark-ness illuminated only by the light of their torches, they became *Bacchoi*. In their original Thracian orgies they experienced 'the joy of the raw feast'—the *omophagia*—tearing in pieces animals embodying Dionysus-Zagreus with their bare hands and devouring the flesh, as the central act of the Bacchanalia.[27]

Ecstatic rites of this nature did not commend themselves to the sober and unemotional Greeks of the Hellenic tradition, but ecstasy is infectious; and in the sixth century B.C., when new forces, political, economic and religious, were rapidly changing the outlook of the masses in Greece, and mystical ideas were gaining ground, the Dionysiac was not without a powerful appeal as a means of obtaining union with the divine. As Professor Nilsson says, 'there exists in every man, however humble his station, a dormant desire to enter into communion with the divine, to feel himself lifted up from the temporal into the spiritual. This form of ecstasy found its herald in the god who, with Apollo, impressed himself most strongly upon the religious feeling of the age—Dionysos.'[28] In his rites his votaries surmounted the barrier which separates man from the supernatural world and unconditionally surrendered themselves body and soul to those mighty powers that transcend time and space, and the personal life of man, and were carried to the timeless, spaceless realm of the eternal. They found salvation and satisfaction in that divine union which is the goal of all mysticism.

The wilder escapades were repressed and sublimated in more sober religious movements, notably Orphism and its Olympian mythology wherein the Bacchic cult incorporated two myths of Persephone, representing her as the daughter of Demeter by Zeus who violated her and so produced Dionysus; and that of her abduction by Pluto to his nether realms. Zeus, having begotten Dionysus, wanted to hand over royal power to his son, but the Titans lured away the child, tore him to pieces and devoured his limbs. Athena, however, saved his heart and gave it to Zeus who ate it, and eventually a new Dionysus was born, the son of Semele, the Phrygian Earthgoddess. The Titans were destroyed by lightning and from their ashes mankind was formed. Thus, the original *omophagia* was transformed into a crime since the Titans as the incarnation of evil were made responsible for the slaying and eating of the divine child, Dionysus-Zagreus, who took the place of the dismembered animal.

This is mentioned in the classical literature only by Pausanias in an Orphic poem. Nevertheless, in the background of Orphism the Titan story is paramount, and although Diony sus is the principal Orphic god the hostility between the wor/ shippers of Orpheus and those of Dionysus is doubtless to be explained by the Orphics having transformed the central Bacchic sacrament, the *omophagia*, into the primeval crime resulting in the evil nature in mankind.[29] Yet the two cults centred in the worship of the same god, Dionysus. The votaries seem to have regarded themselves as having much the same filial relationship with the gods by virtue of their initiation into the Mysteries. Thus, the Orphici appear to have appropriated to themselves the rebirth of Dionysus, and to have entered into a new life by a renewal of the divine (Dionysian) element in their dual nature. The Orphic *Maenad* personated the Eleusin/ ian Maiden or Mother/goddess, and by a sacramental rite in which a serpent was used as the instrument, became herself mystically the mother of the infant god; but she was not actually reborn, like her son.

The primary purpose of the Orphic ritual was to raise the soul to its native divinity through sacraments which conferred divine life on the recipient and so enabled him to attain im/ mortality. This was accomplished by a ritual regeneration which, while it retained the ancient Bacchic conception of man becoming a god, gave a new interpretation of divinity. 'The grace sought was not a physical intoxication but spiritual ecstasy, the means adopted not drunkenness but abstinence and rites of purification.'[30] The votaries were not begotten anew by a god or born again by a goddess, but made immortal and divinely pure. Life was a grim struggle between two opposing elements in human nature demanding rigid asceticism and purifications till at length, through many reincarnations, the Dionysiac soul was freed from its fleshly bondage. An initiate in an Orphic hymn on the Sybaris tablets is represented as being sustained in his perilous journey through the lower world by the conviction that he would be 'god instead of mortal'.[31] He is not reported to have declared himself to be destined actually to become a god because the aim of initiation was to secure union with the divine nature as Bacchos rather than absorption into and unity with static Being as the ultimate zero of existence, as in the Indian conception of Nirvana. Orphism introduced Eastern categories of thought into the West and prepared the way for the welter of oriental Mystery cults in the Graeco-Roman world after the conquests of Alexander the Great in the fourth century B.C.

(c) *The Attis and Kybele Cult.* From Asia Minor came the worship of the Anatolian Magna Mater; this took two distinct forms. In her chief Phrygian sanctuary at Lydia, and in the Troad, Kybele and her son Attis were worshipped together with Bacchic rites reminiscent of the primitive Thracian orgies. By the fifth century she was known in Greece in association with Demeter, and her worship penetrated to Italy through the Sibyls, the prophetic priestesses who had established a centre of Apolline divination at Cumae comparable to those associated with Orphism in Greece. But although in times of distress and anxiety recourse was made to the sacred oracle not only by Etruscans of oriental origin but also by the patrician rulers of Rome, it was not until the Hannibalic war in the third century that the cult of the Anatolian Mother-goddess was brought to Rome officially from her ancient seat at Pessinus, in response to an appeal to the Sibylline oracles after an unusual burst of pebble-rain following the Metaurus battle.[32] Having been established in her temple on the Palatine Hill[33] with her Anatolian castrated *galli*, under the Republic her ecstatic rites were confined to her own precincts except on the festival instituted in her honour on April 4, known as the Megalesia, with its *ludi* (games) and a *lectisternium*. This opened with a procession through the city with Kybele in her car drawn by a yoke of lions and followed by her *galli*. Amid a thunder of timbrels, the clanging of cymbals, and the braying of horns, goaded by the outlandish music of the Phrygian pipe, the *galli* leapt in rhythmic movement, cutting themselves with knives like the priests of Baal on Carmel, 'gladdened at the sight of blood'.[34]

This strange scene, as alien but as fascinating to the Romans as were the Bacchanalian Dionysian revels to the Greeks, was confined to the Phrygian worshippers of the Magna Mater, until, in imperial times, the regulation was relaxed by Claudius when the spring festival of Kybele and Attis was introduced and Roman citizens were permitted to take part in the annual enactment of the death and resurrection of the youthful lover of the Mother of the Gods from March 15 to 25. The proceedings opened with a procession of the *cannophori*, or Reed-bearers, and, after a week of fasting and purifications, on the 22nd the pine-tree, symbolizing Attis, was taken to the temple. Two days later on the *Dies Sanguinis*, his castration and death were enacted by the *archigallus* cutting his arm amid loud lamentation and the clashing of cymbals, the rumbling of drums and the screaming of the pipes, at the point where formerly the neo-phytes were castrated.[35] As night fell a light suddenly shone in the darkness and the tomb was opened to symbolize the rising of the god from the grave. His resurrection was an-nounced, and the following day (25th) the Hilaria was ob-served with feasting and rejoicing. After a day of rest (*Re-quietio*) the festival concluded on the 27th with the washing (*Lavatio*) of the image of Kybele in the Almo below the walls of Rome.

(d) *The Taurobolium.* On the next day (March 28) it appears that initiations were held. Little is known of the manner in which they were performed.[36] At some point in the cere-monies the initiates went down into the παστός, or under-ground bridal-chamber, presumably the cave sanctuary of the Goddess. They are also said to have eaten a sacred meal from a drum and a cymbal.[37] But whether or not they emerged from the chamber 'born again' as the sons of Kybele, and were strengthened and renewed sacramentally by the risen life of Attis can only be conjectured, however likely this may have been. After the time of Antoninus Pius (A.D. 138–161) the grim ritual of the *taurobolium* was performed on March 28 at the sanctuary of the Magna Mater, known as the *Gaianum*, on the Vatican Hill. There the initiate crowned with gold and wreathed with fillets descended into a pit and stood below a grating over which a bull (or a ram in the case of the *crio-bolium*), adorned with garlands of flowers and gold leaf, was stabbed to death, drenching the recipient of the baptism with its life-giving blood. From this ordeal he emerged reborn for twenty years, or as a late inscription records, *renatus in aeternum*.[38]

This crude mode of regeneration originated in Asia Minor and made its way into the West from Cappadocia or Phrygia in the second century A.D. In the next two hundred years it was widely adopted, spreading throughout the Empire from Rome to Gaul, Spain and North Africa, in association with the worship of the Mother-goddess. For those who braved its terrors it must have had a deep personal significance as a 'baptism of blood', though in the earliest inscriptions it is said to have been done on behalf of the Emperor and the Empire. But since according to the Neoplatonist Sallustius the neophyte was himself fed with milk at the vernal equinox like a new-born babe[39] it would seem that in the fourth century A.D. Attis initiates were regarded as having undergone a sacramental process of rebirth as a result of the *taurobolium*. To what extent it was adopted and practised in Mithraism is difficult to determine, but Cumont may be right in thinking that it was taken over from the cult of the Magna Mater.[40]

(e) *The Isiac*. Similarly, the Isiac *mystae* died symbolically to be reborn as the son of the Egyptian Goddess, the wife of Osiris and mother of Horus. In the Hellenistic form of the cult in the Graeco-Roman world this was accomplished by preliminary ablutions of Nile water and fastings followed by an elaborate ritual of initiation, described in considerable detail by Apuleius (A.D. 123-155) in the eleventh book of the *Metamorphoses*. In relating the adventures of Lucius, the hero of the romance, a full account is given of how he 'approached the realms of death' in order to attain his 'spiritual birthday in the service of the sacred rites'. With the aid of a passion play representing the sorrowful search of Isis for the dismembered body of Osiris depicted on a fresco in the museum at Naples from Herculaneum, and other rites he was not permitted to divulge, he underwent, at midnight, a mystic death and was described as having 'set foot on the threshold of Proserpine'. He saw the sun gleaming with bright light and 'entered the presence of the gods and adored them'. The next day, arrayed in the vestures and regalia of an initiate, he was presented to the people of Corinth as a reborn initiate.[41]

Unlike the Kybele-Attis Mystery the Isiac emphasized abstinence from sexual intercourse, wine, flesh and bread, and repeated ablutions designed to rid both initiates and votaries of ritual impurity, as the proper condition to approach 'the purest of religions'.[42] Similarly, those who were invited to 'sup at the couch of the Lord Serapis' in the Serapeum at Alex-andria[43] found behind all the outward purifications and cere-monial observances a deeper meaning which enabled them to gain renewal and strength from Isis in this life and in the world to come everlasting bliss through the immortal glory of Osiris.

(f) *Mithraic Initiation*. The same is true of those who were 'begotten anew' or 'born again' as immortal sons of the Iranian solar deity Mithras when his cult reached Europe at the begin-ning of the Christian era. As we have seen,[44] this Persian Mystery made headway rapidly in the Roman Empire because it combined a developed sacramentalism with a lofty ethic, an ideal of moral purity and the assurance of a bestowal of divine grace in this life with the hope of immortality. Behind the cult-legend lay a death and resurrection motif in which the bull, depicted in the *tauroctonus*, played the part of the dying god by way of substitute. Therefore, although Mithras did not pass through death to life like most male mystery divinities, he was a life-giver by virtue of his sacrificial act. Consequently, as the animals in the *tauroctonus* were represented as sapping the creative vitality of the sacred bull, so the initiates, by identifying themselves with the *sol invictus*, underwent a series of renewal rites, which very likely included the *taurobolium*, to iden-tify the *mystae* with the death of the sacrosanct victim (the bull) before ascending to heaven.

Each stage in this upward course had proper rites, involving mortification, purification, lustrations, ordeals, oaths and vows of secrecy. These are said to have included a baptism of total immersion,[45] and the discovery of natural springs or a water system at many *mithraea* suggests that ablutions played an

important part in the ritual. The sealing of the candidates'
foreheads, probably with a red-hot iron, at the third, or *miles*,
degree when they became soldiers of Mithras and refused the
crown offered to them with the words, 'Mithras is my crown',
was compared by Tertullian with the Christian sacrament of
Confirmation.[46] Their hands and tongues were purified with
honey at the next stage (*Leo*) before undergoing a symbolic
death in order to rise in the last and highest grades to a new
and purified existence.

If we could be sure that the *Mithras Liturgie* published by
Dieterich was in fact the official liturgy of the Mystery there
would be no doubt that the neophyte was 'transformed by the
immortal birth' so that after 'the impending doom' which
pressed hard upon him, he was able to 'look on the immortal
source of his being'. Then when 'the holy *pneuma*' had breathed
on him and he had beheld the prescribed sacred sights, he who
had been 'born mortal from a mortal womb' was 'changed into
something better by a mighty force and an incorruptible right
hand', awaiting 'to see with immortal eyes the immortal Aeon
and Lord of the fiery diadems'. Here, it is affirmed, 'is one that
was born of man: he was brought forth from a mortal womb,
and begotten by human seed. But this day he has been begotten anew by thee; and having, alone among the many myriads
of mankind, been made immortal in this hour, he claims and
requests permission to bow down before thee.'[47]

This treatise, which betrays Hermetic influence,[48] comes to
us, however, from an Egyptian magician who probably was
interpreting current theosophical ideas in Mithraic terms without having any real knowledge of the worship. There are no
adequate grounds for regarding the so-called 'Liturgy' as a
genuine Mithraic production; but it doubtless reflects the
general purpose of Mystery initiations in the Roman Empire at
the beginning of the Christian era. In Mithraism the ceremony
apparently was called *sacramentum* because at each advance
through the seven spheres the initiate took an oath comparable
to that of soldiers on enlistment in the army. Although we do
not know exactly in what the seven sacraments consisted, their

purpose seems to have been to combat the forces of evil in the great cosmic struggle between light and darkness in which man shared, and eventually to partake of the joys and victory of the regenerate in the supreme heaven when their warfare was accomplished. At each stage of initiation ablutions were pre/scribed to remove the defilements that had been contracted, the lustration having a different purpose and effect at each degree. Most of the information, however, acquired by people like Porphyry, Origen and Tertullian was gained from hearsay and from the signs and symbols used in the rites,[49] and therefore was largely conjectural. This applies to all the Graeco/oriental esoteric cults.

Judaeo-Christianity

These cults represent an ancient heritage of Near Eastern and Mediterranean religion which from about the sixth century B.C. gave expression in a sacramental ritual to an intense desire for supernatural strength and renewal in this life leading at length to a blissful hereafter. Now it can hardly be denied that Chris/tianity is in this tradition and that its sacramental system was based to a considerable extent on the same fundamental prin/ciples; with the very important distinction that it was centred primarily in the Incarnation. In Christian theology the sacra/ments were instituted to perpetuate the union of God with man in the historic person of Christ as 'the Word made flesh', in and through a visible organization, the Church, regarded as the Mystical Body of Christ.

BAPTISM

Jewish Proselyte Baptism

Baptism was the act of initiation of the catechumen into the fellowship of the Church, and can be compared to the initia/tion rites in Judaism and the pagan Mysteries. In the Old Dis/pensation the very primitive rite of circumcision was the covenant/sign of the true Israelite,[50] though in spite of its alleged divine sanction it was not regarded as a regenerative rite; nor was divine grace considered to be conferred by it. It was a legal injunction rather than a sacramental ordinance, and as such it became a condition of the participation of Gentiles in the Passover,[51] second in importance to repentance or conversion. In the post-exilic community there arose the idea of a universal kingdom embracing all mankind, and some provision had to be made for the admission of Gentiles into Israel as proselytes without destroying its national character as a theocracy. This was done by an initiatory rite consisting of circumcision, a baptismal immersion in water, and the presentation of an offering in the temple,[52] except in the case of women where nothing equivalent to circumcision was required.

From the literature of the Tannaitic period it is clear that in the first two centuries of the Christian era proselyte baptism was in vogue.[53] In the earlier Maccabaean legislation it was declared that on becoming a proselyte to Judaism a Gentile woman who had had immoral relations with a Jew must submit to a purificatory bath, or *tebilah*,[54] and the Mishna prescribes such a purification. Lustration in the case of a foreigner embracing Judaism seems to have been a long-standing practice before the fall of Jerusalem in A.D. 70, and in the Talmud it is coupled with the offering of a sacrifice.[55] After the fall it became the only means by which women were initiated, and towards the end of the century and the beginning of the second century A.D., the rival claims of baptism and circumcision were in frequent debate among the Rabbis,[56] until finally proselyte baptism alone sufficed.[57]

The Johannine Rite

At the beginning of the Christian era baptismal regeneration took shape in Judaism. Those who received it became 'sons of the covenant like a new-born child of Jewish parents'. To what extent it was a generally accepted practice when John the Baptist made it an integral ordinance in his Messianic movement is less certain. It does not appear to have been a novelty among the Jews, as no indication is given in the Gospel narratives of the rite causing any surprise or comment, it being regarded apparently as a natural sign of repentance at the approach of the Kingdom of God. It was preparatory rather than sacramental in the sense of being a grace-bearing rite, except in so far as it was initiatory and the token of participation in the new age. John combined the role of herald, prophet and baptist, and those who responded to his eschatological message, proclaimed as a divine invitation (μετάνοια), received forgiveness. Therefore, the rite was not devoid of spiritual gifts.

Josephus regarded the Baptist as 'a good man' who exhorted the Jews to exercise virtue both to justice (διχαιοσύνη) towards one another and piety (εὐσέβεια) towards God, and to come to baptism (βαπτισμῷ συνίευαι). Baptism could be acceptable to God if it was received for purification of the body after the soul had been thoroughly purified beforehand by righteousness.[58] If, as is very probable, this passage is substantially authentic,[59] it would suggest that the Johannine rite was a bodily lustration, not necessarily a preparation for the coming of the Messianic Kingdom, and corresponded closely with Jewish proselyte baptism. The Gospel tradition, however, clearly puts the emphasis on its eschatological character as a sign guaranteeing endowment with the Spirit in the approaching Messianic Age.

Mark states that it was 'a baptism of repentance unto remission of sins' apparently connected with the commencement of the reign of God.[60] It also had a prophetic significance as, like the Hebrew prophets, John bore witness to an approaching divine judgment which was now actually at hand—a baptism with fire as well as with water and the Spirit—and by the aid of metaphors derived from the operations of harvest and the felling of trees, he called upon the crowds who went into the desert in expectation of a Messianic theophany to establish a right relationship with Yahweh by repentance.[61] Therefore, while in all the four Gospels and in the Acts of the Apostles he is represented as a preacher of repentance, the eschatological message is predominant in the earlier source from which the Matthaean and Lucan narratives were drawn.[62]

Josephus, on the other hand, appears to have identified the Johannine movement and its rite with the baptismal lustrations of the Essenes, and the Gnostic Mandaean community east of Jordan which also has claimed to have had traditional affinities with the Baptist in spite, or perhaps because, of its subsequent hostility to Christianity.[63] The origin of these sects is very obscure, and the liturgical documents are late, notwithstanding archaic elements in them going back perhaps to the beginning of the Christian era. Their veneration of the Baptist may be the result of their baptismal rites rather than the cause of their observances, but they may have been derived from one of the several allied movements which influenced John. It is not likely that he himself was a member of such a sect. He was essentially a prophetic figure equated subsequently with Elijah, although John denied this role in his lifetime.[64] He was an ascetic of the desert whose mission was to call his countrymen to prepare for the Messianic judgment by a baptism as the outward token of an inward spiritual change of heart. This ethical teaching corresponded more closely with what is known of the preparation of proselytes to Judaism than with Essenic or Mandaean baptisms.

Nevertheless, his mission was located in the district round the Dead Sea where Pliny maintains that the Essenes had persisted for 'thousands of ages',[65] and in the neighbourhood of which, east of Jordan, the Mandaean community was established in the first or second century A.D., and still survives south of Baghdad. Doubtless in this region sacramental ideas were prevalent, and it is reasonable to suppose that the Johannine movement was influenced to some extent by these baptismal sects in the background of its thought and practice. By the beginning of the Christian era the Essenes numbered probably about four thousand in Palestine, organized on a communistic and ascetic basis with a succession of oaths of obedience during the three years' novitiate imposed on those who joined the exclusive brotherhood. They endeavoured to live so far as possible in conformity with nature, emancipated from all worldly affairs and carnal lusts and appetites, including a strict observance of celibacy and the repudiation of blood sacrifice. In all this there were points of contact no doubt with the Johannine movement, the Baptist having adopted the life of a desert ascetic in contrast to his cousin, Jesus, who was accused of being a gluttonous man and a wine-bibber, a friend of publicans and sinners.[66]

Jesus was attracted by the mission and accepted baptism by John, who is said to have recognized him to be the Messiah. At least three of the Twelve Apostles had been John's disciples and Christ himself held his herald in the highest esteem, re- garding him as the last and greatest figure of the Old Dispensa- tion. However, the least in the kingdom about to be established would be greater than he.[67] The equation of the Baptist with the Elijah of Malachi[68] was probably a later insertion by an early copyist from a collection of 'proof texts' in support of Isaiah xl, 3, quoted by Christian controversialists in relation to John, whose movement had continued as a sect with its water- baptism in the Apostolic period after the crucifixion. It was regarded as inadequate by the Apostles. It did not confer the gift of the Spirit, and so necessitated a rebaptism in the name of the Lord Jesus.[69]

The Baptism of Jesus

That Jesus was himself baptized by John, as is explicitly main- tained in all the Gospels, suggests a continuity in the Johan- nine and Christian rites. The emphasis, however, is placed on the anointing of the Spirit for the Messianic role as the Son of God and the Suffering Servant, the prefiguration of the out- pouring of the Spirit on the New Israel at Pentecost. The Jordan baptismal experience of Christ is represented as con- taining the essential elements of a mystery initiation with the addition of the sacramental gifts inherent in the conception of the anointed Messiah being set apart and charismatically endowed for the fulfilment of his vocation. The Johannine purificatory lustration was thereby transformed into the proto- type of the Christian sacrament in which rebirth was effected by the union of water and the Spirit portrayed in the outward and visible signs of immersion, the imagery of the dove, in accordance with Rabbinic symbolism, and the heavenly voice.[70] Eventually it was brought into relation with the death and resurrection of Christ when Baptism and the Eucharist became the two principal Dominical sacraments of the Church, the one prefiguring his Messianic vocation as the Isaianic Servant, the other constituting its perpetual memorial.

It is not certain whether Jesus ever himself baptized any of his converts,[71] but the automatic acceptance of baptism by the Apostolic Church would seem to suggest that it had been in vogue during his public ministry as the method of initiation into the 'new age'. If this were so it must have been practised side by side with the Johannine rite,[72] and this caused confusion after the Pentecostal experience. Then the Church refused to admit the validity of any sacramental initiation which did not include the name of Jesus and the gift of the Spirit to distinguish it from the water-baptism of John.[73] By the end of the century the Trinitarian formula had been established, and from St Matthew xxviii, 19, it would seem that, unless the text is a later interpolation, it had been adopted in the Judaeo-Christian community when the First Gospel was circulated soon after the destruction of Jerusalem, probably about A.D. 80. The first mention of the formula in connexion with the rite is in *The Didache* at the beginning of the second century. It is not likely that such a theological phrase was actually employed by Christ in commissioning his Apostles, and had the command been as clear-cut as the passage indicates, the Apostolic Church would hardly have been so reluctant to admit Gentiles into its fellowship.[74] It may be presumed that had this been the case St Peter would have appealed to the words of Jesus rather than to his own experience with Cornelius in defending his action in baptizing the centurion and those gathered with him in Caesarea.[75] The Matthaean text, therefore, cannot be regarded as reliable evidence for the Dominical institution of baptism in the name of the Holy Trinity.

The Pauline Conception of Baptism

Nevertheless, from the day of Pentecost onwards Baptism was regarded as necessary for salvation, and particularly under

Pauline influence it was given a mystery interpretation in terms of the identification of the initiate with the death and resurrec/ tion of Christ. 'Know ye not', says St Paul in his letter to the Romans, 'that so many of us as were baptized into Jesus Christ were baptized into his death. Therefore we are buried with him by baptism into death, that like as Christ was raised up from the dead by the glory of the Father, even so we also should walk in newness of life.'[76] For the Apostle the sacrament was a *rite de passage* comparable to the crossing of the Red Sea by Israel at the time of the Exodus, uniting the catechumen to Christ and the Church as the Israelites were united to Moses their leader and consolidated into a community.[77] The new life in Christ sacramentally bestowed as a rebirth leads naturally to member/ ship of the New Israel, the Church, and to union with its divine Head from whom justification, sanctification and com/ munion proceed. Thus, Baptism is represented as a mystical experience involving a symbolic identification with the death of Christ—a dying to the old life—and the rising again in new/ ness of life and status, sealed with 'the Holy Spirit of prom/ ise'.[78]

At first St Paul regarded the sacrament as transforming the recipient into a 'new creation'[79] which is virtually a rebirth into a spiritual community so that 'by one Spirit we were all baptized into one body'.[80] This conception he developed in the Epistle of the Romans into his theory of initiation in rela/ tion to the remission of sins and the bestowal of the Spirit as a means to the acquisition of a new character appropriate to the new status of the baptized.[81] By a mystical participation in the death, burial and resurrection of Christ the neophytes were transformed into the children of God, 'washed, sanctified and justified in the name of the Lord Jesus Christ, and in the Spirit of our God.'[82] Later, in writing to the Colossians, he ex/ horted those who had undergone this baptismal regeneration to reveal their union with their Risen Lord by 'seeking those things that are above', for they had 'died' and their lives were hid with Christ in God. By mortification they were 'to put off the old man with his doings', and to 'put on the new man renewed by knowledge after the image of Him that created him'.[83]

These mystery ideas recur throughout the baptismal teaching of St Paul. The notion of passing through a mystic grave to newness of life is, as we have seen, a fundamental theme in these rituals, and must have been familiar to his Gentile con-verts in Rome, Corinth, Colossae and Ephesus. Similarly, suffering in union with the Saviour-god has a parallel in the mutilation of the Attis votaries on the *Dies Sanguinis*. But the Pauline doctrine centred in the sacrificial death of the Re-deemer as the means whereby remission of sins had been secured and moral regeneration effected. The dying and rising again is primarily a resurrection, a *rite de passage* from the old man to the full-grown estate of the glorious liberty of the sons of God.

If St Paul had had a more intimate knowledge of the Mys-teries himself as an initiate, doubtless he would have seen in 'the washing of regeneration' (λουτρόν πουλιγγενεσίας) a purely *ex opere operato* sacramental efficacy, but like the medieval Scholastics he recognized that the grace was con-ditioned by the spiritual disposition of the recipient in the case of the adult catechumen.[84] It was bound up with incorpora-tion in the unity of the Church as the Body of Christ through a process of spiritual rebirth. With the development of mystery theology in Christianity a simulated renewal and a mystic re-birth were fused so that by the end of the first century baptism had become a new birth bestowing the gift of immortality.[85] With the growth of the practice of infant baptism[86] as distinct from the baptism of households which included the children (such as those of Lydia the jailer, Crispus and Stephanas, mentioned in the Acts), the sacrament would naturally appear in the light of a regenerative bath coupled with the charismatic laying-on of hands as the seal of the Spirit following baptism.[87]

Confirmation and the Baptismal Rite

When this 'confirmation' of the baptismal initiation became a separate rite as an 'unction' administered by a priest or bishop after baptism, it assumed a character of its own. From Judaism the Church inherited the laying-on of hands as the outward sign of the bestowal of supernatural power,[88] and in conjunction with baptismal initiation it acquired a new meaning and character derived from the Christian experience and interpretation of the gift and sealing of the Spirit.[89] There was no uniformity concerning the place and precise function of the rite and its relation to baptism in the Early Church. In the Acts of the Apostles the situation is obscure, and the term 'Confirmation' to describe the second part of the initiation rite did not come into general use until the fifth century, and then it was and has remained peculiar to Western Christendom. No mention of it occurs in the *Didache* or in Justin Martyr's *Apology*, but it appears as a separate rite after the threefold immersion in Tertullian.[90] The newly initiated catechumen was then clothed in white garments and fed with milk and honey after receiving Holy Communion. Irenaeus seems to distinguish the grace of baptism as a regeneration from the gift of the Spirit,[91] and in the 'Church Orders' in the third century[92] it is represented as a separate liturgical rite, whether it was conferred by anointing or laying-on of hands.

After a course of instruction which might be continued for three years the conduct of the catechumen was examined. If this was satisfactory he then underwent a more extensive preparation which included a daily laying-on of hands. At either Easter or Pentecost, being the two seasons of initiation, an oath of purity of life was taken in the presence of the bishop. On the fifth day of the week the candidates were washed ceremonially and exorcized, and on the following day (Friday) they fasted in preparation for the solemn imposition of hands by the bishop on Saturday. At cock-crow prayer was said over flowing water and the catechumens renounced the devil. The priest anointed them with 'the oil of thanksgiving' blessed by the bishop, to whom he presented them naked. The deacon thereupon went down into the water with each of them and instructed him in a short creed. The priest then baptized him three times after three interrogations, and anointed him again in the name of Jesus

Christ as soon as he emerged from the water before he had dried and dressed. The newly baptized proceeded to the church where the bishop laid his hands on them with the words, 'O Lord God, Who has made them worthy to receive remission of sins through the laver of regeneration by the Holy Spirit, send on them Thy grace that they may serve Thee according to Thy will.' He then poured oil on their heads saying, 'I anoint thee with holy oil in the name of the Lord Father Almighty and Christ Jesus and the Holy Spirit.' Signing them on their fore﹑heads, he kissed them, and they then took their places among the faithful at the Eucharist that followed.

In the East the same general liturgical pattern prevailed.[93] In Syria up to the fifth century, and among the Nestorians to the end of the sixth century, the threefold acts—unction, baptism and communion—were maintained, but the imposition of hands and the anointing preceded the baptism, till the rite was recast to bring it into line with established custom common to East and West.[94] In the East the entire rite was performed by the priest on infants as on adults, the oil of chrism being conse﹑crated by the bishop and then distributed for subsequent use to the local clergy. In the West the Roman tradition restricted the laying﹑on of hands to the bishop, and as dioceses increased in area it became impossible for the complete ritual to be prac﹑tised at the same time, or for the bishop to baptize in person all the catechumens. The function of immersion (i.e. baptism) was then delegated to the parish priests, the bishop retaining only the anointing and laying﹑on of hands (i.e. Confirmation). The priest baptized the infants immediately after birth, but the episcopal rite of Confirmation was deferred until it could be conveniently administered, though it was not until the six﹑teenth century that the two rites were permanently separated. Indeed, up till that time infant Confirmation was still practised, as for instance in the case of Elizabeth I in England, and sometimes it occurs in Spain today.

This twofold initiation essentially corresponded with the mystery ritual of sacramental regeneration. First the neophyte became an *audiens*, and was instructed in the faith and practice of the Divine Society by a catechist who was set apart for this office, like the mystagogue at Eleusis. When infant baptism became the normal custom the catechumenate was necessarily mainly restricted to the diminishing number of pagans who sought admission to the Church, chiefly in countries where the barbarians had settled. With the separation of Confirmation from Baptism in the West, a period of preparation and instruc' tion for the laying'on of hands, usually at the age of reason, has taken the place of the preliminary exercises of the *audiens*. But in their original form they followed the pattern of Mystery ritual installations, held appropriately on Holy Saturday in conjunc' tion with the Annual Festival of Easter in which the death and resurrection of Christ were dramatically celebrated. The candidates were assembled at night, as at Eleusis, having spent Good Friday in fasting, mortification and exorcisms. The creation story was recited in the Vigil ceremonies in the Gela' sian Sacramentary together with the Prophecies to give the candidates a final résumé of the preparation for the redemption of the world in the Old Dispensation and its baptismal sig' nificance. The triple immersion of the catechumens followed, effecting their ritual death and renewal by anointing with the oil of chrism, and symbolized by the change of garments, the bestowal of a new name, and the subsequent gift of the Holy Spirit through the laying'on of hands by the bishop and the last unction. The process of sacramental regeneration was com' pleted by first Communion and admission into 'the promised land', having crossed 'the waters of Jordan' and become new' born citizens of a heavenly country signified by receiving as tokens milk and honey.

Whether or not the grace bestowed by Baptism and Con' firmation is complementary or independent in the two rites is still in debate. When, in the Middle Ages, Confirmation became one of the seven sacraments in Western Christendom, it was assigned Dominical institution by St Thomas Aquinas[95] and the Dominicans, whereas St Bonaventura regarded it as of Apostolic origin.[96] Similarly, opinions have differed about the 'matter' of the sacrament being the chrism unction or the laying-on of hands. Some have held that they both bestowed the grace of the Holy Spirit, while the elimination of the chrism at the Reformation in the Anglican rite left the laying-on of hands the only sign in the administration of the sacrament of Confirmation, reserved as before to the episcopate, and including a ratification of baptismal vows.

F. W. Puller suggested in 1880 that confirmation was a new relation with the Holy Spirit that was established by the imposition of hands giving in a new way his indwelling presence.[97] This was further stressed by A. J. Mason who maintained that while in Baptism forgiveness and regeneration were effected by the Holy Spirit from without, in Confirmation the soul received the gift of the Holy Spirit's personal indwelling within the life of the believer. So regarded, water-baptism was considered incomplete without 'the seal of the Spirit', and, therefore, unless a man had been confirmed no valid Ordination could be conferred upon him.[98] Dix agrees that it is 'the Baptism of the Spirit that seals a man to eternity, for which Baptism in water is only a preliminary'.[99] But it is not denied that the Spirit was operative before it was 'sealed' and made valid by the laying-on of hands.

Against this view A. T. Wirgman in 1897 argued that the Fathers taught that the indwelling primacy of the Spirit was given by water-baptism, and an increase of grace was bestowed by Confirmation.[100] This has been supported by Professor Lampe, who holds that the seal of the Spirit is given exclusively in water-baptism, Confirmation being merely a pledge of the sanctifying and strengthening work of the Spirit to complete the baptismal gifts, symbolizing a commission to an 'apostolate' for service in the mission of the Church to the world.[101] L. S. Thornton, in a somewhat involved attempt to relate baptismal rites to Biblical idioms and typology, maintains a distinction between the action of the Spirit upon the soul and its indwelling personal presence, but also inclines to regard Confirmation as the sealing of Baptism without which the initial initiation is incomplete. It is by no means clear, however, what precisely is the significance and validity of Baptism in this sealing process, or exactly what is the position of those who do not complete the twofold initiation.[102]

Notwithstanding some confusion in the double anointing during Baptism, and the separation of the rites and their con-ferment at different times in Western Christendom, with differences in the administration of Confirmation, the sacra-ment has come to be regarded as conferring an indelible quality on the soul comparable to that of Baptism and Ordination. It is not repeated after it has once been validly performed, except rarely in the Early Church in the case of heretics and the lapsed. Thus, its fundamental importance has been in no doubt, whatever interpretation may have been placed upon the relation of the two rites to each other. The work of the Holy Spirit in Christian theology is so diverse and all-embracing that it can-not be confined rigidly to specific actions and activities, sacra-mental or otherwise, be it in the form of regenerative 'energizing', or of sanctifying grace. This is manifest not only in the relation of Baptism to Confirmation but also to that of the sacrament of Penance, which emerged out of the system of public penance regarded in the third century as a 'second Baptism', though behind it lay the Christian doctrine of reconciliation.

PENANCE

The Doctrine of Reconciliation

In formulating his conception of justification by faith, in con-trast to the Jewish view of salvation attained by individual effort and obedience to the demands of the Law, St Paul con-tended that the process of reconciliation required a change of status in the first instance.[103] Baptism into the Church as the mystical body of Christ was a *sine qua non*, since until this had been accomplished justification, sanctification and commu-nion with the Risen Christ as mediator could not be realized. But once this new status had been acquired it became possible for the reborn to reckon themselves 'to be dead unto sin but alive unto God in Christ Jesus'.[104] This interpretation of the relationship between God and man raised a number of prac-tical and theoretical problems for the Church, since if 'God

was in Christ reconciling the world unto Himself' this reconciliation had to be made effective and actual in the life of the
individual and in that of redeemed humanity as a whole. In
short, a 'ministry of reconciliation' had to be established to
deal with post-baptismal sin and forgiveness.

The power to 'bind and loose' assigned in the Matthaean
tradition to St Peter in a vice-regental capacity and then collectively to the *ecclesia*, appears to have referred to administration
and arbitration rather than to absolution.[105] The commission
to remit and retain sins bestowed by the Risen Christ on Easter
Day on the apostolic company is, according to the Johannine
narrative,[106] represented as the confirmation of the earlier
Matthaean power of the keys to enable them to carry on the
work of salvation in the world by his delegated authority and
reconciling power. It was generally assumed in the Early
Church that this Johannine commission represented a special
endowment of the apostolic ministry prior to the Pentecostal
afflatus on the whole company after the Ascension to effect and
maintain the reconciliation with the Church, and so with God
through Christ of all its members.

The spiritual life of the Christian was thought to begin with
a baptism closely associated with a confession and remission
of sins in which, as St Augustine said, 'the peace given by the
Church has reconciliation with God connected with it, and
sin is remitted through it, inasmuch as by its force the Holy
Ghost is poured into the soul, through whom is all justification and grace.'[107] As this initiatory rite took shape,
confession and absolution were brought into juxtaposition, together with the laying-on of hands conveying the charismatic
gift to form a whole in the process of rebirth,[108] so that those
who had been cleansed, sanctified and fortified might live in
a state of grace. But this raised a practical difficulty, since in
fact those who had been initiated into the Body of Christ were
capable of contracting actual sin. Therefore, ways had to be
found of securing reconciliation with the Church for the post-
baptismal offender who, by reason of his misdeeds, was in
danger of being excluded from communion with the faithful.

To reinstate the erring and lapsed a penitential discipline was devised which constituted the nucleus of the penitential rites of the Church. Those who voluntarily, or under threat of ex/ communication, applied to the bishop for public penance having undergone their period and course of prayer, fasting and alms/giving, were reconciled and rejoined the congregation of the faithful as a normal procedure. Very occasionally, however, certain deadly sins (e.g. adultery, apostasy and homicide), like the blasphemy against the Holy Ghost,[109] incurred excom/ munication and required special treatment before reconciliation could be attained.

Penitential Exercises and Rites

Since deadly sins, like lapses into paganism during the perse/ cutions, were of a public character, they demanded public penance, graded according to their gravity if they were to be followed eventually by reconciliation. This involved con/ fession followed by penitential exercises administered under episcopal authority, or in the East by a special penitentiary appointed by the bishop. The discipline known as *exomologesis* included fasting, prostration, the wearing of sackcloth, lying in ashes, mortification in food and drink, and exclusion from the sacraments. If the sin involved public scandal the sinner, as St Augustine declared, should do penance 'in the sight of many even of the people at large'.[110] But it rested with the confessor to determine whether or not the penance should be publicly performed and the confession published, though at first even private sins demanded some form of public penance. The pro/ cedure followed much the same threefold division as the initia/ tion rite: (1) admission to the status of a penitent; (2) the penitential period and its exercises; (3) reconciliation (i.e. re/ admission into the congregation of the faithful and release from excommunication). Each stage had its own liturgical rite associated with the Ash Wednesday penitential ceremonies and those of Maundy Thursday.[111]

That confession to a priest in private was the normal prac/ tice is suggested by the counsel of Origen urging penitents to consider the character of the priest to whom they should show their sin and seek the remedy.[112] Having made the choice the first duty was to confess to the priest or bishop in private and leave it to him to decide the subsequent procedure. In the case of an adulteress who had made confession through piety, as St Basil states, to avoid the matter becoming public knowledge she should be admitted to the Eucharist but debarred from receiving Communion.[113] In the West, Leo the Great appealed to the 'Apostolic rule' against 'the recitation of the nature of particular sins in a written statement (*libellus*)', maintaining that 'it sufficed that the accusation of conscience be indicated to the priests alone in secret confession'.[114]

Confession and Absolution

This ordinance, issued in 461, marks the end of public confession in the Western Church, and in the East the office of *poenitentarius* already had been abolished by Nestorius in 390 because of the scandal occasioned by the practice. The four 'stations', or grades of penitents—'weepers' stationed outside the church; 'hearers' in the narthex; 'prostrators' between the door and the chancel or ambo; and 'bystanders' present at the liturgy awaiting restoration to the status of a communicant—soon fell into abeyance. Penitents tended to be treated as catechumens, the priest assigning to them the penitential exercises required,[115] administered very largely with the aid of the Penitential Books of Celtic origin ascribed to St Patrick in the fifth century.

In the Middle Ages Penance consisted generally of fasts, continence, flagellations, and pilgrimages to the Holy Land or to the shrine of St James at Santiago de Compostella in Spain, or of equipping a soldier to go on a Crusade. As pilgrimage and similar penances were not always reasonably possible a system of commutation grew up in the form of payments of money to cover the penitential discipline by redemption. This led to abuses, and the familiar scandals connected with the traffic in indulgences by 'alms-gatherers', and the treasury of merit, until they were finally abolished, and the doctrine reformulated at the Council of Trent in 1551.[116] As the system of public penance gave place to the practice of private confession, absolution alone was regarded as effecting the forgiveness of sins. Thus, the Fourth Lateran Council in 1215 imposed on every Christian in the West who had reached maturity the obligation to confess to a priest at least once a year at Eastertide, and to fulfil the penance imposed by the confessor.

Long before this requirement was enjoined on all the faithful, recourse to the sacrament of Penance had been widely adopted by the devout, largely under Celtic and AngloSaxon influences where the custom first arose in certain Celtic monasteries, and after the cessation of the rigorist attitude to postbaptismal sin and the system of graded penances it came into general use. Then absolution followed immediately upon a good confession instead of being delayed until the penance had been fulfilled, and it assumed a more authoritative form. The priest pronounced the forgiveness of the sin confessed with the words *ego auctoritate te absolvo*, imparted with the sign of the cross and the invocation of the Holy Trinity. The exercise of this 'ministry of reconciliation' could only be undertaken by the delegated authority, or 'faculty', of the diocesan bishop or the superior of a Religious Order. The general commission to absolve sins given at ordination to the priesthood bestowed sacramental power (*potestas sacramentalis*) to declare divine forgiveness and reconciliation on behalf of the Church, but for regular and valid absolution to be given episcopal jurisdiction (or its monastic equivalent) must first be conferred upon the priest by institution to a benefice or licence (faculty) to minister in this capacity. And when this had been granted, certain sins in 'reserved cases' might have to be submitted to a higher tribunal and absolved only by the bishop, or some other superior authority to whom a *specialis facultas* had been issued.[117]

Penance during and after the Reformation

The valid administration of the sacrament of Penance requires both 'the power of the keys' and internal jurisdiction, either 'ordinary' or 'delegated'. It presupposes the Catholic constitution of the Church as the ultimate authority in the pro, cess of 'binding' and 'loosing', When this conception of divine forgiveness and reconciliation was repudiated by the Protestant Reformers in the sixteenth century, the sacrament of Penance and the penitential system were abandoned as having no right, ful place and function in the 'reformed faith'. Luther took his stand against the practice of indulgences, so closely associated with the principle of vicarious satisfaction for the penalties attached to sin. He asserted that justification was acquired by the sinner surrendering himself wholly and unconditionally to Christ and the merits of his sacrificial death, quite apart from the atoning power of his Mystical Body the Church. Justifying faith and the regenerative ministry of the Word alone sufficed though voluntary private confession survived for a time in Lutheranism as a pious custom. Divorced from efficacious sacramental absolution it soon died out and was replaced by a service of public confession and promise of amendment as a preparation for Communion. Zwingli instituted a court of discipline for the exclusion of unworthy communicants from the Lord's Supper, leaving formal excommunication to the State. In Geneva, where Calvin in conjunction with the State maintained a rigid discipline over the moral and religious con, duct of households within its domain, private confession was permitted only for the purpose of consultation in a Consistory Court.

The Puritans in England and the Presbyterians in Scotland adopted a similar attitude to penitential discipline, but the Acts of Uniformity between 1549 and 1762 were abortive attempts to enforce a common faith and worship rather than to impose penalties on sinners and the lapsed. Public Penance survived in the Commination drawn up in 1549 for use on Ash Wed, nesday in place of the medieval 'Greater Excommunication' at the beginning of Advent, Lent, on Trinity Sunday and within the octave of the Assumption. The Caroline divines urged its enforcement in the case of 'open and notorious evil livers' and Pepys records a declaration of penitence of a man who had undergone 'the Church's censure for his wicked life' which he witnessed on July 16, 1665. In 1686 a verger of Durham Cathedral did public penance for drunkenness, and several similar cases are on record in the eighteenth century.[118]

As regards the sacrament of Penance, the vesting of the Anglican priesthood with the power of absolution at their ordination was retained in the Book of Common Prayer from 1549 onwards where the Johannine commission was included in the Edwardian Ordinal and its successors. Cranmer in his injunctions in 1538 recognized private confession as a regular part of the sacramental discipline of the Church, and although he thought the practice was not enjoined in Scripture, he recommended those with troubled consciences to seek 'consolation, counsel and absolution *singulatim a sacerdote*'. According to the pamphlet *Recontaeyans*, published privately from a manuscript in the Bibliothèque Nationale in Paris, found among the Harpfield papers, he made his confession to a priest on the morning of his execution. In the Order for the Visitation of the Sick, based on that in the Sarum Manual, a rubric was inserted requiring the priest to urge the sick person to make a special confession if his conscience was troubled by any weighty matter, and supplying an absolution in the indicative form—'by his authority committed to me I absolve thee from all thy sins, in the name of the Father, and of the Son and of the Holy Ghost'.

This formula was not adopted until the eleventh century, and then it only gradually replaced the earlier precatory form, praying that God would absolve the penitent. Since it was incorporated in the Anglican office there can be little doubt that the purpose was to exercise the sacrament of Penance in the normal medieval manner. Stress has always, however, been laid on the voluntary nature of auricular confession in the Church of England. Since the Reformation it has never been obligatory. Nevertheless, the sacrament appears to have been widely used both before and after the Restoration in 1660. Whitgift (1530–1604) regarded the giving of absolution as 'the principal duty of a minister'[119] and Hooker (1554–1600) maintained that 'confession to man, not to God only' is 'both lawful and behoveful for God's people',[120] and himself received absolution and the Viaticum on the day before his death,[121] as did Charles I before his execution. In the post-Restoration period the practice was continued, especially among the Caroline divines and the Non-jurors.[122] In the eighteenth century it lingered on, but with the decline in sacramental religion absolution lost much of its earlier significance, and by the beginning of the nineteenth century it had ceased to be an integral part of the Anglican tradition. Its revival by the Tractarians after 1833 met with strenuous opposition and misrepresentation[123] in spite of its having been so firmly embedded in the Prayer Book and in the official formularies, as well as in the teaching and practice of many of the most eminent Anglican divines. However, since it meets a very real human need, in the intervening period resort to the sacrament of Penance has been increasingly exercised and dispensed under delegated episcopal jurisdiction, in accordance with the provisions of Canon Law, by confessors properly trained and duly qualified in 'the direction of souls' as in the rest of Catholic Christendom.

MARRIAGE

Christ's teaching about Matrimony

In the domestic domain the natural institution of marriage was raised to the level of a sacrament by Christ and the Church when it was claimed to have been restored to its original place in the divine ordering of the family and society. On the basis of monogamy as the established form of marriage in the Roman Empire and the general rule in Judaism at the beginning of the Christian era, Jesus affirmed the divine origin and indissolubility of the union, abrogating the Deuteronomic toleration of divorce as a concession displeasing to God and man.[124] From the beginning, he declared, man and woman had been joined together by divine ordinance in an indissoluble monogamous 'one-flesh' relationship,[125] and only because of 'the hardness of men's hearts' had the Mosaic legislation departed from this primeval condition. The Matthaean exceptive clause (Matt.

xix, 9) permitting divorce and remarriage in the case of adul/
tery, in accordance with the practice of the Rabbinic School of
Shammai, very likely represents a later interpolation introduced
by the Jewish section of the Christian community, perhaps in
Antioch about A.D. 80, as otherwise the adherence of Jesus to
the Shammaite position would have hardly caused great sur/
prise. St Paul leaves no room for doubt about his adherence to
the rigorist Marcan view,[126] and he made the nuptial bond un/
equivocally the symbol of the mystical union of Christ with
the Church.[127]

The Pauline Nuptial Union

Behind this imagery lay the ancient conception of the sacred
marriage of heaven and earth so familiar in the Graeco/oriental
Mystery cults and in agrarian fertility ritual everywhere. St Paul
likened the husband to the soul and the wife to the body very
much as in the Ancient Near East the creative process was
represented as the union of the life/giving sky and the fertilized
earth personified in the connubium of the king and queen.[128]
The New Covenant in the Pauline analogy was interpreted as
a spiritual union between Christ as the heavenly bridegroom
and the Church as his earthly spouse. As the baptized collec/
tively were 'the body of Christ and severally members there/
of',[129] so the husband and wife were sacramentally united in
an indissoluble nuptial relationship for the generation of life
and the continuance of the human race. To meet the require/
ments of the human situation this involves the psycho/
physical bond of permanent wedlock in an enduring biological,
emotional, sexual and spiritual association vital for the pro/
creation, nurture and training of children.

In making the matrimonial union symbolic of this mystical
relationship of Christ and the Church with the duty of love
in the foremost place,[130] St Paul went beyond the Jewish
imagery based on the covenant between Israel and Yahweh
since it was a permanent and indissoluble sacramental bond
within a sacred community like the ἱερός γάμος. Nevertheless,
the introduction of the so/called 'Pauline privilege' permitting

a baptized Christian to dissolve a marriage with a pagan part‑
ner when the unbelieving spouse refuses 'to abide' with the
Christian partner, cut across the principle of the indissolubility
of marriage, and had serious effects when pagans flocked into
the Church in the fourth century. The intention of the Apostle
appears to have been to encourage the convert to continue the
original marriage,[131] and, as St Augustine maintained, to
labour for the conversion of the partner.[132] But opinion among
the Fathers and the decrees of Councils have been no more
clear and conclusive than the Pauline ambiguous language,
though after the thirteenth century the 'Privilege' was brought
into Canon Law by Innocent III.[133]

The Christian Nuptial Rite

Although the Church could not exercise its jurisdiction over
the unbaptized, the West adopted a more rigorist attitude than
the East in its efforts to maintain the stability of marriage as a
natural institution and to give it a sacramental status for the
baptized. In essence the nuptial union always has been in the
nature of a contract between two individuals, and provided it
had been contracted monogamously before conversion to
Christianity it could be elevated to the level of the Christian
sacrament by the baptism of the two parties. But as a Divine
Society the Church devised its own nuptial ceremonial to
give expression to its conception of the ordinance. It added to
the Roman *Sponsalia* (betrothing) a Christian benediction, and
the eucharistic oblation to hallow the alliance.[134] Ignatius
affirmed that it behoved Christian men and women 'to form
their union with the approval and blessing of the bishop, that
it might be according to God'.[135] The betrothal was usually
supplemented by the plighting of the troth (*nuptiae*), the
delivery of the pledges (*subarrhatio arrhae*), and the dowry,
accompanied by the veiling of the bride, the crowning, the
giving of the ring, and the handing over of the bride to the
bridegroom *in facie Ecclesiae*, followed by the benediction and
the Nuptial Mass with the Communion of the contracting
parties.

In this way the secular *Sponsalia* was transformed into *Matri-monium* as a sacramental ordinance, though for some time the betrothal and the nuptial rite continued to be distinct obser-vances, the one a civil responsibility, the other an ecclesiastical consecration to the marriage state. This being effected by the solemn benediction (*velatio nuptialis*) during the Mass, it could only be given once. It was not repeated at a second marriage nor bestowed on a mixed marriage. Occasionally it was deferred until the day after the first bridal night when the union had been consummated. Since this nuptial rite was essentially a sacrament the presence of a priest at its solemniza-tion was required. Charlemagne, in fact, enjoined that without a sacerdotal blessing no marriage should be regarded as valid.[136] Even betrothal was made by the Church, though not in a sacred building (i.e. usually in the home), until the cere-monies were incorporated in the religious service as an integral part of the Nuptial Mass. But the espousals were then per-formed before the door of the church or in the narthex, as directed, for example, in the Sarum *Ordo faciendum*.

Sponsalia

When the wedding rites became a composite sacramental ordinance the several adjuncts acquired their own symbolism. The ring (*annulus pronubus*), originally a royal ornament indica-tive of the union of the sacral king with his kingdom, like that of the bishop with his see, was associated with the *arrhae* given in the *Sponsalia* as a pledge of the contract.[137] Later it became the sign of constancy, mutual trust and intimate vision; a seal of faith and a token of the vow and covenant made between them. The joining of hands typified the sacramental union of the bride and bridegroom. The giving of gold and silver to the bride was a relic of the dowry, and earlier of the life-giving qualities with which gold was associated. The crowning, as in the coronation rite, signified the victorious transition to the married state and all that it involved.[138] In the West it was replaced by the veiling of the bride, and from being a protec-tion against the evil eye it became a symbol of constancy and of

dedication in an indissoluble sacramental union. The exchange of consent, or marriage contract, belonged originally to
the betrothal preliminaries rather than to the actual solemniza-
tion of the alliance, but it is the essential element inasmuch as
it is the sole requirement for a valid marriage. The presence of
a priest at the rite has been required to prevent clandestine
unions since the betrothal became an integral part of the wedding ceremony. The priest is also required to say the Nuptial
Mass and give the special blessing and consent of the Church
to the marriage and its ratification.[139]

The Contract and its Permanence

Although the contracting parties 'marry themselves' by their
mutual consent, Holy Matrimony has been regarded as a
sacramental ordinance by virtue of the grace given and received
to render the vinculum indissoluble, and to enable them to fulfil its purposes and ends, as summed up for example in the
preface to the rite in the English Book of Common Prayer. In
spite of the Henrician breach with the Holy See over the king's
sordid divorce proceedings, the indissoluble sacramental nature
of marriage was not called in question in England, and its
canonical regulation remained singularly unchanged after the
Reformation, despite the facilities for divorce in vogue among the
Continental Reformers. In the Anglican Canons of 1604 divorce
a vinculo was forbidden, and this enactment has been retained
in Canonical legislation ever since, notwithstanding the introduction of civil marriage and the Matrimonial Causes Act in
1857.

HOLY ORDERS

The Apostolic Ministry

The Apostolic ministry like marriage is a sacramental state or
vocation. It is divinely ordained and conferred, when it is
regarded as a duly commissioned succession deriving its
authority and functions from Christ through his apostles.[140]
Whatever view may be taken about the highly controversial
problem of the episcopal succession during the first two

centuries of the Church,[141] the laying-on of hands with prayer appears to have been the normal method of appointment for the exercise of ministerial functions from apostolic times.[142] This involved the bestowal of a special charismatic endowment whether or not any distinction was made between a 'local' or a settled ministry and an itinerant charismatic ministry,[143] or of an 'essential' and 'dependent' ministry, as Kirk and his colla-borators suggest.

The Development of Holy Orders

In the Apostolic Church the sacred ministry took shape under the influence of the synagogal pattern from which emerged a sacerdotal hierarchy corresponding to the Judaic priesthood but centred upon the eucharistic oblation. This required, as it developed, an increasing number of Minor Orders which by the third century consisted of sub-deacons, acolytes, exorcists, lectors and door-keepers, with diversities of functions.[144] Ex-cept in the case of the sub-deacons, these minor offices were conferred without the imposition of hands and so they have been regarded as sacramentals rather than as a true sacramental status, though since the thirteenth century the sub-diaconate became a Major Order derived from the diaconate, with a clerical status. Varying degrees of sacramental power have been thought to be bestowed in Holy Orders according to the nature and requirements of the diaconate, the priesthood, and the episcopate, and the subordinate offices associated with them.

When the threefold ministry was definitely established in the second century the bishop retained the plenitude of apos-tolic sacramental power and authority, and he was the ordinary minister of Holy Orders and Confirmation as well as the president of the Eucharist and of the presbyterate. Occasionally a priest was authorized to ordain as an episcopal deputy,[145] but this was soon allowed in the West only by special papal permission. From the eighth century Abbots within their monasteries gave the tonsure[146] as the form of admission to the clerical state, as well as Minor Orders, and this indult has been widely exercised from time to time in cases of special need.

The Ordination Rite

Sacramental power to ordain, confirm, absolve, consecrate and bless can be given, taken away, or suspended for sufficient reason, but this does not effect the indelible character of the Major Orders. Once the quality and status have been con-ferred a permanent imprint, it is held, is left on the soul so that ordination to the same office cannot be repeated. Below the level of the sub-diaconate the functions of the Minor Orders have now become combined or laicized altogether, and the diaconate has been made a preparation for the priesthood with a graded outpouring of sacramental grace appropriate to each order as it is attained and its particular duties specified and symbolized in the rite. In the case of the diaconate the bishop alone lays his hands on the candidates because they were ordained originally to the service of the bishop, as Hippolytus affirmed. At the ordination of priests, on the other hand, after the ordinands have been anointed, vested, endowed with power to absolve sinners and offer the Holy Sacrifice, symbolized by the presentation of the chalice and paten, the priests as well as the bishop have laid their hands on them since the thirteenth century. Then the newly ordained priests concelebrate with the bishop, reciting with him the Canon of the Mass.[147] As these sacerdotal powers can only be exercised under episcopal authority and jurisdiction the ordinands are required to swear allegiance to the bishop, placing their hands between his as their liege lord.

The Consecration of Bishops

A bishop has been consecrated according to ancient custom by the laying-on of the hands of the Metropolitan with two other members of the episcopate as conconsecrators, after having been duly elected either by the Pope,[148] or in non-papal jurisdic-tions by the Dean and Chapter of the cathedral of the dio-cese.[149] In the Gallican rite, anointing with the oil of chrism was introduced while the *Veni Creator* was sung, an open book of the Gospels being placed on the shoulders of the bishop-elect during the consecration prayer. This ancient practice became a permanent feature when the Gallican and Roman pontificals were fused,[150] and further ceremonies were added which included the anointing of the hands with chrism, the presentation of the episcopal insignia: the pastoral staff, the ring, and later, after the blessing at the end of the Mass, the mitre and the gloves. At the Offertory two loaves, two casks of wine and two large wax candles were given to the consecrating bishop. Enthronement followed; this has now become a separate ceremony when the newly consecrated diocesan is installed in his cathedral, and takes possession of the see. In the English Pontificals there is a good deal of variation and duplication in the later ceremonies. In the first Edwardian rite (1549) the unctions were omitted and the delivery of the instruments was confined to the pastoral staff and the laying of the Bible upon the neck.

THE LAST RITES

Anointing of the sick and dying as the last initiatory rite conforms to the general pattern of the sacramental principle. From birth to death the series of *rites de passage* has been celebrated from time before memory to effect the transition from one state of life to the next, comparable to the succession of the seasons in nature exemplifying the process of growth, decline and renewal. All life is in a state of flux, 'never continuing in one stay'; a perpetual dying to be born again. So at birth, adolescence, marriage and death, as at seed-time and spring, summer and harvest, sacramental rites have been required to secure supernatural power and spiritual grace to ensure divine protection and aid against the forces of evil rampant, as it has been believed, at these critical junctures, and to obtain a fresh outpouring and renewal of life and power.

The Anointing of the Sick

At no time has this been more essential than at the final transition and dissolution. Death is the gateway to the after-life; and as the new-born babe has had to be reborn in this world by baptismal regeneration and initiation, so the departing soul requires *rites de passage* through the dark and dangerous 'valley of the shadow of death' to enable it to be securely launched on its new career in the fuller life beyond the grave. In its Christian setting this transitional sacramental ritual has consisted in anointing with episcopally consecrated oil the sick and dying, together with prayer and absolution. In the New Testament reference is made to the practice in relation to the sick,[151] and in the Early Church it was continued, becoming increasingly prominent in and after the fifth century.[152] It was not until the eighth and ninth centuries that it became a definitely established custom, and in the twelfth century it was included in the seven sacraments by Peter Lombard under the title *unctio extrema*, being the last of the three anointings administered at the hour of death.

Extreme Unction

In Eastern Christendom it has never been confined to those *in extremis*, nor has the blessing of the oil by a bishop been required. Indeed, in the Middle Ages, as in former times, this episcopal requirement was not in vogue, and the validity of the sacrament can hardly be made to depend upon it. Nor should it be confined exclusively to the dying if ancient precedent is to be followed, since for the first seven centuries at least it was administered for 'the health of soul and body'. When it became essentially the sacrament of the dying—the first stage in the last *rite de passage*—the penitential character of the rite was stressed as part of the process of expelling and keeping at bay the forces of evil, which were so dominant on this occasion, both in the background of the ritual, and in the thought of the later Middle Ages. Confession made and absolution given, the anointing and laying-on of hands followed, and then Communion, to provide strength for the passage into the eternal world. This completed the *Viaticum*, fortifying the soul against the assaults of the Devil. Eventually the anointing tended to be placed after the Communion of the sick on the assumption that it was the final initiation into the next life, and should only be administered when recovery was thought to be impossible. If by any chance death did not ensue the rite could not be repeated in the same illness though the anointing and Communion might be given daily for a week in the same illness. The earlier sequence has now been restored,[150] and restoration to health still underlies the three closing prayers.

In the English Prayer Book of 1549 unction was retained in a simplified form, but only as an optional addition to the rite. The prayer requested the healing of body and mind, and forgiveness and strengthening of the soul. The omission of any provision for the sacrament in the 1552 and 1662 Office of the Visitation and Communion of the Sick has now been supplied by the restoration of unction in the Scottish, American and South African Prayer Books, and in a special form issued by the Convocations of Canterbury and York in 1935, following the earlier use. The Council of Trent, on the other hand, reaffirmed the medieval doctrine of the last of the seven sacraments.

NOTES

CHAPTER I

1. Pliny, Bk. X, xcvi.
2. Tertullian, *Ad Martyres*, 3.
3. *Adv. Nationes*, i, 3.
4. *Summa Theol.*, q.v., lx, art. 1. *IV. Sent.*, i, 1, 5.
5. Rom. i, 20.
6. *The Christian Sacraments*, 1925, p. 45.
7. *Religion of the Semites*, 3rd ed., 1927, pp. 245 ff., 345 ff.
8. Cf. Spencer and Gillen, *Native Tribes of Central Australia*, 1938, pp. 167 ff.; Frazer, *Totemism and Exogamy*, 1910, vol. iv, p. 231.
9. Gen. xxxiii, 19; xxxiv, 2–26; xxxvi, 20–30; Jud. ix, 28; Jos. xxiv, 26.
10. Nöldeke, *Die altestamentliche Litteratur*, Leipzig, 1868, p. 40; Lagrange, *Études sur les religions sémitiques*, 1903, chap. vii.
11. 'Essai sur la nature et fonction du sacrifice', *L'Année Sociologique*, 1898, ii, 29 ff.
12. Durkheim, *Elementary Forms of the Religious Life*, 1915, pp. 327 ff.; Spencer and Gillen, *Native Tribes of Central Australia*, pp. 193 ff.
13. Spencer and Gillen, pp. 170 ff.; *The Arunta*, 1927, vol. i, pp. 148 ff.
14. *Native Tribes of Central Australia*, pp. 181 ff.
15. *Op. cit.*, pp. 184 ff.
16. Malinowski, in *Science, Religion and Reality*, 1927, p. 42.
17. Breuil, *La Caverne d'Altamira*, Monaco, 1909, p. 139.
18. Breuil, *Four Hundred Centuries of Cave Art*, Montignac, 1952, pp. 38 ff.
19. Lalanne and Breuil, *L'Anthrop.*, xxii, 1911, pp. 257 ff.; xxiii, 1912, pp. 129 ff.; cf. Passemard, *Les statuettes féminines dites Vénus stéatopyges*, Nîmes, 1938, pp. 121 f.
20. Capitan, *Les Combarelles aux Eyzies*, 1924, pl. vi.
21. Begöuen, *L'Anthrop.*, xxiii, 1912, pp. 657 ff.
22. Breuil, *Four Hundred Centuries of Cave Art*, p. 176; cf. Begöuen, *Antiquity*, iii, 1929, p. 12.
23. James, *Origins of Sacrifice*, 1932, p. 33.
24. *Essai historique sur le sacrifice*, 1920, p. 22.
25. Decle, *Three Years in Savage Africa*, 1898, p. 157.
26. G. Gouldsbury and C. H. Sheane, *The Great Plateau.*
27. Ellis, of *Northern Rhodesia*, 1911, pp. 294 ff.; *Tshi-speaking Peoples*, 1887, pp. 147 f.
28. J. Batchelor, *The Ainu and their Folklore*, 1901, pp. 204 ff., 483 ff.
29. J. de Acosta, *Natural and Moral History of the Indies*, Hakluyt Society, London, 1880, vol. ii, Bk. v, ch. 24, pp. 356 ff.

30. Bancroft, *Native Races of the Pacific States*, 1875–76, vol. iii, pp. 297 ff.; Brasseur de Bourbourg, *Histoire des nations civilisées du Mexique et de L'Amérique Centrale*, Paris, 1857–59, iii, pp. 531 ff.

31. Bancroft, *op. cit.*, p. 316; Brasseur de Bourbourg, *op. cit.*, p. 535.

32. J. R. Swanton, *23rd Bulletin Bureau of American Ethnology*, Washington, 1911, pp. 115 ff.

33. F. C. Speck, *Ethnology of the Yuki Indians*, Philadelphia, 1909, pp. 86 ff.

34. W. Mannhardt, *Mythologische Forschungen*, Strassburg, 1884, p. 317.

35. *Op. cit.*, p. 136.

36. Cabo, *Historia del nuevo mundo*, Sevilla, 1895, iv, 25 ff.

37. J. G. Campbell, *Superstitions of the Highlands and Islands of Scotland*, Glasgow, 1900, pp. 243 ff.

38. Grönbech, in *Chantepie*, iii, 3.

CHAPTER II

1. *P.T.*, 316–18.

2. Cf. Gardner, *J.E.A.*, ii, 1915, pp. 122 ff.; xxxi, 1945, p. 24; xxxix, 1953, p. 23; Frankfort, *Kingship and the Gods*, Chicago, 1948, pp. 101 ff.

3. Sethe, *Dramatische Texte zu altaegyptischen Mysterienspielen*, Leipzig, 1928, i, ii.

4. Blackman, *Journal of Manchester Egyptian and Oriental Society*, 1918–19, pp. 30 ff.; Moret, *Le rituel du culte divin journalier en Egypte*, Paris, 1902, pp. 5 f.

5. Erman, *Handbook of Egyptian Religion*, 1907, pp. 46 f.

6. Blackman, *Recueil de Travaux*, vol. xxxix, pp. 67, 71; *P.T.*, 222.

7. *Zeitschrift für Aegyptische Sprache und Altertumskunde*, Leipzig, 1884, p. 38.

8. Budge, *The Gods of the Egyptians*, 1904, vol. ii, p. 216.

9. Pausanias, x, 32, 18; Budge, *Osiris and the Egyptian Resurrection*, 1911, vol. ii, p. 278.

10. Davies and Gardiner, *The Tomb of Amenemhet*, 1915, pp. 79 ff.

11. Laws of Manu, vii, 3–7; ix, 303–11; cf. v, 96.

12. *Rig-Veda*, iv, 42.

13. *Satapatha Brahmana*, v, 1, 1, 2; iii, 2, 2, 4.

14. *Op. cit.*, vi, 5, i ff.; i, 9, 2, 29.

15. *Op. cit.*, vi, 1, 1, 7.

16. Hocart, *Kingship*, Oxford, 1927, p. 115.

17. *Sat. Brah.*, x, 6, 4, 1.

18. *Sat. Brah.*, x, 5, 4, 16.

19. *Brhad. Upan.*, I, i, ii; iv, 10; III, ix, 6, 21.

20. *Eastern Religions and Western Thought*, Oxford, 1939, pp. 357 ff.

21. *Op. cit.*, p. 358.

22. 2 Kings, xviii, 1–8; 2 Kings, xxii, 8 ff.

23. 2 Sam., viii, 18; 1 Kings, iv, 5; Jud. xvii, 5; 1 Sam., vii, 1.
24. Ex. xxxiii, 11; Gen. xlix, 5–7; J. T. Meek, *Hebrew Origins*, 1950, pp. 121 ff.; Waterman, *J.A.O.S.*, lvii, 1937, pp. 375 ff.; *American Journal of Semitic Languages and Literature*, lv, 1938, pp. 25 f.; lvi, 1939, pp. 113 ff.; E. B. Gray, *Sacrifice in the Old Testament*, Oxford, 1925, pp. 181 ff., 244 f.
25. Num. xii, xvi–xviii.
26. Num. xviii, 2–7; xxv, 11–13; Lev. viii; 1 Chron. xxiv, 3.
27. Ezek. xliv, 10 ff.
28. Mowinckel, *Psalmenstudien*, vol. iii, Kristiana, 1924, p. 17; Johnson, *The Cultic Prophet in Ancient Israel*, Cardiff, 1944, pp. 59 f.; M. Weber, *Ancient Judaism*, Illinois, 1952, pp. 169 ff.
29. Ezek. xliv, 17 ff.; xlvi.
30. Mal. i, 6–8, 12–14; ii, 10, 13; iii, 1–12.
31. Ps. xliii, 5; lxxxiv; cxxii; li, 7, 10; xl, 7–12; lxix, 31 f.; cxli, 2.
32. Ber., 55a; Suk., 55 b; *Midrash Lev.*, 16, 2; Yoma, 19 a.
33. Mark xiii, 2; John iv, 20 ff.
34. Matt. ix, 13; xii, 7; Hos. vi, 6.
35. Matt. xxvi, 17 ff.; Mark xiv, 12 ff.
36. Heb. v, 5 ff., 24; viii, 1; ix, 25 f.; Rev. xiii, 8; Rom. v, 8.
37. Heb. vii, 25; x.
38. Heb., ix, 23; cf. vi, 5.
39. Heb. iv, 3.
40. Heb. viii, xi.
41. Heb. ix, 12.
42. Acts xi, 30; xiii, 23; xv, 22; xx, 17 f.; Phil. i, 1; Titus, i, 5.
43. Clement, 44; Hippolytus, *Apos. Trad.*, iii, 4; ix, 11; Ignatius, *Smyrn.*, 8.
44. Cf. Chap. I; cf. *Apostolic Constitutions*, viii, xxiv, 43 f.; *Older Didascalia*, ii, 57; Ignatius, *Magn.*, vi, 1; *Smyrn.*, viii, 1–2; G. Dix, *The Apostolic Ministry*, 1946, pp. 246 (ed. K. E. Kirk).
45. *Didascalia, Apostol.*, xxvi, 4–8, ed. R. E. Connolly, 1929, pp. 80 f.
46. *Dogmengeschichte*, 4th ed., vol. ii, p. 103.

CHAPTER III

1. Chap. I, p. 22.
2. Gen. xxxv, 18; 2 Sam. i, 9; 1 Kings xvii, 21; 2 Kings iv, 34; Job xl, 19; Cant. v, 6.
3. Lev. xvii, 11.
4. Cf. Chap. I, p. 18.
5. Ex. xxiv, 6–8.
6. Gen. xxxi, 54; Ex. xxiv, 11; Lev. ii, 13; Num. xviii, 19.
7. C. Trumbull, *The Blood Covenant*, 1887.

8. Hewitt, *Handbook of American Indians North of Mexico*, ii, 790.

9. L. von Steinen, *Unter den Naturvölkern Zentral-Brasiliens*, Berlin, 1894, p. 201; cf. E. F. Im Thurn, *Among the Indians of Guiana*, 1885, pp. 350 ff.

10. *Les fonctions dans les Sociétés Inférieures*, Paris, 1915; *La Mentalité primitive*, 1921; *L'Expérience mystique et les symboles chez les primitifs*, 1938.

11. Seligman, *Cult of the Nyakang and the Divine Kings of the Shilluk*, Khartoum, 1911, p. 222; *The Pagan Tribes of the Nilotic Sudan*, 1932, pp. 90 ff.

12. *The Divine Kingship of the Shilluk of the Nilotic Sudan*, Cambridge, 1948, p. 21.

13. O. S. Oyler, *Sudan Notes and Records*, 1920, pp. 296 ff.

14. *Op. cit.*, p. 18.

15. Cf. P. Munro, *Sudan Notes and Records*, 1918, pp. 147 ff.; Howell and Thompson, *ibid.*, 1946, pp. 41 ff.

16. Zimmern, *Der Alte Orient*, xxv, 1926, p. 12.

17. Pallis, *The Babylonian Akitu Festival*, 1926, p. 198.

18. Moret, *Du caractère religieux de la royauté Pharaonique*, Paris, 1902, pp. 256 ff.; Murray, *Ancient Egypt*, ii, 1906, p. 185.

19. Seligman, *Egypt and Negro Africa*, p. 2; Petrie, *Researches in Sinai*, 1906, p. 185.

20. Frankfort, *Kingship and the Gods*, pp. 79 ff.; A. E. Gardiner, *J.E.A.*, ii, 1925, pp. 124 f.; Moret, *op. cit.*, p. 105.

21. Breasted, *Development of Religion and Thought in Ancient Egypt*, 1914, p. 39; Frazer, *G.B.*, vol. vi, pp. 153 ff.; Petrie, *op. cit.*, pp. 186 ff.; Seligman, *op. cit.*, p. 2; Mercer, *Religion of Ancient Egypt*, 1945, pp. 122, 362 f.

22. *J.E.A.*, xxviii, 1942, p. 71; cf. Gardiner, *op. cit.*, p. 71.

23. Moret, *Mystères Egyptiens*, Paris, 1913, pp. 187 ff.

24. Moret, *Royauté*, p. 256.

25. Herodotus, 7, 197, 1; Apollodorus and Hyginus, i, 9 ff.

26. Plutarch, *Quaest. Graec*, 38; Ovid, *Metam.*, iv, 1 ff.

27. Ex. xiii, 13; xxii, 20–2; xxxiv, 19.

28. *G.B.*, pt. iv, p. 176.

29. Ex. xxxiv, 19 f.; xiii, 12 f.

30. 1 Sam. xiv, 25.

31. Jud. xi, 30 ff.

32. 2 Kings xvi, 3; xxi, 6; cf. xvii, 17.

33. Deut. xviii, 10; Lev. xviii, 21; xx, 2–4; 2 Kings xxiii, 10; xxxii, 35.

34. Ezek. xxiii, 29, 37 ff.; cf. Jer. xii, 31; xix, 51.

35. Gen. xxii, 1–14.

36. Ezek. xxxiv, 24; xxxvii, 25; Mic. v, 2; Zech. vi, 9 ff.; Haggai, ii, 23 f.

37. Cf. Rowley, *The Servant of the Lord*, 1952, pp. 61 ff.

38. Chap. IV, pp. 114 ff; cf. Snaith, *Studies in Old Testament Prophecy*, 1950, p. 191.

39. Mark viii, 31–3; Matt. xvi, 21–3.

40. Matt. xxvii, 27 ff.; Mark xv, 15 ff.

41. Dio Chrysostom, *Orationes*, vol. i, iv, p. 96 (Dindorf).
42. Bultmann, *Die Geschichte der Synoptischen Tradition*, 1931, p. 294; Frazer, *G.B.*, vol. ix, pp. 412 ff.
43. Matt. xxvii, 37.
44. Matt. xxvii, 37.
45. Rev. v, 6 ff.; xii, 7 ff.; xiii, 8; xix, 9.
46. Luke xxii, 20; Matt. xxvi, 28; 1 Cor. xi, 25.
47. John i, 29; xix, 14, 36; 1 Cor. v, 7; xv, 3; Ephes. v, 2; 1 Peter i, 19; Rev. xiii, 8.
48. Chap. V, pp. 117 ff.
49. Heb. ix, 24.
50. *Ber.*, 32b; *Midr. Shamuel*, i, 7.
51. M. Gaster, *The Prayer Book and Order of Service of the Spanish and Portuguese Jews*, 1902, i, 11.
52. *Ber.* 17a.
53. Hos. xiv, 2; Ps. xl, 6–8; li, 16 f.; Mal. 1, 11.
54. Matt. v, 23 f.; viii, 4 f.; ix, 13; xii, 7.
55. Mark xiii, 2; John iv, 20 ff.
56. Ephes. ii, 2; Heb. ix, 14; xiii, 11; Rom. iii, 25; viii, 3; 1 Cor. x, 16.
57. 1 Cor. xv, 7; Heb. ix, 11 ff.; x, 8 f.
58. Cf. Chap. V, pp. 126 ff.
59. Rom. iii, 25; v, 9.
60. *Kingship*, Oxford, 1927, p. 243.

CHAPTER IV

1. Cf. Chap. III, pp. 63 ff.
2. Brasseur de Bourbourg, *Le Popol Vuh*, Paris, 1861, pp. 215 ff.
3. Bancroft, *Native Races of the Pacific States*, San Francisco, 1882, vol. v, p. 440.
4. Sahagun, *Historia General de las Cosas de Nuova España*, Mexico, 1938, vol. v, chaps. 38, 64, 70; Seler, 28th *B.B.A.E.*, 1904, pp. 276 f.
5. Sahagun, *op. cit.*, pp. 57 ff.
6. Sahagun, *op. cit.*, pp. 61 ff., 96 ff.; Bancroft, *op. cit.*, ii, 319 ff.; iii, 422; Brasseur de Bourbourg, *Histoire des nations civilisées du Mexique et de l'Amér-ique-Centrale*, Paris, 1859, iii, 510 ff.
7. Bancroft, *op. cit.*, ii, 325 ff.
8. Sahagun, *op. cit.*, pp. 66 f., 126 f.
9. Sahagun, *op. cit.*, pp. 18, 68 ff., 133; Bancroft, *op. cit.*, iii, 353–9.
10. Sahagun, *op. cit.*, pp. 141 ff.
11. *Op. cit.*, pp. 71 ff., 148 ff.
12. *Op. cit.*, pp. 164 f.
13. Caso, *El Teocalli*, 1927; L. Spence, *The Gods of Mexico*, 1923.

14. Cf. Chap. III, p. 64.
15. La Jeune, *Jesuit Relations*, vol. xiii, pp. 37–79; xvii, p. 75; lxi, p. 65.
16. *Op. cit.*, xiii, pp. 37 ff.
17. Wissler, *19th Internat. Congress of Americanists*, Washington, 1917, p. 367.
18. Du Pratz, *Histoire de la Louisiana*, Paris, 1758, pp. 314 f.; Swanton, 43rd *B.B.A.E.*, Washington, 1911, pp. 138 ff.
19. De Molina, *Relación de los fabulas y ritos de los Ingas*, Lima, 1916, pp. 90 f.
20. J. Rankin, *The Conquest of Peru and Mexico*, 1827, pp. 229 f.
21. Molina, *op. cit.*, pp. 90 f.
22. Joyce, *South American Archaeology*, 1912, p. 162.
23. Cobo, *Historia del nuevo mundo*, Sevilla, 1895, iv, 31, 79.
24. Cieza de Leon, *Travels*, E.T. by C. R. Markham, 1864, p. 203; Juan de Velasco, *Histoire du Royaume de Quito*, Paris, 1840, i, 121 f.
25. H. R. Schoolcraft, *Indian Tribes of the U.S.*, Philadelphia, 1853–6, v, 77 ff.; J. de Smet, in *Annales de la Propagation de la Foi*, xi, 1838, pp. 493 ff.; xv, 1843, pp. 277 ff.; G. B. Grinnell, *Pawnee Hero Stories and Folk-tales*, New York, 1889, pp. 362 ff.
26. J. Campbell, *Wild Tribes of Khondistan*, 1864, pp. 54 ff., 113, 120 f., 187.
27. Westermarck, *Origin and Development of Moral Ideas*, 1908, vol. i, pp. 443 ff.
28. *G.B.Pt.* vii, vol. i, p. 250.
29. E. B. Cross, *Journal of the American Oriental Society*, iv, 1834, pp. 311 ff.; Fox, *The Threshold of the Pacific*, 1924, pp. 230, 249; Hutton, *J.R.A.I.*, lxviii, 1928, pp. 403 ff.
30. C. Hose and W. McDougall, *The Pagan Tribes of Borneo*, 1912, vol. i, pp. 114; vol. ii, pp. 20 ff.; H. I. Marshall, *The Karen People of Burma*, Ohio, 1922, p. 22.
31. J. G. Scott and J. P. Hardiman, *Gazetteer of Upper Burma and the Shan States of Rangoon*, 1900–1, i, 430, 496.
32. A. Schadenburg, *Zeits. für Ethnol.*, xx, 1888, p. 39.
33. Hose and McDougall, *op. cit.*, ii, 20, 23.
34. Hose, *Natural Man*, 1926, pp. 145 f.
35. W. K. H. Furness, *Home-Life of Borneo Head-Hunters*, Philadelphia, 1902, p. 141.
36. *Op. cit.*, p. 399.
37. *History of Melanesian Society*, Cambridge, 1914, vol. ii, p. 259.
38. Mills, *The Ao Naga*, 1926, p. 279.
39. H. Baudesson, *Indo-China and its Primitive People*, 1919, p. 314.
40. Scott and Hardiman, *Gazetteer of Upper Burma and the Shan States*, vol. i, Pt. i, pp. 493 ff.
41. Turner, *Samoa*, 1884, pp. 342 f.
42. E. Best, *Journal of Polynesian Society*, xii, 1903, pp. 195 ff.
43. Lev. i, 8, 12, 15; iv, 11; cf. viii, 17.
44. W. R. Smith, *Kinship and Marriage in Early Arabia*, 1903, p. 296.
45. J. Roscoe, *J.A.L.*, xxxi, 1901, p. 129.

46. Weeks, *Folk-Lore*, xx, p. 36.
47. Sahagun, *op. cit.*, pp. 203 ff.
48. W. H. Keating, *Narrative of an Expedition to the Source of the St Peter River*, Philadelphia, 1824, i, 412.
49. J. L. Wilson, *Western Africa*, 1856, p. 167.
50. 2 Kings vi, 28 f.
51. Budge, *Osiris and the Egyptian Resurrection*, 1911, vol. i, pp. 167 ff.
52. Budge, *op. cit.*, i, 197 f., 201.
53. 1 Sam. xv, 32 f. It is said that Agag was slain 'before Yahweh', but was it as a sacrificial victim or as the spoils of war?
54. Budge, *op. cit.*, pp. 207, 209.
55. *Op. cit.*, pp. 222 ff.; Müller, *Egyptian Mythology*, 1924, pp. 196 f.
56. Diod. Siculus, 1, 45, 88.
57. *De Abstinentia*, ii, 55.
58. *De Bello Pers.*, i, 19.
59. *Ars Amator*, i, 647.
60. *Historia Ecclesiastica*, ii, 24.
61. Herod., ii, 45; cf. Plutarch, *De Iside et Osiride*, 73.
62. Woolley, *Excavations at Ur*, 1954, vol. ii, pp. 33 ff.
63. IV Rawlinson, 28, no. 6; III *ibid.* 61; Zimmern, *Die Keilinschriften und das Alt. Test.*, 1903, pp. 597, 599.
64. C. H. W. Johns, *Assyrian Deeds and Documents*, Cambridge, 1901, vol. iii, p. 345.
65. 2 Kings xxiii, 10.
66. Macalister, *Gezer*, 1912, vol. ii, pp. 402 ff.
67. Gen. xxii, 1–14.
68. 2 Kings iii, 27.
69. 1 Kings xvi, 34.
70. Neh. xii, 43.
71. Jud. xi, 30 ff., 40.
72. Micah vi, 7; 2 Kings xxiii, 10.
73. Lev. xviii, 21; xx, 2.
74. 2 Kings xvi, 3; xxi, 6; cf. xvii, 17.
75. Jer. xxxii, 35; Ezek. xvi, 20; xx, 31.
76. Jer. xix, 5; xxxii, 35; Ezek. xxiii, 39; cf. Lev. xxvii, 1 ff.; Num. xviii, 15 ff.
77. Diodorus Siculus, 13, 86; Plutarch, *De Superst.*, 171; Sophocles, *Frag.*, 132; Dionysius Halicarnasensis, i, 38.
78. Herodotus, iv, 71.
79. Aeschylus, *Agam.*, 184 ff.
80. Cypria Euripides, *Iphigenia Taurica*.
81. Brit. Mus. Catalogue of Vases, iii, 188, no. E, 246; cf. Cook, *Zeus*, Cambridge, 1914, vol. i, pp. 654 f.
82. Scholiast, Clement of Alexandria, *Protr.*, i, 2, 1 f., p. 3, 26 ff.
83. Guthrie, *Orpheus and Greek Religion*, 1935, p. 132.

84. Plutarch, *Themistokles*, 13.
85. Pausanias, viii, 38, 7, cf. 2, 6.
86. Pausanias, vi, 82.
87. Farnell, *C.G.S.*, 1909, vol. v, pp. 171 ff.
88. Euripides, *Heraclides*, 404 ff.
89. Apollodorus, iii, xv, 8.
90. Paroem., i, 402.
91. Scholiast on Aristophanes, *Frogs*, 734.
92. Strabo, x, 2, 9, pp. 453, 542.
93. Hipponax, *Frag.*, 37; Athenaeus, ix, 9, pp. 370B; Lysias, 6, 537.
94. Tzetzes, *Chiliades*, 6, 736.
95. Strabo, 452, 683; Ovid, *Ibis*, 467; Scholiast on Euripides, *Phoen.*, 1408.
96. Livy, xxii, 57, 6.
97. Wissowa, *Religion und Kultur der Römer*, Leipzig, 1912, pp. 354, 420 f.
98. Minucius Felix, *Octav.*, 22, 30; Tertullian, *Apol.*, ix; Lactantius, i, 21.
99. Strabo, v, 250; Festus, 321; Livy, xxii, 10.
100. Ovid, *Fasti.*, v, 621–62; Varro, *De lingua Latina*, vi, 45; vii, 44; Dionysius Halicarnasensis, *Antiq. Rom.*, i, 37, 3.
101. *Fasti* iv, 91; Wissowa, 'Argei' in PaulyWissowa, *RealEncyclopaedie der classischen Altertumswissenschaft*, ii, 689–700.
102. Wissowa, *Gesammelte Abhandlungen*, p. 227.
103. *Roman Festivals*, 1899, pp. 112 ff.; *The Religious Experience of the Roman People*, 1922, pp. 322 ff.
104. *Antike Wald und Feldkulte*, Berlin, 1877, pp. 265 ff.
105. Deubner, *Archiv für religionswissenschaft*, xxiii, 1925, pp. 299 ff.
106. Strabo, xv, i, chap. 30.
107. xiii, 6.

CHAPTER V

1. *Origin and Development of Moral Ideas*, 1906, vol. i, pp. 65, 440.
2. *Op. cit.*, p. 140.
3. Lev. i, 4; iv, 26, 31, 35; v, 10, 13; Ezek. xlv, 15, 17.
4. *Babyloniaca*, iii, 16.
5. Langdon, *Babylonian Penitential Psalms*, Paris, 1927, pp. 40 ff.; Zimmern, *Babylonische Busspsalmen*, Leipzig, 1885, iv, 19–21, 42 ff.
6. Jastrow, *Religion of Babylonia and Assyria*, 1898, p. 291.
7. Stephens, *A.N.E.T.*, p. 385.
8. Zimmern, *Bab. Busspsalmen*, iv, 100–6; Langdon, *op. cit.*, pp. 43 f.; Stephens, *op. cit.*, p. 392.
9. Zimmern, *Die Keilinschriftliche und Das A.T.*, 1903, pp. 609 ff.; *Der alte orient*, 1903, vii, 3, pp. 27 ff.; *A.N.E.T.*, pp. 434 ff.; Langdon, *Babylonian Wisdom*, 1923, pp. 35 ff., 67 ff.
10. Lev. xvi.

11. Langdon, *Expository Times*, xxiv, 1912, p. 11.
12. *Cuneiform Texts*, Brit. *Mus.*, xvi, 10 f.; R. Campbell Thompson, *Semitic Magic*, 1918, p. 203.
13. F. Thureau-Dangin, *Rituels Accadiens*, 1921, pp. 140 ff.
14. Ex. xxx, 33, 38; xxxi, 15; xxxv, 2; Lev. v, 2, 6; xiv, 40, 52; xvii, 4, 9, 14; Num. xxxv, 31; xix, 12 f., 19 f.
15. 1 Sam. iii, 14; Lev. 18; xvi, 6 ff.; Is. vi, 7.
16. Cf. Gray, *Sacrifice in the Old Testament*, 1925, pp. 69 ff.; Langdon, *Expository Times*, 1911, pp. 320 ff.
17. Ezek. xlv, 18 ff.; Zech. viii, 19; Neh. ix, 1 f.
18. Lev. xvi, 5–10.
19. The scene is laid in the desert because the observance is referred back to the time of Moses and Aaron to give it a divine origin and sanction.
20. Lev. xvi, 11–28.
21. Lev. xvi, 29–34a.
22. Lev. viii, 14 f.; xvii, 11; Deut. xii, 23.
23. Lev. xiv, 4 ff.; Zech, v, 5, 11.
24. Is. lv, 6, 7; xliv, 22; Ps. xlv, 7; li, 16 ff.; lxix, 30 ff.
25. Yoma, viii, 9.
26. Yoma, viii, 8; cf. Lev. xvi, 30.
27. *Shabbat shabbaton*, Lev. xxiii, 32.
28. Abot de R. Nathan, 4, 5; Bacher, *Tannaiten*, i, 39.
29. *Studies in Sin and Atonement*, Oxford, 1928, p. xiv.
30. C. G. Montefiore, *Jewish Quarterly Review*, old series, xvi, 1904, pp. 215 ff.
31. *Hilkhoth Teshubah*, Venice, ed. 1615.
32. Jos. vii, 10–15.
33. 2 Sam. xxi, 1–14.
34. Is. xliii, 1–4; xlix, 1–6, 4–9; lii, 12–liii.
35. Is. liii, 10 ff.
36. liii, 10, cf. 5, 8; Num. xix, xxi; Josephus, *Ant.*, IV, iv, 6.
37. Num. xx, 23 ff.; *Jer. Yoma*, 38b.
38. Deut. xxi, 1–9.
39. Cf. Chap. II, pp. 55 f.
40. Is. liii, 5, 8.
41. H. H. Rowley, *The Servant of the Lord*, 1952, pp. 61 ff.
42. Is. xlii, 1.
43. Mowinckel, *De Senere profeter*, 1944, p. 195.
44. Ezek. xxxiv, 23 f.; xxxvii, 24; Jer. xxiii, 5 f.; xxxiii, 15 f.
45. Cf. R. S. Driver and A. Neubauer, *The 53rd Chapter of Isaiah according to the Jewish Interpreters*, Oxford, 1877, pp. lxvi ff.; Strack-Billerbeck, *Kommentar zum Neuen Testament aus Talmud und Midrasch*, vol. ii, 1924, p. 274.
46. Mark viii, 31–3; Matt. xvi, 21–3.

47. Cf. Snaith, in *Studies in Old Testament Prophecy*, ed. by H. H. Rowley, 1950, p. 191.

48. W. Manson, *Jesus the Messiah*, 1943, pp. 99 ff., 171 f.

49. Mark viii, 27–33; Matt. xvi, 13–23; Luke ix, 18–22.

50. Rev. v, 6 ff.; xii, 7 ff.; xiii, 8; xix, 1–9.

51. Rom. vi, 3 ff., 20 f.; xi, 15; Gal. ii, 20; 2 Cor. v, 18 ff.

52. Rom. vi, 11.

53. Cf. Chap. II, p. 56.

54. 1 Cor., i, 8; vi, 20; vii, 23; Gal. ii, 17; iii, 15 f.; iv. 5–7; Rom. iii, 24; viii, 1, 17, 33; 2 Cor. v, 21.

55. Rom. ii, 14–16; iii, 9–25; 1 Cor. xv, 3.

56. Heb. ix, 13 f.

57. Mark x, 44 f.; Matt. xx, 28.

58. Rashdall, *The Idea of the Atonement in Christian Theology*, 1920, pp. 49 ff.; V. Taylor, *The Atonement in New Testament Teaching*, 1940, pp. 87 ff.

59. *De Incarn.*, 54.

60. H. N. Oxenham, *Catholic Doctrine of the Atonement*, 1865, pp. 114 ff.; Moberley, *Atonement and Personality*, 1901, pp. 324 ff.; J. K. Mozley, *The Doctrine of the Atonement*, 1915; L. W. Grensted, *A Short History of the Doctrine of the Atonement*, 1920.

61. J. McLeod Campbell, *The Nature of the Atonement*, 1886; R. W. Dales, *The Atonement*, 1875; J. Scott Lidgett, *The Spiritual Principle of the Atonement*, 1901.

62. *Summa Theol.*, P. iii, Q. xlviii, Art 1, 2.

63. *Institutes*, 1553, vii, 29; 1602, II, xvi, 2.

64. *Christianae Religionis Brevissima Institutio*, 1656, tom. i, pp. 664 ff.

65. F. H. Bradley, *Ethical Studies*, 2nd ed., 1928, pp. 28 ff.

66. Rev. xii, 2 ff.

67. Cf. *Den Kristna forsoninggstanten*, Lund, 1930, E.T. by A. G. Hebert, *Christus Victor*, 1931.

68. Heb. ix, 11–28.

69. Heb. ii, 10, 14.

CHAPTER VI

1. Lalanne and Breuil, *L'Anthropologie*, xxii, 1911, pp. 259 ff.; lxxiii, 1912, p. 431; Passemard, *Les statuettes féminines dites Vénus stéatopyges*, Nîmes, 1938, pl. ii, fig. 8, pl. iii, pp. 121 ff.

2. Verneau, *Les Grottes de Grimaldi*, Monaco, 1906, vol. xi, pp. 23, 260, 277 f., 298 ff.

3. *Comptes-Rendus de l'Acad. des Sciences*, lxxiv, 1872, pp. 1060 f.; Boule and Vallois, *Fossil Men*, London, 1957, pp. 274 f.

4. *Antiquity*, xxx, 1956, pp. 132 ff.; cf. pp. 184 ff.

5. Kenyon, *Digging up Jericho*, 1957, pp. 51 ff.

6. M. E. L. Mallowan and J. Cruikshank Rose, *Iraq*, vol. ii, pt. i, 1935, pp. 79 ff., 87, 95.

7. Tobler, *Excavations at Tepe Gawra*, Philadelphia, 1950, ii, pp. 165 ff., pls. lxxxi, cliii, figs. 1–10.

8. *Iraq*, ix, 1947, pp. 156 ff.

9. Garstang, *Prehistoric Mersin*, Oxford, 1953, pp. 71, fig. 39.

10. Ghirshman, *Fouilles de Tepe-Giyan*, Paris, 1933, p. 50, pl. vi; *Fouilles de Sialk*, Paris, 1938, i, 19.

11. Piggott, *Prehistoric India*, 1950, p. 127.

12. *Mohenjo-daro and the Indus Civilization*, 1937, vol. i, p. 339.

13. Vats, *Excavations at Harappa*, Delhi, 1940, pp. 51, 55, 116, 140, 368 ff.

14. Mannhardt, *Mythologische Forschungen*, Strassburg, 1884, pp. 317 ff.

15. Mannhardt, *op. cit.*, pp. 318 ff.

16. J. G. Campbell, *Superstitions of the Highlands*, Glasgow, 1900, pp. 243 ff.

17. A. Polsen, *Our Highland Folk-lore Heritage*, Dingwall, 1926, p. 150; G. Henderson, *Survivals in Belief among the Celts*, Glasgow, 1911, p. 284.

18. Batchelor, *The Ainu and their Folk-lore*, 1901, pp. 471 ff.; cf. Chap. I, p. 28.

19. *Op. cit.*, pp. 204 ff.

20. L. Grout, *Zululand*, Philadelphia, 1864, p. 161.

21. J. R. Swanton, 43rd *B.B.A.E.*, Washington, 1911, pp. 113 f.

22. F. G. Speck, *Ethnology of the Yuki Indians*, Philadelphia, 1919, pp. 86 ff.; C. MacCauley, 5th *B.B.A.E.*, Washington, 1887, pp. 522 ff.

23. Lev. xix, 24 f.

24. Num. xviii, 27; cf. Ex. xxii, 28.

25. Ex. xii, 12; xvi, 1–8.

26. Ex. xiii, 15 ff.; xxii, 18; xxiv, 25.

27. Ex. xii, 6; Deut. xvi, 6; Ex. xiii, 4; xxiii, 15.

28. The sprinkling of the blood of the lamb on the lintel and doorposts was a later apotropaic rite to repel demons. It had nothing to do with the Passover.

29. Num. i, 1–14.

30. Deut. xvi, 8.

31. Lev. xxiii, 4–8; Num. xxviii, 16–25.

32. Ex. xxxiv, 22; Lev. xxiii, 17; Deut. xvi, 9-12.

33. Ex. xxiii, 14 f., 17.

34. Lev. xxiii, 15–21; Deut. xvi, 9.

35. Deut. xvi, 10 f.; xxvi, 1 ff.

36. Num. xviii, 12 f.

37. Deut. viii, 8; Num. x, 35, 37; xii, 44.

38. Zech. xiv, 16 ff.; 1 Kings viii, 2; xii, 32; 2 Chron. vi, 26; Jud. xxi, 19; P. Volz, *Das Neujahresfest Jahwas*, Tübingen, 1912, p. 15.

39. Lev. xxiii, 33, 36, 39 ff.; Neh. viii, 15.

40. Jud. ix, 2, 4, 27.

41. Jud. xxi, 15–25.
42. 1 Kings viii; Neh. viii, 14; Num. xxix, 12 (LXX).
43. Josephus, *Ant.*, IV, viii, 22.
44. Lev. ii, 14–16.
45. Amos iv, 4.
46. Gen. xxviii, 22.
47. Gen. xiv, 20; 1 Sam. viii, 17.
48. Deut. xii, 17; xiv, 22; xvi, 10.
49. Lev. xxvii, 30–3; Num. xviii, 25–32; Neh. x, 27 f.
50. Neh. x, 36–40; xii, 44; xiii, 5.
51. Mal. iii, 8, 10; 2 Chron. xxxi, 5 ff.
52. Ex. xxxiv, 19 f.; cf. xiii, 12 f.
53. *Corpus Inscrip. Atticarum*, i, 226, 210; Plutarch, *Quaest. Gr.*, 35.
54. Diodorus, xi, 65.
55. *C.I.A.*, ii, 984 f. *Bulletin de Correspondance Hellénique*, vi, 41, 114; xiv, 408; xxvii, 90, 43; xviii, 103; xx, 695 f.
56. Callimachus, *Hymn to Delos*, 278 ff.; *C.I.A.*, iv, 276.
57. Theocritus, *Idyl*, vii, 31; Homer, *Iliad*, ix, 534; Rouse, *Greek Votive Offerings*, 1902, p. 43.
58. Nilsson, *Greek Popular Religion*, 1940, p. 26.
59. Nilsson, *Griechische Feste von religiöser Bedeutung, mit Ausschluss der Attischen*, Leipzig, 1906, pp. 106 ff.
60. Plutarch, *Theseus*, 22.
61. Plutarch, *Quaest. Rom.*, 68; Romulus, 21; Servius, *Ecl.*, 8182.
62. Dionysius Halicarnasensis, *Ant. Rom.*, ii, 66.
63. Varro, s.v. 'Aulus Gellius', i, 12, 9; Ovid, *Fasti.*, vi, 2691 ff.
64. Cf. Chap. IV, pp. 99 f.
65. Diodorus Siculus, iv, 21, 3, 4; cf. Dionysius Hal., *Antiq. Rom.*, i, 40, 6.
66. Pliny, *Nat. Hist.*, xviii, 7.
67. Ovid, *Fasti*, iv, 409, 679 ff.
68. *Fasti*, iv, 681 ff.
69. Ovid, *Metamorphoses*, x, 431 ff.; *Amores*, iii, 10, 1 ff.; Festus, s.v. 'Graeca sacra', p. 86 (ed. Lindsay).
70. Ovid, *Meta*, x, 431 ff.
71. Cf. Wissowa, *Religion und Kultus der Römer*, p. 301.
72. *Tammuz and Ishtar*, Oxford, 1914, pp. 4 f.
73. Langdon, *Sumerian and Babylonian Psalms*, Paris, 1909, p. 160; i, 14, p. 338, n. 9.
74. *A.N.E.T.*, 1955, p. 56.
75. W. R. Dawson, *Egyptian Mummies*, 1924, pp. 45 ff.; Budge, *The Opening of the Mouth*, 1909, vol. i, pp. 9 ff. For a similar ceremony in Babylonia see Blackman, *J.E.A.*, vol. v, 1918, pp. 117 ff.; x, 1924, pp. 47 ff.; S. Smith, *J.R.A.S.*, 1925, pp. 37 ff.
76. Blackman, *Journal of Manchester Egyptian and Oriental Society*, 1918–19, pp.

30 ff.; *Recueil de Travaux*, xxix, 1920, pp. 44 ff.; Moret, *Le Rituel du culte Divin Journalier en Egypte*, Paris, 1920, pp. 9–66.

77. Budge, *Osiris and the Egyptian Resurrection*, 1911, pp. 133 f.

78. P.T. *Ut*, 222, 563.

79. Deut. viii, 7 ff.

80. 1 Kings xvii; cf. Gen. xii, 10; x, 1 ff, 57; Ruth i.

81. *A.B.* (Anat-Baal Texts), viii, 40–2; 51, i, 13; 51, iv, 52 ff.; 49, vi, 27 ff.

82. Schaeffer, *The Cuneiform Texts of Ras Shamra-Ugarit*, 1939, p. 8.

83. *Op. cit.*, p. 68.

84. 1 Kings xviii, 30 ff.

85. Gen. vii, 11; Is. xxiv, 18; Job xxxviii, 25; Enoch, xli, 4.

86. 1 Kings vii, 23 ff.; 2 Chron. iv, 2 ff.

87. 1 Sam. vii, 6.

88. 2 Sam. xxiii, 16.

89. Joel, i, 13; ii, 14.

90. *Sukkah*, v, 1–4; 50a; *Rosh ha-Shanah*, 16, 9.

91. *Sukkah*, iv, 9, 10.

92. Widengren, *Sakrales Königtum im Alten Testament und im Judentum*, Stuttgart, 1955, pp. 34–43, 112.

93. *Iliad*, xxi, 130–2.

94. Athenaeus, p. 261D; Servius on Vergil, *Georg.*, i, 13.

95. Nilsson, *Minoan-Mycenaean Religion*, 1950, pp. 147 ff.; Evans, *J.H.S.*, xlv, 1925, pp. 21 ff.

96. Evans, *Palace of Minos*, vol. iv, p. 453, fig. 377.

97. Evans, 'Mycenaean Tree and Pillar Cult', *J.H.S.*, xxi, 1901, pp. 110 f.

98. P. Gardner, *J.H.S.*, xvi, 1896, pp. 275 ff.; fig. 1, pl. 12; Roehl, *Inscrip. Graec. Ant.*, no. 70.

99. Pollux, 6, 15.

100. Evans, *Palace of Minos*, vol. iv, pp. 140 ff.

101. B. E. Williams, *Gournia*, Philadelphia, 1908, pp. 47 ff.; Nilsson, *Minoan-Mycenaean Religion*, p. 82, fig. 4.

102. Nilsson, *op. cit.*, p. 113; Froedin and Persson, *Asine* (1939), p. 298, fig. 20B.

103. Pausanias, *Description of Greece*, ii, 125.

104. i, 424.

105. v, 10, 12.

106. i, 26, 5.

107. v, 15, 10.

108. Cato, *De agni. Cult.*, i, 41.

109. Servius on Vergil, *Aen.*, vii, 603; viii, 3, 285.

110. Festus, 'Lustratio', 120 (Lindsay, p. 107).

111. E. Hull, *Folklore of the British Isles*, 1928, pp. 288 ff.

112. *Fasti*, iv, 735–82.

113. Chap. IX, pp. 257 f.

114. Tertullian, *De Baptismo*, iv, v.

115. A. A. King, *Holy Water*, 1926.
116. Canon XLVIII of Council of Elvira (c. A.D. 300).

CHAPTER VII

1. D. Black, *Fossil Man in China*, Pekin, 1938, pp. 5, 60; Obermaier, *Fossil Man in Spain*, 1925, pp. 136 f., 339; Wernert, *Histoire générale de religion*, i, 56 f.; Oppenoorth, *Early Man*, Philadelphia, 1937, pp. 349 ff.; Breuil and Obermaier, *L'Anthropologie*, xx, 1909, p. 523.
2. Breuil, *L'Anthrop.*, xxxi, 1921, pp. 343 ff.
3. Hauser, *Archiv. für Anthropologie*, vii, 1909, p. 290.
4. Sollas, *J.R.A.I.*, xliii, 1913, pp. 325 ff.; Verneau, *Les Grottes de Grimaldi*, Monaco, 1906, pp. 23, 260, 277 ff., 298 ff.
5. W. R. Dawson, *Egyptian Mummies*, 1924, p. 26.
6. Budge, *The Liturgy of Funerary Offerings*, 1909, cf. *Bibl. Egypt*, ii, 283–324.
7. Cf. Chap. II, pp. 37 f.
8. J. A. Wilson, *J.N.E.S.*, iii, 1944, pp. 205 ff.
9. *P.T.*, 9 ff., 144, 153, 1002 f., 1046 ff., 1747 f.
10. *P.T.*, 723, 904.
11. *P.T.*, 614.
12. Cf. Chap. IV, pp. 92 f.
13. Waterlin, *Kish.*, vol. iv, Paris, 1934, pp. 17 ff.
14. Seton Lloyd and Fuad Safar, *J.N.E.S.*, iv, 1945, pp. 267 f.; A. L. Perkins, *The Comparative Archaeology of Early Mesopotamia*, Chicago, 1949, p. 5.
15. Tobler, *Excavations at Tepe Gawra*, Philadelphia, 1950, ii, 51 ff.; Speiser, vol. i, 1935, pp. 25, 142.
16. Woolley, *Ur Excavations*, 1934, vol. ii, pp. 135 ff.
17. Woolley, *Excavations at Ur*, 1954, pp. 187 ff.
18. Cf. Chap. III, pp. 66 f.
19. Speiser, *A.N.E.T.*, p. 87.
20. Kramer, *J.A.O.S.*, lxiv, 1944, pp. 11 ff.
21. Kramer, *Sumerian Mythology*, Philadelphia, 1944, pp. 36 ff., 79 f.
22. Speiser, *A.N.E.T.*, pp. 101 ff.; Heidel, *The Babylonian Genesis*, Chicago, 1951, pp. 148 ff.
23. H. Vincent, *Canaan d'après l'exploration récente*, Paris, 1914, pp. 227 f., fig. 159.
24. Tobit iv, 17.
25. D. Mackenzie, *Palestine Exploration Fund Annual*, ii, 1912–13, pp. 58, 67; Macalister, *Excavations at Gezer*, 1912, pp. 300 ff.; E. Grant, *Beth Shemesh*, Haverford, 1929, pp. 56 ff.; Kenyon, *Digging up Jericho*, 1957, pp. 195, 212 ff., 235 ff.
26. *Mitteilungen und Nachrichten des deutschen Palaestina-vereins*, 1906, pp. 9, 19, 23, 60; Vincent, *op. cit.*, p. 223.

27. 1 Sam. xxvi; 1 Kings i, 34; 2 Sam. ii, 32; xvii, 23.

28. 1 Kings xi, 23; xiv, 31; xv, 8, 24; 2 Chron. xxxii, 33; xxxv, 24; 2 Kings xxi, 18, 26; xxiii, 30.

29. Gen. xxiii, 17 ff.; xxv, 9, 19 ff.; xlix, 31; xxxv, 8; 1 Sam. x, 2; Jos. xix, 32.

30. Gen. xxxv, 8, 14, 20.

31. Jer. xxiv, 5; 2 Chron. xvi, 14; xxi, 20.

32. 1 Kings xvii, 21 f.

33. 2 Sam. xxi, 1–14; Gen. iv, 11 ff.

34. 1 Sam. xxviii, 3–25; Is. xxix, 4; cf. xix, 3; Deut. xviii, 10–12.

35. 2 Kings xxi, 6; 2 Chron. xxxiii, 6.

36. Job xxvi, 6; xxviii, 22; Is. xxvi, 14; Ps. lxxxviii, 11 ff.; Job vii, 9; xiv, 12; Eccles. ix, 5, 10.

37. Deut. ii, 10 ff., 20 ff.; Is. xiv, 9 f.; xxvi, 14.

38. Gen. xiv, 5; xv, 18 ff.; Jos. xii, 4; xiii, 12; xvii, 15.

39. Oesterley, *Immortality and the Unseen World*, 1921, pp. 63 ff.

40. Ps. lxxiii, 24 ff.; Wisdom, iii, 1–9; iv, 17–19; v, 5; Is. xxvi, 19; Dan. xii, 2.

41. 2 Enoch xxii, 2.

42. Acts ix, 37; *Shabboth*, xxiii, 5; Mark xvi, 1; Luke xxiv, 1; John xii, 7; xix, 40.

43. Gen. xlvi, 4; John xi, 44.

44. Matt. xxvii, 50; Mark xv, 46; Luke xxiii; John xl, 44; xx, 6 f.

45. Josephus, *Ant.*, XVII, viii, 3.

46. *Op. cit.*, XV, iii, 4.

47. Lev. xx, 14; xxi, 9; Jos. vii, 25; 2 Kings iii, 27.

48. Maimonides, *Yad, 'Ebel*, xii, 1; *Shabb.*, 105b.

49. 2 Sam. iii, 35; Jer. xvi, 7; Hos. ix, 4.

50. Nilsson, *Minoan-Mycenaean Religion*, pp. 425 ff.

51. Mylonas and Papademetriou, *Archaeology*, v, 1952, pp. 194 ff.; Wace, *Bulletin British School of Athens*, xlviii, 1953, pp. 7 ff.

52. *Greek Hero Cults and Ideas of Immortality*, Oxford, 1921, pp. 5 f.; Foucart, *Le Culte des Héros chez les Grecs. Men. de l'Acad. des Inscr.*, xlii, 1918, p. 40.

53. Nilsson, *op. cit.*, p. 587; Oeconomus, *De profusionum receptaculis sepulcralibus*, Athens, 1921, pp. 8 ff.

54. Wace, *Chamber Tombs at Mycenae*, 1932, pp. 129, 136.

55. W. Dörpfeld, *Mélanges Nicole*, 1905, pp. 95 ff.; Xanthondides, *The Vaulted Tombs of Mesara*, 1924, pp. 6 ff., 90, 129, 135.

56. Persson, *The New Tombs at Dendra*, Lund, 1942, pp. 165 ff.

57. Wace and Blegen, *Klio*, 1939, p. 147.

58. *Iliad*, xvi, 456, 674; xxiii, 50; Nilsson, *Homer and Mycenae*, 1933, p. 153.

59. *Iliad*, xxiii.

60. *Op. cit.*, p. 155.

61. *Iliad*, xxiii, 43.

62. xxiv, 664–710; 237, 245.
63. *Odyssey*, xi, 140 ff.
64. *Od.*, x, 494; iv, 561 ff.; v, 135 ff., 209 ff.; xxiii, 335 ff.
65. Ridgeway, *The Early Age of Greece*, 1931, p. 507; Rhode, *Psyche*, pp. 20 ff.; Nilsson, *History of Greek Religion*, p. 99.
66. Myres, *Who were the Greeks?*, p. 445; Herodotus, vi, 58; Plutarch, *Lyk-ourges*, 25.
67. Mylonas, *American Journal of Archaeology*, 52, 1948, pp. 67 ff.
68. Sophocles, *Trachiniae*, pp. 1191 f.; Hyginus, *Fab.*, 36.
69. *Od.*, xi, 29 ff.
70. *De anima*, *Frags.*, viii, 23; Stabaeus, ed. Meineke, iv, 107.
71. *Panegyricus*, 6.
72. Pindar, *Frag.*, 102; Plutarch, *De audiendis poetis*, 4; Clement of Alex., *Strom.*, iii, 3, 17, p. 518, ed. Potter.
73. *Homeric Hymn to Demeter*, 480 ff.
74. *Refutatio omnium haeresium*, v, 8. This is accepted by Frazer, Jane Harrison, Foucart and Loisy, but rejected by Farnell, *C.G.S.*, iii, 183 ff.
75. *De Legibus*, ii, 14.
76. Cf. Chap. VII, p. 168.
77. Angus, *The Mystery Religions and Christianity*, 1925, p. 206.
78. D. Randall-MacIver, *Villanovans and Early Etruscans*, Oxford, 1924, pp. 5 ff.; *The Iron Age in South Italy*, 1927, pp. 2 ff.
79. Horace, *Satirae*, viii, 8.
80. *Religious Experience of the Roman People*, 1922, pp. 380 ff.
81. Lucretius, iii, 94 ff., 417 ff., 830 ff.
82. Festus, s.v. 'Mundus', pp. 144 ff., ed. Lindsay; Cicero, *de Leg.*, 2, 9, 22; *In Pisonem.*, 16; Ovid, *Meta.*, 9, 407.
83. Ovid, *Fasti*, ii, 533–70.
84. *Fasti*, ii, 533–70.
85. *Fasti*, ii, 617–38.
86. Cato, *De Agricultura*, 143; Horace, *Epodi.*, 2, 65; *Sat.*, ii, 5, 12, 65 f.
87. Festus, p. 68 (ed. Lindsay); Cicero, *de Leg.*, ii, 22, 57; in *Vat.*, 12, 30.
88. Horace, *Sat.*, i, viii, 8–16.
89. 1 Cor. iii, 16; vi, 19; xv, 42; Rom. xii, 1; Rev. vii, 13.
90. Acts ix, 27 f.; Mark xv, 46; xvi, 1; John xi, 44; xix, 39 f.; xx, 5 ff.
91. Matt. ix, 23; Luke viii, 52; Acts viii, 2.
92. 1 Thess. iv, 15 f.; John xi, 13, 38; xix, 41; Acts vii, 60; 1 Cor. xv, 18 f.
93. Tertullian, *De Corona*, iii; *ad Scapulam*, ii; St Cyprian, *Ep.*, xxxiv.
94. 1 Cor. xv, 29.
95. T. Mommsen, *Abhandlungen der philosophisch-philologischen*, i, 1850, pp. 547 ff.
96. Eusebius, *Vita Const.*, iv, 60, 66, 72.
97. Tertullian, *De Cor.*, 3; *De Exhort. Cast.*, ii; *De Monog.*, 18; Eusebius, *Vita Const.*, iv, 60–72.

98. Gregory of Nazianzus, *Panegyric on Basil*, 80.
99. Origen, *Works*, ed. Lommatzsch, vol. xvi, p. 238.
100. *De Mortalitate*, c. xx.
101. *Iliad*, xvi, 855 ff.; Gen. i, 10; Judith xvi, 29; Num. xx, 29; Deut. xxxiv, 8.
102. A. le Braz, *La légende de Morten Basse-Bretagne*, Paris, 1893, pp. 280 ff.
103. Reinsberg-Duringfeld, *Calendrier Belge*, Brussels, 1861–2, ii, 236 ff.; *Fest-Kalender aus Böhmen*, pp. 493 ff.; E. H. Meyer, *Badisches Volksleben im neunzehnten Jahrhundert*, Strassburg, 1900, p. 601.
104. Rom. vi, 23; John xvii, 3; Dante, *Inferno*, iii, 4 ff.

CHAPTER VIII

1. *Yasna*, 44, 20; cf. 51, 14; 32, 12.
2. *Yasna*, 32, 14.
3. Amos iv, 4, 5.
4. Portions of a victim were still offered to the angel Hem until the middle of the last century, and on the third day after death a goat was slain by the Parsee priest (M. N. Dhalla, *Zoroastrian Theology*, 1914, p. 355).
5. Denkart (Madan), 466, 12 ff.; Zaehner, *Zurvan, A Zoroastrian Dilemma* 1959, p. 52; *Yasna*, 29, 1.
6. *Yasna*, 32, 14.
7. *Yashts*, xi, 4, 17, 1; Herodotus i, 132; Strabo, XV, iii, 15.
8. Athenaeus, iv, 10; Herodotus, vii, 43.
9. Xenophon, *Cyr.*, VIII, iii, 9 ff.
10. *Yasna*, 9–11, 19, 20; *Yashts*, x, 88–90; *Ashi*, xvii, 5.
11. *Yashts*, xiii, 116.
12. *Yasna*, 11, 4.
13. *Yashts*, ix, 26; x, 89.
14. *Yasna*, 9, 1, 17; 10, 90.
15. Rig-Veda, x, 119.
16. J. J. Modi, *The Religious Ceremonies and Customs of the Parsees*, Bombay, 1922, pp. 306 ff.
17. *Datastan i Dinik*, chap. 47.
18. *Yasna*, 11, 4; *Yashts*, 10, 89; cf. *Yasna*, 9, 1, 4–5.
19. *Datastan i denik*, chap. 47.
20. *Yashts*, 10, 88 f.
21. Cumont, *Mystères de Mithra*, Brussels, 1899, vol. i, p. 321.
22. *Yashts*, 10, 16.
23. Cumont, *Textes et Monuments figurés relatifs aux mystères de Mithra*, Brussels, 1896–9.
24. 1 Cor. xi, 17, 34; xv, 3.
25. 1 Cor. xi, 20 f., 29.

26. 1 Cor. xi, 23–29.
27. Acts ii, 42, 46.
28. Westcott and Hort, *The New Testament in the Original Greek*, Cambridge, 1881, Appendix, pp. 63 f., Introd., p. 175.
29. F. L. Cirlot, *The Early Eucharist*, 1939, pp. 236 ff.; G. Dix, *The Shape of the Liturgy*, 1945, pp. 48 ff.
30. Mark xiv, 21; Matt. xxvi, 18; Luke xxii, 13.
31. John xiii, 1.
32. John xix, 31 f.; cf. 14; xviii, 28.
33. *Das letzte Passamahl Christi*, Leipzig, 1908, pp. 11 ff.
34. *Die Abendmahlsworte Jesus*, 1949, pp. 18 ff.
35. *San.*, xi, 3.
36. Mark xiv, 2; Matt. xxvi, 5.
37. Cf. Burkitt and Brooke, *Journal of Theological Studies*, ix, 569 ff.; Oesterley, *The Jewish Background of the Christian Liturgy*, Oxford, 1925, p. 181.
38. Cf. M. Braun and J. Elbogen, *Festschrift zu Israel Lewys Siebzigsten Geburtstag*, Breslau, 1911, pp. 173 ff.
39. *Tosephta Berakhoth*, vi, 14.
40. Luke xxii, 15.
41. John vi, 4.
42. Schweitzer, *Quest of the Historical Jesus*, 1919, p. 374.
43. John vi, 23.
44. Mark vi, 52.
45. John vi, 26.
46. *Messe und Herrenmahl*, Bonn, 1926, p. 221.
47. 1 Cor. v, 7, 8; x, 16; xi, 26; xv, 24 f.
48. Heb. ix, 11, 12, 28; x, 10, 12.
49. Mal. i, 11.
50. Luke xxiv, 30; John xxi, 12 ff.; Mark xvi, 14; Acts i, 4.
51. 1 Cor. x, 1–5.
52. Acts xx, 7–12; 1 Cor. xi, 20.
53. Box, *Journal of Theological Studies*, iii, 1901–2, pp. 361 ff.; A. J. Maclean, *The Doctrine of the Twelve Apostles*, 1922; F. E. Vokes, *The Riddle of the Didache*, 1938, with bibliography.
54. *Smyrn.*, viii, 1.
55. Justin Martyr, *Dial. cum Tryphone*, 41–70; 117, 7–10; Irenaeus, *Adv. Haer.*, iv, 17 f.
56. Ex. xxix, 39; cf. Lev. ix, 7; xxiv, 7; Num. x, 10; Ps. lxvi, 15; Lock, *Theology*, 1923, vii, 284 ff.
57. 1 Peter ii, 5.
58. *The Mediaeval Stage*, Oxford, 1913, vol. ii, pp. 3 ff.
59. *Ep.*, lxiii, 4, 14, 17.
60. *Catecheses Mystagogicae*, v.
61. *Ep. ad Heb.*, hom. xiii, 3; xiv, 1, 2; xvii, 3.

62. *Cat.*, xxiii, 7.
63. *Liturgies Eastern and Western*, 1896, p. 469.
64. *The Shape of the Liturgy*, 1945, p. 198.
65. *Cat.*, xxii.
66. Brightman, *op. cit.*, vol. i, pp. 353 ff., 470.
67. Bicknell, *Messe und Pascha*, Mainz, 1872, p. 68; Lietzmann, *Messe und Herrenmahl*, pp. 125 ff.; Cabrol, *Les origines liturgiques*, pp. 328 ff.
68. *De Mysteriis*, ix, 52–4; *De Sacramentis*, iv, 4, 14; *De Fide*, iv, 10, 124.
69. *Serm.*, cclxxii; *De An. et Orig.*, i, 11, 13; ii, 15, 21; cf. *Confess.*, ix, 12, 32.
70. *Summa Theologiae*, iii, lxxiii–lxxxii, 6.
71. *De sacrificia Missae*, Tract 3, 1, 2, 3.
72. 1 Peter ii, 5; Rom. xii, 1.
73. Tertullian, *De Cor.*, 3; *De Monogam*, 10; Cyprian, *Ep.*, i, 2; xxxix, 3; Augustine, *Serm.*, 1591, 325; *Confess.*, ix, 12.
74. Leonine Sacr., xxxiii; Gelasian, III, xcii–cv.
75. Council of Trent, Session XXII, cap. i, ii, Anglican Article XXXI.
76. C. Jenkins, *Journal of Theological Studies*, 1922, pp. 1–30.
77. Thorndike, *Works*, vi, pp. 107 ff.; Andrews, *Minor Works*, p. 20; Cosin, *Works*, v, pp. 119, 351 ff.
78. C. J. Stranks, *Church Quarterly Review*, 1940, pp. 31 ff.
79. Jeremy Taylor, *Works*, ed. R. Heber, iii, pp. 296 f.
80. *Apology of the Church of England*, pt. vi.
81. *Ecclesiastical Polity*, Preface IV, 4; V, xxviii, 1.
82. *Report*, Resolution 33c, p. 49.
83. *Lambeth Report*, p. 136.
84. Session XXII, can. iii (Denzinger n. 950).
85. O. Rousseau, *Histoire du mouvement liturgique*, Paris, 1945; J. H. Srawley, *The Liturgical Movement*, Alcuin Club Tracts, xxvii, 1954; Dom Laporta, *La piété eucharistique*, Louvain, 1929; Dom Beauduin, *La piété de l'église*, Louvain, 1914.
86. J. A. Jungmann, *The Mass of the Roman Rite*, E.T. 1959, pp. 103 ff.

CHAPTER IX

1. O. Casel, *Jahrbuch für Liturgiewiss.*, viii, 1928, p. 232.
2. *Symbolism and Belief*, 1938, pp. 11 f.
3. Cf. Chap. I, p. 28.
4. *J.A.L.*, xxiv, 1895, pp. 187 f.
5. Cf. Chap. I, pp. 17 f.
6. Krujt, *Maesa* (By der agen Taal-Land-en Volkenkunde van Nederlandsch-Indie), The Hague, 1918, i, 74; 1919, p. 75; 1920, p. 76.
7. Batchelor, *The Ainu and their Folk-lore*, 1901, pp. 486 ff.
8. F. H. Cushing, *The Century Illustrated Monthly Magazine*, 1883, pp. 45 ff.

9. Chap. III, pp. 60 ff.
10. Cf. Chap. III, pp. 66 ff.
11. *Admon.*, 12, 1. Cairo, 34501.
12. Chap. II, pp. 37 f.
13. Chap. VI, pp. 149 f.
14. E. Chiera, *Sumerian Ritual Texts*, xxxi, Upland, Pa., 1924, 24; i, 22–5.
15. Chap. VI, p. 139.
16. Chap. II, pp. 37 f.
17. *P.T.*, 222.
18. Pausanias, x, 32, 18.
19. Chap. VII, pp. 179 f.
20. Hippolytus, *Refutatio omnium haeresium*, v, 8; Clement of Alexandria, *Protrept*, ii, 12, p. 12, ed. Potter.
21. *C.G.S.*, iii, 1906, pp. 176 ff., 252 f.
22. *Introduction to the History of Religion*, 1911, p. 214.
23. Noack, *Eleusis, die baugeschicthliche Entwicklung des Heiligtums*, 1927, pp. 11 ff.
24. Strabo, 10, 3, 10.
25. Deubner, *Attische Feste*, 1932, pp. 73 ff., 93 ff.; Höfer, Roscher, Lexikon 'Iakchos'.
26. Scholiast, Aristophanes, *Frogs*, 316; Lucian, *De Salt.*, 39.
27. E. R. Dodds, *Euripides Bacchae*, Oxford, 1960, pp. xi ff.; *Harvard Theo-logical Review*, xxxiii, 1940; Farnell, *C.G.S.*, vol. v, chaps. iv–vii; Guthrie, *The Greeks and their Gods*, 1950, pp. 145 ff.; Rhode, *Psyche*, 2, p. 43.
28. *A History of Greek Religion*, Oxford, 1925, p. 205.
29. Nilsson, *Harvard Theological Review*, xxviii, 1935, p. 204.
30. J. Harrison, *Prolegomena to the Study of Greek Religion*, p. 476.
31. *Op. cit.*, p. 589.
32. H. Graillot, *Le Culte de Cybele*, Paris, 1912, pp. 25 ff.
33. Livy, xxix, 10–14; Ovid, *Fasti*, iv, 179 ff.; Dionysius, *Hal. Ant. Rom.*, 2, 19, 3–5.
34. Lucretius, ii, 600–43; Ovid, *Fasti*, iv, 181–6.
35. Julian, *Orat.*, v, 168C, 169C; Catullus, lxiii; Hepding, *Attis. Sein Mythen und sein Kult*, Giessen, 1903, pp. 147 ff.
36. Hepding, *op. cit.*, pp. 146–67.
37. Clement of Alex., *Protrept*, ii, 15; Firmicus Maternus, *De err, prof. relig.*, xviii, xix; Hepding, *op. cit.*, p. 185.
38. *Corpus Inscriptionum Latinarum*, vi, 510; viii, 8203; cf. 4152; Prudentius, *Peristephanon*, x, 1011–50; Firmicus Maternus, xxviii, 8.
39. *De Diis et Mundo*, iv (*Fragmenta Philosophorum Graecorum*), ed. Mullach, iii, 33; cf. G. Murray, *Five Stages of Greek Religion*, Oxford, 1925, p. 246.
40. *Textes et monuments figurés relatifs aux mystères de Mithra*, Brussels, 1896, vol. i, pp. 334 f.
41. *Metam.*, xi, 3, 21 ff., 30.
42. *Metam.*, xi, 21.

43. *Oxyrhynchus Payri.*, nos. 110, 523.
44. Chap. VII, pp. 196 f.
45. Porphyry, *De Antro Nymph.*, 15; Tertullian, *De Bapt.*, 5.
46. Tertullian, *De Praescr. Haer.*, 40; *De Corona*, 15; cf. Gregory of Nazianzus, *Orat.*, iv, 70.
47. Dieterich, *Eine Mithrasliturgie*, ed. R. Wunsch, Berlin and Paris, 1910.
48. *Corpus Hermeticum*, xiii, c. A.D. 300.
49. Porphyry, *De Abstin.*, iv, 16.
50. Gen. xvii, 13 f., 25; Mekhilta, Bahodesh, 2.
51. Ex. xii, 48; Num. ix, 14.
52. Sifre Num., 108; Mekhilta de R. Simeon ben Yohai in Ex. xii, 48.
53. Mekhilta, *Yebbamoth*, 45–7; *Gerim.*
54. Büchler, *Jewish Quarterly Review*, N.S., July 1926, p. 15.
55. Num. xix, xxxi, 19–24; Lev. xiv, 8; xv; *Pesahim*, viii, 8; *Josefta Pes*, vii, 13, ed. Zuckermandel, p. 167; cf. Abrahams, *Studies in Pharisaism and the Gospels*, Cambridge, 1917, vol. i, p. 37.
56. *Sotah*, 126; Sifra, *Ahave Perek.*, 12.
57. *Yebamot*, 48b; 62a.
58. *Ant.*, xviii, v, 2.
59. *Jewish Encyclopaedia*, vii, p. 218.
60. Mark i, 4, 15; cf. Matt. iii, 2.
61. Matt. iii, 12; Luke iii, 17.
62. Matt. iii, 2; xi, 10 f.; Luke iii, 15 f.; x, 9; xvi, 16.
63. Abrahams, *op. cit.*, vol. i, p. 34; Drower, *Water into Wine*, 1956, pp. 229 f.
64. Matt. xvii, 13.
65. *Historia Naturalis*, v, 17.
66. Matt. xi, 19.
67. Matt. xi, 11.
68. Mal. iii, 1; Mark i, 2 f.
69. Acts xviii, 26; xix, 1–7.
70. Luke iii, 22; Mark i, 11; Matt. iii, 17; Talmud, *Hagigah*, 15a; Abrahams, *op. cit.*, vol. i, pp. 47 ff.
71. John iii, 22; iv, 2.
72. John iii, 25; iv, 1–9.
73. Acts ii, 38; x, 48; xix, 5.
74. Acts x, xv.
75. Acts x, 34 ff.
76. Rom. vi, 3–5; cf. Gal. iii, 27; Col. ii, 12.
77. 1 Cor. xii, 13.
78. Ephes. i, 13; cf. Gal. iii, 2; Rom. x, 17; 1 Cor. ii, 4; iv, 15; xii, 15, 27.
79. 2 Cor. v, 17.
80. 1 Cor. xii, 13.
81. Rom. v–viii.
82. Rom. viii, 15 ff.; 1 Cor. vi, 11.

83. Col. iii, 1–10; Rom. vi, 3.
84. Flemington, *The New Testament Doctrine of Baptism*, 1948, pp. 79 f., 82.
85. John iii, 5, 7; 1 Peter i, 23; Titus iii, 5, 7; 1 Tim. iv, 12; Acts xiii, 46.
86. Tertullian, *De Baptismo*, xviii.
87. Acts viii, 14–17.
88. Num. xxvii, 18–20; Deut. xxxiv, 9; cf. Matt. xix, 13.
89. 2 Cor. i, 20 f.; Heb. vi, 2; Ephes. i, 13; iv, 30.
90. *De Baptismo*, vi; *De Res. Carnis*, viii; *Adv. Marc.*, i, 14.
91. *Haer.*, III, xvii, 2; IV, xxxviii, 1, 2; *Dem.*, iii, 41 f.
92. e.g. *The Apostolic Tradition of Hippolytus in the Egyptian Ordo*, c. A.D. 217.
93. Cyril, *De Myst.*, III, iv, 7.
94. R. H. Connoly, *Liturgical Homilies of Narsai*, Cambridge, 1909, pp. 43 ff.; *Older Didascalia*, iii, 12; H. Denzinger, *Ritus Orientalum*. Würzburg, 1863, i, p. 273.
95. *Summa Theol.*, iii, q. 72.
96. *In Sent.*, IV, dist. vii, art. 1.
97. *What is the Distinctive Grace of Confirmation in relation to Baptism?*, 1880, pp. 11 f.
98. *The Relation of Confirmation to Baptism*, 1891.
99. *The Theology of Confirmation in relation to Baptism*, 1946, p. 21.
100. *The Doctrine of Confirmation considered in Relation to Holy Baptism*, 1897.
101. *The Seal of the Spirit*, 1951, pp. 196 ff., 223 ff., 297 ff., 322.
102. *Confirmation. Its Place in the Baptismal Mystery*, 1954, pp. 18, 134, 139, 156, 173.
103. Gal. ii, 20; Rom. vi, 3 ff.
104. Rom. vi, 1–11; 1 Cor. xii, 13.
105. Matt. xvi, 13–20; xviii, 18; Acts x, 47; *Ep. Clementis ad Jacob*, 2, 6; Migne, *Pat. Graec.*, ii, 26, 41.
106. John xx, 19–23.
107. Galtier, *De Poenitentia*, ed. 2a, 1931, p. 111, n. 161.
108. Tertullian, *De Baptismo*, 7, 8, 20.
109. Mark iii, 28–30.
110. *Refutatio omnium haeresium*, ix, 7.
111. L. Eisenhofer and J. Lecher, *The Liturgy of the Roman Rite*, E.T. 1961, pp. 374 ff.
112. *Homil. in Ps. xxxvii*, n. 6; Migne, *Pat. Graec*, xii, 1386; in Lev. ii, 4; P.G., xii, 418.
113. *Ep. Can.*, ii, 34.
114. *Ep.*, 1682.
115. St Innocent I, *Ep.*, 25, ad Decentium Eugub.
116. Session XXI, *de reform.*, ch. 9, Session XXV.
117. A. Lehmkuhl, *Theologia Moralis*, Freiburg, 1896, 8th ed., 410, 418; Alphonsus de Liguori, *Theologia Moralis*, Ratisbonem, 1846, vi, n. 560, 561.

118. Thorndike, *Just Weights and Measures*, 1662, p. 120; *Memoirs of William Wordsworth*, 1851, vol. i, p. 8; cf. J. Wickham Legg, *English Church Life*, 1914, pp. 258 f., 278.

119. Whitgift, *Works*, vol. i, p. 489.

120. *Eccles. Polity*, iv, 4.

121. Church and Paget, *Hooker*, Oxford, 1888, i, 85.

122. *The Remains of Dennis Granville*, 1865 (Surtees Society), xlvii, pp. 49 f.; *Life of John Sharp*, 1825, vol. i, p. 301; Fielding, *Tom Jones*, Bk. 5, chap. viii; Cosin, *Collection of Private Devotions*, 8th ed., 1681.

123. Liddon, *Life of Dr Pusey*, iv, 1898, pp. 266 ff.

124. Mal. ii, 16; Matt. v, 27–32; Mark x, 2–12; Luke xvi, 18.

125. Gen. ii, 18 f., 24.

126. 1 Cor. vii, 2, 10 f.; Rom. vii, 3; vi, 18–vii, 6.

127. Ephes. v, 23 f.

128. Cf. Chap. III, p. 67.

129. 1 Cor. vii, 27.

130. Ephes. v, 28 ff.

131. 1 Cor. vii, 12 f., 15 ff.

132. *De Conjugiis Adulterinis*, lib. i, c. 13.

133. Codex, Iuris Canonici. cons., 1120–7; G. H. Joyce, *Christian Marriage*, 1948, pp. 477 ff.

134. Tertullian, *Ad Uxor.*, ii, 9; *De Padis*, 4.

135. *Ep. ad Polycarp*, v.

136. Beauchet, *Nouvelle Revue de Droit Français*, vi, 381 ff.

137. Clement of Alex., *Paed.*, lib. iii, c. xi, p. 243.

138. Cf. Martène, *De Antiquis Ecclesiae Ritibus*, Venice, 1783, p. 609; Goar, *Euchologion*, Paris, 1647, pp. 396 ff.

139. *Rituale Romanum*, Appendix, *De Matrimonie*, I, II.

140. Matt. x, 1–3; xxviii, 19 f.; Mark iii, 13 ff.; Luke vi, 12 ff.; Acts ii, 14; iii, 1–10.

141. K. E. Kirk, *The Apostolic Ministry*, 1946; R. Dunkerley, *The Ministry and the Sacraments*, 1947; Ehrhardt, *The Apostolic Succession*, 1953; T. W. Manson, *The Church's Ministry*, 1948.

142. Acts vi, 1–6; xiii, 1–3; 1 Tim. iv, 14; v, 22; 2 Tim. i, 6.

143. 1 Cor. xii, 28; Ephes. iv, 11.

144. Eusebius, *Historia Ecclesiastica*, vi, chap. 43.

145. Lennerz, *De Sacramento Ordinis*, 2nd ed., Rome, 1953, pp. 139 ff.

146. *Op. cit.*, pp. 145 ff.

147. *Leonianum*, 122.

148. *Acta Apostolicae Sedis*, Rome, 1944, 37, pp. 131 ff.

149. In the English Establishment a *congé d'élire* is issued by the Crown to the Chapter before the election and the royal assent is given after the election has been completed. Phillimore, *Ecclesiastical Law of the Church of England*, 1895, vol. i, pp. 33 ff.

150. *Apostolic Constitutions*, VIII, c. 5; Durandus, *Rationale divinorum*, Lyons, 1592, lib. 2, c. ii, n. 8.
151. Mark vi, 13; x, 9, 17 ff.; James v, 14 f.
152. *Canons of Hippolytus*, 53, 54; St Serapion, *Euchologion*; Innocent I, *Ep. ad Decentius Eugobium. Ep.*, 25, 8; Caesarius of Arles, *Sermo.*, 13, 3; 19, 5; 50, 1; 184, 5.
153. *Rituale Roman-Germanicum*, Regensburg, 1950.

ABBREVIATIONS

A.B.	*Anat-Baal Texts.*
A.N.E.T.	*Ancient Near Eastern Texts relating to the Old Testament,* ed. by J. B. Pritchard, Princeton, 2nd ed., 1955.
B.B.A.E.	*Bulletin Bureau of American Ethnology,* Washington.
E.R.E.	*Encyclopaedia of Religion and Ethics,* ed. Hastings, 1908–26.
C.G.S.	*Cult of the Greek States,* L. R. Farnell. O.U.P., 1896–1909.
C.I.A.	*Corpus inscriptionum Atticarum.*
G.B.	*The Golden Bough,* J. G. Frazer, 3rd ed., 1911–27.
J.A.O.S.	*Journal of the American Oriental Society,* New Haven.
J.E.A.	*Journal of Egyptian Archaeology.*
J.H.S.	*Journal of Hellenic Studies,* London.
J.N.E.S.	*Journal of Near Eastern Studies,* Chicago.
J.R.A.I.	*Journal of the Royal Anthropological Institute.*
J.R.A.S.	*Journal of the Royal Asiatic Society.*
P.G.	*Patrologia Graecia,* Migne.

BIBLIOGRAPHY

CHAPTER I

Bancroft, H. H., *Native Races of the Pacific States*, 1875–6.
Brasseur de Bourbourg, *Histoire des nations civilisées du Mexique et de l'Amérique-Centrale*, Vol. iii, Paris, 1857–9.
Breuil, H., *Four Hundred Centuries of Cave Art*, Montignac, 1952.
Durkheim, E., *Elementary Forms of the Religious Life*, E.T. 1915.
Evans, Pritchard, E. E., 'The Meaning of Sacrifice among the Nuer', *J.R.A.I.*, 1954, vol. lxxxiv. *Nuer Religion*, Oxford, 1956.
Frazer, J. G., *Totemism and Exogamy*, 1910.
Hubert, H., and Mauss, M., *Mélanges d'histoire des religions*, Paris, 1909; 'Essai sur la Nature et la Fonction du Sacrifice', *L'Année Socio-logique*, t. 11, 1897–8.
James, E. O., *Origins of Sacrifice*, 1933.
Loisy, A., *Essai historique sur le sacrifice*, Paris, 1920.
Luquet, G. H., *The Art and Religion of Fossil Man*, Oxford, 1930.
Mannhardt, W., *Mythologische Forsungen*, Strassburg, 1884.
Marett, R. R., *Sacraments of Simple Folk*, Oxford, 1933.
Quick, O. C., *The Christian Sacraments*, 1925.
Smith, W. R., *Lectures on the Religion of the Semites*, 3rd ed., 1927.
Speck, F. C., *Ethnology of the Yuki Indians*, Philadelphia, 1909.
Spencer, B., and Gillen, F. J., *The Native Tribes of Central Australia*, 1938; *The Arunta*, 1927.
Swanton, J. R., *23rd Bulletin, Bureau of American Ethnology*, Washington, 1911.

CHAPTER II

Barth, A., *Religions of India*, E.T. 1882.
Bloomfield, M., *The Religion of the Veda*, 1889.
Box, H. S., *Priesthood*, 1937.
Deussen, P., *The Philosophy of the Upanishads*, E.T., Edinburgh, 1906.
Dix, G., 'The Ministry in the Early Church', in *The Apostolic Ministry*, ed. K. E. Kirk, 1946.
Eliot, C., *Hinduism and Buddhism*, new ed., 1954.
Erman, A., *Handbook of Egyptian Religion*, 1907.
Frankfort, H., *Kingship and the Gods*, Chicago, 1948.

Gray, E. B., *Sacrifice in the Old Testament*, Oxford, 1925.

Griswold, H. D., *The Religion of the Rig Veda*, Oxford, 1923.

Hastings, J., Articles on 'Priesthood' in *E.R.E.*

Hubert, H., and Mauss, M., *Mélanges d'histoire des religions*, Paris, 1909.

James, E. O., *The Nature and Function of Priesthood*, 1955.

Kennett, R. H., *Old Testament Essays*, 1928.

Lévy, S., *La Doctrine du sacrifice dans les Brahmanas*, Paris, 1889.

Monier-Williams, M., *Brahmanism and Hinduism*, 4th ed., 1891.

Radhakrishnan, S., *Indian Philosophy*, 1951.

Renou, L., *Religions of Ancient India*, 1953.

Sethe, K., *Dramatische Texte zu Altaegyptischen Mysterienspielen*, Leipzig, 1928.

Stevenson, S., *The Heart of Jainism*, 1915.

Welch, A. C., *King, Prophet and Priest in Old Israel*, Oxford, 1953.

Zimmer, H., *Myths and Symbols in Indian Art and Civilization*, New York, 1953.

CHAPTER III

Engnell, I., *Studies in Divine Kingship in the Ancient Near East*, Uppsala, 1945.

Evans-Pritchard, E. E., *The Divine Kingship of the Shilluk of the Nilotic Sudan*, Cambridge, 1948.

Frankfort, H., *Kingship and the Gods*, Chicago, 1948.

Gaster, Th., *Thespis*, New York, 1950.

Hooke, S. H., *Myth, Ritual and Kingship*, Oxford, 1958.

Johnson, A. R., *Sacral Kingship in Ancient Israel*, Cardiff, 1956.

Labat, R., *Du caractère religieux de la royauté Assyro-Babylonienne*, Paris, 1939.

Lévy-Bruhl, L., *Les Fonctions Mentales dans les Sociétés Inférieures*, Paris, 1912; *La Mentalité Primitive*, Paris, 1922.

Moret, A., *Du caractère religieux de la royauté Pharaonique; Le rituel du culte divin journalier en Egypte*, Paris, 1902.

Oesterley, W. O. E., *Sacrifice in Ancient Isreal*, 1937.

Oesterley, W. O. E., and Box, G. H., *The Religion and Worship of the Synagogue*, 1911.

Pallis, S. A., *The Babylonian Akitu Festival*, Copenhagen, 1926.

Rowley, H. H., *The Servant of the Lord*, 1952.

Seligman, C. G., *Cult of the Nyakang and the Divine Kings of the Shilluk*, Khartoum, 1911; *The Pagan Tribes of the Nilotic Sudan*, 1932; *Egypt and Negro Africa*, 1934.

Thackeray, H. St John, *The Septuagint and Jewish Worship*, 1921.
Trumbull, C., *The Blood Covenant*, 1887.

CHAPTER IV

Bancroft, H. H., *Native Races of the Pacific States*, 1875–6.
Brasseur de Bourbourg, *Le Popol Vuh*, Paris, 1861.
Campbell, J., *Wild Tribes of Khondistan*, 1864.
Fowler, W. Warde, *Roman Festivals*, 1899; *The Religious Experience of the Roman People*, 1922.
Fox, C. E., *The Threshold of the Pacific*, 1924.
Furness, W. K. H., *Home-life of Borneo Head-Hunters*, Philadelphia, 1902.
Guthrie, W. K. C., *Orpheus and Greek Religion*, 1935.
Haddon, A. C., *J.R.A.I.*, vol. xix, 1890.
Hose, C., and McDougall, W., *The Pagan Tribes of Borneo*, 1912.
Joyce, T. A., *South American Archaeology*, 1912; *Mexican Archaeology*, 1914.
Keating, W. H., *Narrative of an Expedition to the Source of the St Peter River*, Philadelphia, 1824.
Macalister, R. A. S., *Excavations at Gezer*, 1912.
Marshall, H. L., *The Keren People of Burma*, Ohio, 1912.
Mills, J. P., *The Ao Naga*, 1926.
Molina, C. de, *Relaciòn de los fabulas y ritos et los Ingas*, Lima, 1916.
Payne, E., *History of the New World called America*, Oxford, 1892.
Rankin, J., *The Conquest of Peru and Mexico*, 1827.
Rivers, W. H. R., *History of Melanesian Society*, Cambridge, 1914.
Sahagun, B. de, *Historia General de las Cosas de Nuova España*, Mexico, 1938.
Schoolcraft, H. R., *Indian Tribes of the United States*, Philadelphia, 1953–6.
Spence, L., *The Gods of Mexico*, 1923; *The Myths of Mexico and Peru*, 1913.
Talbot, A. M., *Some Nigerian Fertility Cults*, Oxford, 1927.
Wissowa, G., *Religion und Kultur der Römer*, Leipzig, 1912.
Woolley, L., *Excavations at Ur*, 1954.

CHAPTER V

Aulen, G., *Den Kristna forsoninggstanten*, Lund, 1930, E.T. by A. G. Hebert, *Christus Victor*, 1931.
Büchler, A., *Studies on Sin and Atonement*, Oxford, 1928.

Franks, R. S., *History of the Doctrine of the Work of Christ*, 1918.

Gray, E. B., *Sacrifice in the Old Testament*, Oxford, 1928.

Grensted, L. W., *A Short History of the Doctrine of the Atonement*, 1920.

Jastrow, J., *Religion of Babylonia and Assyria*, Boston, 1898; *Religious Belief in Babylonia and Assyria*, New York, 1911.

Langdon, S. H., *Babylonian Penitential Psalms*, Paris, 1927.

McLeod Campbell, J., *The Nature of the Atonement*, 1856.

Manson, W., *Jesus the Messiah*, 1943.

Moberley, R. C., *Atonement and Personality*, 1901.

Montefiore, C. G., 'Rabbinic Conception of Repentance', *Jewish Quarterly Review*, O.S., vol. xvi, 1904.

Mozley, J. K., *The Doctrine of the Atonement*, 1915.

Oxenham, H. N., *Catholic Doctrine of the Atonement*, 1865.

Rashdall, H., *The Idea of the Atonement in Christian Theology*, 1920.

Rowley, H. H., *The Servant of the Lord*, 1952; *Studies in Old Testament Prophecy*, 1950.

Taylor, V., *Jesus and His Sacrifice*, 1937.

Thompson, R. Campbell, *Semitic Magic*, 1918; *Devils and Evil Spirits in Babylonia*, 1904.

Thureau-Dangin, F., *Rituale Accadiens*, Paris, 1921.

Westermarck, E., *The Origin and Development of Moral Ideas*, 1906.

Zimmern, H., *Babylonische Busspsalmen*, vol. iv, Leipzig, 1885; *Beiträge zur Kenntnis der Babylonischen Religion*, Leipzig, 1899.

CHAPTER VI

Budge, E. A. W., *The Opening of the Mouth*, 1909; *Osiris and the Egyptian Resurrection*, 1911.

Campbell, J. G., *Superstitions of the Highlands*, Glasgow, 1900.

Dawson, W. R., *Egyptian Mummies*, 1924.

Evans, Sir A., *The Palace of Minos*, vol. iv, 1935; *Mycenaean Tree and Pillar Cult*, 1901.

Fowler, W. Warde, *Roman Festivals*, 1899.

Garstang, J., *Prehistoric Mersin*, Oxford, 1953.

James, E. O., *Seasonal Festivals and Feasts*, 1961.

Kenyon, K., *Digging up Jericho*, 1957.

Langdon, S. H., *Tammuz and Ishtar*, Oxford, 1914; *Sumerian and Babylonian Psalms*, Paris, 1909.

Mannhardt, W., *Mythologische Forschungen*, Strassburg, 1884.

Marshall, Sir J., *Mohenjo-daro and the Indus Civilization*, 1937.

Nilsson, M. P., *Greek Popular Religion*, 1940; *Minoan-Mycenaean Religion*, Lund, 1950; *Griechische Feste von religiöser Bedentung mit Ausschluss der Attischen*, Leipzig, 1906.

Piggott, S., *Prehistoric India*, 1950.

Rouse, W. H., *Greek Votive Offerings*, 1902.

Schaeffer, C. F. A., *The Cuneiform Texts of Ras Shamra*, 1939.

Speck, F. G., *Ethnology of the Yuki Indians*, Philadelphia, 1919.

Tobler, A. J., *Excavations at Tepe Gawra*, Philadelphia, 1950.

Vats, M. S., *Excavations at Harappa*, Delhi, 1940.

Verneau, R., *Les Grottes de Grimaldi*, Monaco, 1906.

Volz, P., *Das Neujahresfest Jahwas*, Tübingen, 1912.

Widengren, G., *Sakrales Königtum im Alten Testament und im Judentum*, Stuttgart, 1955.

Williams, B. E., *Gournia*, Philadelphia, 1908.

Wissowa, G., *Religion und Kultus der Römer*, Leipzig, 1912.

CHAPTER VII

Angus, S., *The Mystery Religions and Christianity*, 1925.

Black, D., *Fossil Man in China*, Peking, 1938.

Braz, A. le, *La légende de Morten Basse-Bretagne*, Paris, 1893.

Breasted, J. H., *Development of Religious Thought in Ancient Egypt*, 1914.

Budge, E. A. W., *The Liturgy of Funerary Offerings*, 1909; *The Book of the Dead*, 1951; *Osiris and the Egyptian Resurrection*, 1911.

Farnell, L. R., *Greek Hero Cults and Ideas of Immortality*, Oxford, 1921.

Fowler, W. Warde, *Religious Experience of the Roman People*, 1922.

Frankfort, H., *Ancient Egyptian Religion*, Columbia Press, 1948.

Heidel, A., *The Babylonian Genesis*, Chicago, 1951; *Gilgamesh and Old Testament Parallels*, Chicago, 1946.

James, E. O., *Seasonal Festivals and Feasts*, 1961.

Kenyon, K., *Digging up Jericho*, 1957.

Kramer, S. N., *Sumerian Mythology*, Philadelphia, 1944.

Lods, A., *La Croyance à la Vie Future et le Culte des Morts dans l'Antiquité Israélite*, Paris, 1906.

Luquet, G. H., *The Art and Religion of Fossil Man*, Oxford, 1930.

Macalister, R. A. S., *Excavations at Gezer*, 1912.

Nilsson, M. P., *Minoan-Mycenaean Religion*, Lund, 1950; *Homer and Mycenae*, 1933.

Obermaier, H., *Fossil Man in Spain*, Yale Press, New Haven, 1925.

Oesterley, W. O. E., *Immortality and the Unseen World*, 1921.

Oppenoorth, W. F. F., *Early Man*, Philadelphia, 1937.
Persson, A. W., *The New Tombs at Dendra*, Lund, 1942.
Tobler, A. J., *Excavations at Tepe Gawra*, Philadelphia, 1950.
Wace, A. B., *Chamber Tombs at Mycenae*, 1932.
Woolley, Sir L., *Ur Excavations*, vol. ii, 1932; *The Royal Cemetery*, 1934.

CHAPTER VIII

Addleshaw, G. W. O., *The High Church Tradition*, 1941.
Brightman, F. E., *Liturgies Eastern and Western*, 1896.
Cabrol, F., *Les origines liturgiques*, 1906.
Chambers, E. K., *The Mediaeval Stage*, Oxford, 1913.
Chwolson, F., *Das letzte Passamahl Christi*, Leipzig, 1908.
Cirlot, F. L., *The Early Eucharist*, 1939.
Cumont, F., *Textes et monumenta figurés relatifs aux mystères de Mithra*, Brussels, 1896–9; *Mystères de Mithra*, Brussels, 1899.
Dhalla, M. N., *Zoroastrian Theology*, New York, 1914.
Dix, G., *The Shape of the Liturgy*, 1945.
Frere, W. H., *The Anaphora, or Great Eucharistic Prayer*, 1938.
Hicks, F. C. N., *The Fullness of Sacrifice*, 1930.
Jeremias, J., *Die Abendmahlsworte Jesu*, 2nd ed., 1949.
Jungmann, J. A., *The Mass of the Roman Rite*, E.T. 1959.
Koenker, E. B., *The Liturgical Movement in the Roman Catholic Church*, Chicago, 1954.
Lietzmann, H., *Messe und Herrenmahl*, Bonn, 1926.
Maclean, A. J., *The Doctrine of the Twelve Apostles*, 1922.
Modi, J. T., *The Religious Ceremonies and Customs of the Parsees*, Bombay, 1922.
More, P. E., and Cross, F. L., *Anglicanism*, 1935.
Moulton, J. H., *Early Zoroastrianism*, 1913; *The Treasure of the Magi*, 1917.
Oesterley, W. O. E., *The Jewish Background of the Liturgy*, 1925.
Proctor, F., and Frere W. H., *Edward VI and the Book of Common Prayer*, 1890.
Rousseau, O., *Histoire du mouvement liturgique*, Paris, 1945.
Srawley, J. H., *The Liturgical Movement* (Alcuin Club Tracts, xxvii), 1954.
Taille, M. de la, *Mysterium Fidei*, 1921.
Vokes, F. E., *The Riddle of the Didache*, 1938.
Vonier, A., *A Key to the Doctrine of the Eucharist*, 1925.

Zaehner, R. C., *Zurvan, a Zoroastrian Dilemma*, Oxford, 1959. *The Dawn and Twilight of Zoroastrianism*, 1961.

CHAPTER IX

Apuleius, *Metamorphoses*, E.T. by H. E. Butler, 1910.
Batchelor, J., *The Ainu and their Folklore*, 1901.
Bevan, E., *Symbolism and Belief*, 1938; *Holy Images*, 1940.
Chiera, E., *Sumerian Ritual Texts*, Upland, Pa., 1924.
Crehan, J., *Early Christian Baptism and the Creed*, 1950.
Cumont, F., *Textes et monuments figurés aux mystères de Mithra*, Brussels, 1896.
Dix, G., *Confirmation, or Laying-on of Hands*, 1936.
Dodd, E. R., *Euripides Bacchae*, Oxford, 1960.
Eisenhofer, L., and Lechner, J., *The Liturgy of the Roman Rite*, 1961.
Elland, G., *Ordination Anointings of the Western Church since A.D. 1000*, Cambridge, Massachusetts, 1933.
Flemington, W. F., *The New Testament Doctrine of Baptism*, 1948.
Graillot, H., *Le Culte de Cybele*, Paris, 1912.
Guthrie, W. K. C., *The Greeks and their Gods*, 1950.
Harrison, J. E., *Prolegomena to the Study of Greek Religion*, Cambridge, 1903.
James, E. O., *Marriage and Society*, 1952.
Joyce, G. H., *Christian Marriage*, 1933.
Kern, J., *De Sacramento Extremae Unctionis*, Ratesbon, 1907.
Lampe, G. W. H., *The Seal of the Spirit*, 1951.
Leeming, B., *Principles of Sacramental Theology*, 1960.
Puller, F. W., *The Anointing of the Sick in Scripture and Tradition*, 1904.
Quick, O. C., *The Christian Sacraments*, 1952.
Roguet, A., *Le sacrament des malades*, Paris, 1957.
Thornton, L. S., *Confirmation: its Place in the Baptismal Mystery*, 1954.
Tixeront, J., *Holy Orders and Ordination*, St Louis, 1932.
Watkins, O. D., *Holy Matrimony*, 1895; *A History of Penance*, 1920.
Whitaker, E. G., *Documents of the Baptismal Liturgy*, 1960.
White, R. E. O., *The Biblical Doctrine of Initiation*, 1960.

INDEX

Purification rites, 108 ff., 149 ff.
See also Lustrations
Purusha, 43, 50, 102 f.
Pythia, the, 156

QUETZALCOATL and human sacrifice, 29, 78
Quick, O. C., 16, 281, 306, 312

RADHAKRISHNAN, S., 282, 307
Ras Shamra, 153
Re, 36 ff., 150, 151, 238, 240
Reconciliation, 118, 120, 263 ff.
Renou, L., 307
Reformation, the, 122, 215 ff.,
225 ff.
Reinach, S., 20
Rephaim, 172, 174
Requiem, Mass of, 189 f., 214
Rig-Veda, the, 42, 45, 101 f.
Rite de passage, the, 139, 168 f., 180,
190, 238, 240, 258, 278
Rousseau, O., 299, 311
Rowley, H. H., 284, 289, 307,
309

SACRAMENT, definition of, 14, 232
Sacramental principle, the, 14 ff.,
232 ff.; meal, the, 17 f., 39, 41,
89, 143, 194, 200 ff., 206 f., 233,
242; signs, 25, 233 ff.; regeneration, 38, 130, 237 ff., 248;
union, 17, 24, 62, 234 f., 236
Sacramentals, 232 ff.
Sacramentum, 232, 237, 250
Sacrifice, definition of, 13; gift
theory, the, 13, 25 f.; communion theory of, 17 f., 24;
piacular, 14, 105 ff.; do-ut-des,
13, 26; human, *see* Human sacrifice; bestowal of life, 17, 26,
33, 60 ff., 128, 237; first-fruits,
13, 17, 26; funerary, 162 ff.;
expiation and atonement, 33 f.,

see also Atonement; and priest-
hood, 36 ff.; Christian con-
ception of, 72 ff.; Vedic, 18, 31,
34, 41 f.; Jewish, 74 f.
Sacrificium, 13, 157
Salii, the, 158
Salvation, doctrine of, 126 f. *See
also* Atonement
Satisfaction, doctrine of, 121 ff.,
126
Saul, 172 f.
Scapegoat, 34, 55, 105
Schaeffer, C. F. A., 153, 293, 310
Sed-festival, the, 68
Servant, the Suffering, 72, 114 f.,
116
Sethe, K., 282, 307
Shades, 176, 182
Sheol, 170, 173, 176
Sin, conception of, 104, 118; offer-
ing, 107, 113. *See also* Piacular
Skulls, cult of, 88 f.
Smith, W. R., 17 f., 19, 63, 281,
306
Snaith, N. H., 290
Socinians, 123
Soma sacrifice, 31, 193 f.
Sol invictus, 197, 249
Soul-substance, 20, 26, 60, 62,
136, 236
Speck, F. C., 282, 306
Spencer, B. and Gillen, F. J., 281,
306
Spence, L., 308
Sponsalia, the, 273 f.
Srawley, J. H., 311
Substitution, 63 f., 68 f., 104
Swanton, J. R., 282, 306
Symbol, sacramental, 25, 62, 131 f.,
134, 233 ff., 235

TABERNACLES, Feast of, 142 ff.,
154
Talmud, the, 54, 154